HOGGY

HOGGY

Welcome to My World

HarperSport

An Imprint of HarperCollinsPublishers

First published in 2009 by
HarperSport
an imprint of HarperCollins
77–85 Fulham Palace Rd
London W6 8JB
www.harpercollins.co.uk

© Matthew Hoggard 2009

1

A CIP catalogue record for this book is
available from the British Library

HB ISBN 978-0-00-728129-9
PB ISBN 978-0-00-729246-2

Printed and bound in Great Britain
by Clays Ltd, St Ives plc

All photographs provided courtesy of Matthew Hoggard and Mark
Swinford with the exception of the following plate section images:
Action Images 10b, 11; Getty Images 5cr, 6t, 6cl, 7, 8t, 8c, 8b,
12, 13t, 13c, 14tl, 14tr, 15tc, 15tr; John Hipkiss 15bl;
PA Photos 5cl, 9tl, 9tr, 9b, 10tr, 10c, 13b, 14b, 15tl, 15br;
Patrick Eagar 6cr; Phil Brown 5b.

What you'll find inside ...

To Sarah and Ernie

My strength and salvation

'He's just a bit silly. He rings you up and leaves daft messages and silly noises on your phone. It's just madness. He's a good lad though.'

Ashley Giles

'He gives you it straight. If he thinks you're a pillock, he'll tell you. He won't ask for anything that he wouldn't do himself, that's the way he is. Hoggy is Hoggy.'

David Byas, former Yorkshire captain

ForePaw-word

By the HOGGY DOGGIES,
BILLY the Doberman and MOLLY the Border Collie

BILLY: So what's all this about, then?

MOLLY: Apparently, this is the bit of a book where important people or animals are asked to say nice things about the bloke on the front cover.

BILLY: About him? Why I should say nice things about him? All he ever does is shout at me.

MOLLY: That's because you play too rough half the time, Billy, and you don't do as you're told.

BILLY: Whenever I try to play with you, you don't give me the time of day. You can be a cantankerous old bitch sometimes.

MOLLY: You forget that I'm an old lady. If I was five years younger, I'd still be able to run rings round you.

BILLY: Like to see you try. Anyway, I still don't see why I should be so nice about the bloke. What does he ever do for us?

MOLLY: He takes us for lots of long walks.

BILLY: I'll give him that.

MOLLY: Even when it's raining. And he feeds us most of the time.

BILLY: Well, yes, you've got a point. Sometimes I want to bite him, but I'm worried that the walks and the food might stop if I do. Shall we gang up on him and both bite him?

MOLLY: He's in charge, Billy boy, whether we like it or not.

BILLY: But if he's so tough and reckons he's top dog, why does he always send me outside first if he hears a noise in the garden? I can never understand that.

MOLLY: Strange creatures, these humans, Billy. I'm still trying to work them out.

BILLY: They must be strange if they want to read a book about him. What's so interesting about him?

MOLLY: Apparently he's quite good at some weird game they play. They throw a red ball, someone hits it and they chase it around a field. It goes on for hours.

BILLY: Well, I chase a ball around a field with him all the time and I'm much better at it than him. This book should be all about me.

MOLLY: I'm inclined to agree with you, Billy. But like I said, he's in charge.

BILLY: He talks a load of rubbish as well. He makes up words of his own that nobody else ever uses, words like 'ridonculous'.

MOLLY: Yes, I've always wondered what that means. Any ideas?

BILLY: Haven't got a clue. Do you think they're all as odd as him?

MOLLY: I very much doubt it.

Introduction

Go on, admit it, you turned to the photo pages first, didn't you?

Before I had the chance to say even a word in my defence, you plunged straight into the middle of the book to check out my dodgy haircuts from when I was younger. Don't worry, though; everybody does it, me included. Those embarrassing old photos are sometimes the best bit of the book, aren't they? I tried to get the publishers to let me have a book full of pictures, but they insisted I put a few words in here as well. Sorry about that.

Anyway, at least you have now made it as far as my first page. I bet there are some buggers who'll pick up the book in a shop, have a quick look at the dodgy photos, then put the book back down again with no intention whatsoever of buying it. I'm thinking of putting on a disguise one day and spending a few hours hanging out in a bookshop to see how many people do that.

When we first started talking about writing a book, it was suggested that I should try to give the reader a feel for what it would be like to sit next to me in the England dressing-room. That's what these books are supposed to do, I was told; to give a flavour of what it is *really* like to play for your country.

But I didn't think that would really be fair, because most people don't find it a particularly pleasant experience to sit alongside me for the duration of a five-day Test match. I've got very smelly kit, for starters. My cricket bag begins a Test match in a pretty disorganised state, with everything just thrown in. And by the end of the fifth day there will be stuff strewn everywhere and it'll take me an age to find all my kit when it's time to go home. It's not a pretty sight, so I think I'll spare you that experience.

Actually, one thing about sitting next to me in the dressing-room that may be worth sharing is my vast store of completely useless information. Sitting on the balcony during a Test match, watching our batsmen pile on the runs, the conversation may flag from time to time. And to while away a bit of time, I have been renowned in the England team for nudging whoever is sitting next to me and producing a random fact to start a discussion of some kind.

Such as: 'Did you know that peanuts are used in the manufacture of dynamite?'

'Really, Hoggy? How interesting.'

'And did you know that peanuts aren't actually nuts?'

'Well, I never did.'

Andrew Strauss has always been especially keen on my little factoids. He says that my ability to produce these pearls of wisdom is evidence of my **HIDDEN INTELLIGENCE**, however well concealed it might be. But I only know so much rubbish because I've got some very good trivia books in the loo at home. How dare he call me intelligent?

So you might find yourself being nudged at various points during the book and being offered a little HogFact or two. Prepare to be amazed. Other than that, this book is a bit of a higgledy-piggledy ramble through my career, with the odd stop off for refuelling along the way (the way a good walk should be). The wife has blagged a chapter or two, because it wouldn't seem right to tell a tale about my life without a contribution from her. She's never been known to miss out on the opportunity to put her two penn'orth in before.

And also, as a special treat, if he's a really good boy, our little lad, Ernie, might even get to say a few words.

Originally, I'd wanted to throw a bit of scandal into the book and tell you about such scrapes as the time the entire England team ■■■■■■■■■■■■■■■■■■■■■■■ and ended up ■■■■■■■■ ■■■■■■■■! But lawyers will be lawyers and the wise men in wigs told me to tone it down a touch.

If you find you're getting bored at any point during this book, I've scribbled a few puzzles between Chapters Two and Three to give you a break. I'll understand if you feel the need to recharge the brain cells for a while before diving back into my deep and meaningful writing. And if you're still struggling after the puzzles, well, you could go away and find someone to tell about a startling new fact that you've just learned.

Failing that, you can always turn back to have a look at those dodgy haircuts, just one more time.

1
My Family and Other Animals

by Matthew 'oggard, aged 8½

Hello. My name is Matthew and I am eight narf years old. I was born on 31st December 1976 in St Mary's Hospitull and I go to Lowtown Primary School. I live in Pudsey in Yorkshire quite near Leeds and Bradford. They named that teddy bear on Children in Need after Pudsey. I don't know why. I'm not really into teddy bears myself. I prefer animals and insects.

When we do show-and-tell at school I like to take in something slimy or stinky. Once I took a slow-worm that I brought back from camping with mum and dad. I showed it to the boys and girls in my class and everybody just went: 'EEEUUURRGHHHH! IT'S A SNAKE!' Especially the girls. So I said: 'No it's not. Don't be so daft. It's only a slow-worm.'

I'm dead lucky cos we've got some fields over our back wall where I can go and look for animals and insects. I love exploring and the fields at the back of our house are brilliant. We call them the blue fields cos some of the soil is blue. It's summat to do with the chemicals on them. My dad told me what but I've forgotten now.

There are two marker posts in the blue fields and mum says I'm not allowed to go past them. At the side of the marker posts there

is a meadowy bit where there are loads and loads of insects. Over the other side there is a big old gas cylinder and the banana. The banana is a big steep dip where bigger boys ride their bikes.

Past the banana there is a flat bit where you can see a family of foxes. I like to go and watch the big foxes playing with the baby foxes. The baby foxes are called cubs. Just below the flat bit there is a pond. Sumtimes I find a frog or a toad from the pond and take it home. I run into the kitchen and shout: 'Mum, Mum, look what I've found!' And she'll say: 'That's very nice, Matthew. But please will you take it out of the kitchen.'

I've brought all sorts of animals home from the blue fields. I've brought toads and frogs and voles and fieldmice and worms. But my favourite are devil's coach-horses. These are little beetles that chomp on worms for their tea. I've got lots of them in an old milk churn at home. Dad has taken the top off the milk churn and I put loads of soil and stones in there for my devil's coach-horses. I give them worms to eat and watch the worms get munched up. It's great. I think I want to be a vet when I grow up.

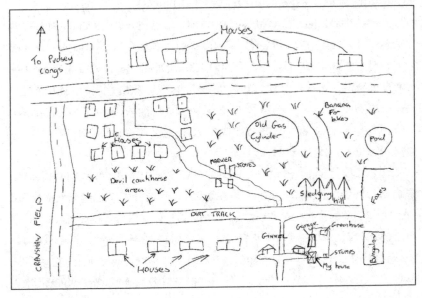

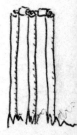

I also like dogs and cats. I like going up to dogs and giving them a stroke. Mum always says: 'Be careful Matthew, they might bite.' But I say: 'No it won't bite me, Mum. Dogs like me.' We have had some cats as pets but they kept dying. Now we've got Smudge and I think he'll be okay.

My Dad is a teacher. He teaches bigger boys to do sums. My Mum used to be a lollipop lady but now she works at a school as well. She works with the science teachers and she wears a white coat. As well as my mum and dad I live with my older sisters Karen and Julie. I like being the youngest cos when Karen and Julie fall out they both start being really nice to me and trying to get me on their side.

Sumtimes I think my sisters wish I was a girl. When it's fancy dress at school they always make me wear stupid stuff. Like being a St Trinian girl which makes me look a right prat. Last time I went to school dressed as a St Trinian I played rugby at morning break and laddered my tights.

The other thing that I love to do apart from looking for animals is playing games with my dad. We play loads and loads of different games with balls. We play chuck and catch, French cricket, Frisbee, rugby and football. We go up to the rugby posts at the top field sumtimes and throw or kick a rugby ball and try to hit the crossbar and posts. Dad gives us points when we hit and we see who can get the most points. We also play a lot in our back garden but we've got to be careful there cos we're always knocking plants over and Mum gets cross.

I always really want to beat my dad when we're playing games and he always really wants to beat me. He wins most of the time cos he's a grown-up. Sumtimes I win and I love it when I do.

I like it when we play proper cricket. But bowling is really difficult. I'm good at standing still and bowling and I'm good at running in super fast. But it's tricky doing them both together. I

run in really fast then hop and skip and jump but I never know where my feet are so I can't bowl when I've stopped hopping and skipping and jumping. I get really angry sumtimes.

So one Sunday morning Dad decided to sort out my bowling. It took us ages and ages and ages. I just ran in and jumped and bowled loads and loads of times and I tried not to do any hopping or skipping. Run jump bowl run jump bowl run jump bowl. I got it wrong a lot but Dad told me to keep trying. Suddenly just before it was time to go in for our lunch I got good at it. So I tried it a few more times and I was still good at it.

Now I really like bowling. It's my favourite bit of cricket. And Dad says that when I bowl the ball swings a lot.

I don't really know what that means but it sounds cool.

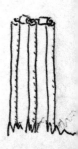

WHY CRICKET IS A BATSMAN'S GAME

1. EFFORT

They stand there and hit balls for a living, and run when it's actually going to be worth something to them. A bit like someone that won't get out of bed unless they're being paid for it. Bowlers put more effort into bowling a dot ball than batsmen do into hitting a six.

2. FIELDING POSITIONS

Where do batsmen normally field? In the slips, chatting away while the bowlers do the running around elsewhere. If you're fielding at fine leg and the batsman snicks a ball through the slips for four, the slips just turn round and look at you to fetch it, even though it's probably closer to them. You've just stood there for twenty overs, you f***ing fetch it.

3. PRACTICE SESSIONS

Once they've had their turn to bat, some batsmen can't be bothered to bowl at us tail-enders. And if they are gracious enough to turn their arms over, they just stroll up and bowl some filthy off-spin.

4. CAPTAINCY

Captains are almost always batsmen, so they don't know what it's like to be a bowler, to be aching and groaning at the end of a hard day. Can you give us one more over, Hoggy? You can't ever say no.

5. SMALL STUMPS

Let's face it, not many dismissals come from a brilliant ball that pitches leg and hits off. Most batsmen get themselves out, through boredom or a daft shot. If we had bigger stumps, there would be more genuine dismissals for the deserving, long-suffering bowlers.

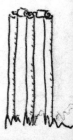

2
Gardens, Gags and Games

In case anyone is wondering, I never did quite make it as a vet. All those ball games I was playing rather got in the way and I ended up doing that for a living instead.

So if you're a dog-lover who saw the front of this book and thought it was for you, well, the dogs will be featuring from time to time, but I'm afraid there will be a bit of cricket along the way as well.

If you really don't like cricket, you can always look up Billy and Molly in the index and skip to those bits. And there's always the photos for you to have a good laugh at. Everyone likes looking at those.

Anyway, sorry if you don't feel you've had your money's worth.

It's mainly my dad's fault, I think, that I became quite so keen on cricket. He hadn't played much himself – the odd staff match here and there – but there was hardly a sport that he wasn't interested in. And there really was no end to those games we played together for years when I was a lad.

Wherever we went, we would take a ball with us and Dad would think up some game or other and invent a set of rules to turn it into a contest. When we were up at the top field by the rugby posts, throwing a tennis ball or kicking a rugby ball at the crossbar, Dad would devise a points system of some sort to turn it into a proper game. We got one point for hitting a post below the crossbar, two for hitting a post above the crossbar and a jackpot of five points for hitting the crossbar itself.

I remember the first time I was given a hard ball. My nan and grandad had bought it for me from a flea market for 20p and I spent ages bowling with it in the back garden. I was desperate to have a bat against it as well, so Dad took me up to Crawshaw playing fields, where they had a concrete wicket covered with green rubber matting, which made the surface quite bouncy.

I was really excited about going up there and I ran up the dirt path that led up the side of the field. I couldn't wait to play on that pitch with a **PROPER HARD BALL**. We were going to start with one of us bowling and the other one catching, just to get a feel for the ball, so Dad got ready to bowl and I got ready to catch. He ran in, turned his arm over and the ball pitched halfway down the wicket. Because of the green matting, it bounced a bit more than I expected and it leapt up and smacked me right in the chops. There was blood everywhere, I bawled my eyes out and we went straight home. So much for playing with a hard ball.

That might not have been quite as much fun as I had hoped, but the best cricket games I played with my dad were with a red Incrediball down at Post Hill, a short walk from our house. This was an overgrown field with trees all around it, and it was the place we used to go when I got my first dog, Pepper (there's another dog to look up in the index). I'd been pestering Mum for years to let me have a dog and she finally let me when I was 13. Pepper was a crossbreed, part Staffordshire bull terrier, part Labrador, with a few more breeds thrown in as well, but he looked very much like a Rottweiler.

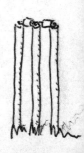

He was a lovely dog, very loyal and friendly, and he generally did as he was told. I trained him to fetch my socks and shoes for me, and when we went camping on a week-end (which was almost every weekend in summer), Pepper would bed down in my tent alongside me. We were very good pals. But probably the best thing about him was that he absolutely loved to chase and fetch a ball. So when we took him for walks down to Post Hill, Pepper became our fielder. Wherever we hit the ball, he'd sprint after it and bring it back to us. He was an absolutely brilliant fielder. He made Jonty Rhodes look like Monty Panesar.

Those games at Post Hill with my dad (and occasionally my mum) were incredibly well organised and we developed hundreds of rules over the years. As a bat, we used a stick that I'd found in the woods and ripped the bark off, about the size of a baseball bat. I think it was bent in the middle as well. Batting was a tricky business, because the pitch was nowhere near flat, there were stones all over it, so one ball could bounce over your head, then the next could roll along the floor.

Not only that, but we had the biggest set of stumps in the world. Whoever was batting would stand in front of a sapling that must have been three feet wide and six feet high. That was our stumps. So if Dad bowled me a bouncer, there wasn't much point in me ducking underneath it because I'd be bowled out. And if the ball hit me on the shoulder, I could be lbw. As I said, batting was far from easy.

If you managed to connect with the ball, and sent it flying into the trees for Pepper to fetch, there were some trees that were out and other trees that were six. If you hit the ball over a track behind the bowler, that was six as well. And if you edged the ball, there was a bigger tree behind the sapling that served as a slip cordon. If you nicked it past the tree, you were okay, but if it so much as clipped a leaf, you were out.

As you can imagine, wickets fell at regular intervals in this game, so we played ten-wicket innings. I would bat until I'd been out ten times, then Dad would do the same and try to beat me. Fifty or sixty[†] all out could well be a match-winning score. I'm not sure who won the most games. I think that I did, but my dad would probably say that he did. Actually, why don't I go and ask him? Or better still, I'll ask my mum as well. I've a feeling that we might need an independent adjudicator.

Me: Mum, who do you think won the most games when we played down at Post Hill?

Dad: I definitely won the most games.

Me: I wasn't asking you.

Mum: Oh, I don't know, it probably ended up about even. But it was always very competitive. Not just when you were playing cricket, either. Whatever you played together was competitive, even if you were just whanging a ball to each other on the beach. Most people just do that to play catch, but with you two there was always some sort of competition involved.

Dad: That's the way it should be. *All* games are competitive.

Me: Did we have many arguments about the rules?

Dad: No, because I was the sole umpire, so there were never any arguments. You just had to put up with that.

Me: I must have won most games, though. You were useless.

Dad: I wasn't, I was absolutely brilliant. Unorthodox, maybe, but brilliant all the same.

Me: You couldn't bat for toffee. And you bowled like my mother.

[†]**HOGFACT:** By the time they reach the age of SIXTY, most people's sense of smell is only half as effective as in their younger days. As you can tell by the aftershave that old blokes wear.

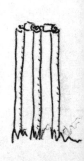

Mum: Erm, excuse me, Matthew. When I went down to Post Hill with you, I was going to walk the dog. I didn't want to have to play cricket as well.

Me: It was boring playing with you, Mum. I could just smack it anywhere when you bowled.

Mum: Cheeky sod.

Dad: My bowling was good enough for you most of the time, anyway.

Me: That was because half the time you didn't bowl it, you threw it.

Dad: You've got a point there. I did throw it from time to time.

Me: Yes, whenever there was a danger of me beating you.

Dad: Well, if you've got a lad who can hit every ball when I bowled it, what was the point? I wanted to keep challenging you. And I didn't just throw it, by the way, I sometimes threw it with sideways movement, so it spun as well. It was a good test for you.

Me: Especially when the stumps were six feet high. And I bet when you were batting you wished that you'd never sorted out my bowling action in the garden that time.

Dad: No, that was well worth the trouble. It was hard work, it took all Sunday morning, but we got there in the end. I got the run and jump sorted out, then I asked Bob Richardson about some of the more technical stuff. Bob taught at my school and he used to play in the Bradford League, so I'd ask him during the day about how to use the front arm, or how to hold the ball, and then I'd come home and tell you about it in the evening. You were a quick learner, but Bob deserves some credit.

Me: Yes, he deserves some credit for me bowling you out all the time.

Mum: Anyway, there were never any hard feelings when the two of you came back. You always seemed to have had a

good time. And at least when you were playing down there, you weren't throwing the ball against the kitchen wall or destroying the garden.

Me: Oh yes, I smashed a lot of plants down, didn't I?

Mum: You smashed everything, even in the bits you weren't supposed to go near. Anything with a head on it would come off. The daffodils never got near flowering, the gladioli never got a chance to come out. In the end, I just got some very low plants that didn't have heads on them, so it didn't make a difference whether they were hit or not.

Me: I remember one time with the flowers as though it happened in slow motion. It was in the part of the garden that I wasn't allowed to go in, but I'd been throwing the ball against the wall and bowled myself a wide, juicy half-volley. I really smacked the ball and it went directly towards some really nice flowers that you had. I knew as soon as I hit it that I was in bother. The ball seemed to travel in slow motion and it went 'Pop', straight against the flower, and the head fell straight off and tumbled to the ground.

Mum: Funnily enough, I remember that as well.

Me: Whenever I knocked the head off a flower, I'd pick it up and stick it back on top of the leaves, so it looked as though the flower hadn't come off. I just hoped you wouldn't notice.

Mum: I always noticed, Matthew. Always.

I'm not sure that leaves us any the wiser about who won the most games, but this is my book so I get the final word. I won the most games, but I might not have done if Dad hadn't sorted my bowling action out in the garden. That seems fair enough.

Once I had got the hang of jumping rather than hopping, I used to spend ages practising in the garden, running in down the side

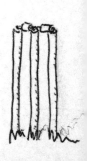

of the greenhouse and bowling into a netting fence that we had. I had to be careful, though, because we lived in a semi-detached house and there was another garden right next door. I once bowled one that hit a ridge, bounced over the fence and smashed next door's garage window.[†]

Mum and Dad still live in the same house and I was round there recently having a look at the garden, and it occurred to me that the layout there is probably responsible for a quirk that I have in my bowling action. I have a bit of a cross-action, in that my front foot goes across to the right too far when I bowl, across my body (compared with how a normal person bowls, anyway). It actually helps me to swing the ball and has helped in particular against left-handers, enabling me to get closer in to the stumps bowling over the wicket, giving me a better chance of getting an lbw.

In the layout opposite, the main set of arrows from top to bottom show my run-up and pitch in the garden. The two-way arrows towards the bottom show where I threw the ball against the kitchen wall and smacked it back across the patio. You can see there wasn't a straight line coming down from the side of the greenhouse to the fence where the wickets were on the other side of the garden, so I had to adjust and come across myself in my action. It had never occurred to me until recently, but that could well have led to the way I have bowled ever since. So perhaps every time I dismissed Matthew Hayden when I was playing for England, I should have been thanking my dad for putting the greenhouse in such a daft place.

Not so far from our house, about a ten-minute walk (fifteen if you had a heavy bag), was our local cricket club, Pudsey Congs, which is where I went to start playing some proper cricket. I

[†]**HOGFACT:** In Massachusetts, snoring is prohibited unless all bedroom windows are closed and securely locked. I'm led to believe that a man's punishment for this crime is a slap from the wife.

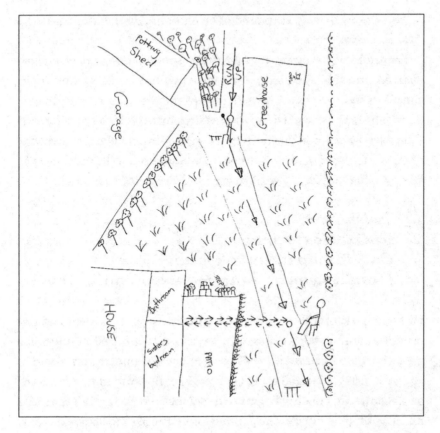

started going down there at the age of 11 and, to begin with, we played eight-a-side, sixteen overs per team, with four pairs of batsmen going in for four overs at a time, and losing eight runs every time one of them was out. From the first time I went, I was really keen, and I think Mum was even keener to have me out of the house. Soon enough, the cricket club became the centre of my little universe.

I was lucky to have such a good club just down the road. I suppose that anywhere you go in Yorkshire you'll never be far from a decent cricket club, but I certainly couldn't have done much better than having Pudsey Congs – or Pudsey Pongos, as we were known – right on my doorstep. It was a friendly place with a good family atmosphere, the bar would be full most nights and the first team

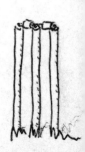

played a very decent standard of cricket, in the Bradford League first division.

I worked my way up through the junior sides and was then drafted into the third team for a season when I was 15. I played a couple of second-team games as well that year, but to my amazement, the next season I was fast-tracked into the first team by Phil Carrick, the former Yorkshire left-arm spinner who was captain of the club. Ferg, as he was known to everyone (think 'Carrickfergus'), had obviously seen something in me that he liked.

♫ *I wish I was*
In Carrickfergus
Only for nights in Ballygran
I would swim over the deepest ocean ... ♫ ♪

I'd been a bit of a late developer up to this point. As well as my cricket, I'd done some judo and played quite a bit of rugby, but I gave those up because all the other lads were bigger and broader than me. From the age of 16, though, I really started to grow and, as a result, my bowling began to develop. To this day, I'm not sure exactly what Ferg saw in me, maybe just a big fast bowler's arse and an ability to swing the ball.

I certainly used to swing the ball in the nets at Congs, but that might have had something to do with my special ball. There was one ball in particular that I used to keep for bowling with in the nets and I looked after it lovingly. At home, I would get Cherry Blossom shoe polish out of Mum and Dad's cupboard, put a dollop of that on the ball and buff it up with a shoebrush. Then before nets on a Wednesday night I would give the ball one last polish with a shining brush, and make absolutely sure that nobody else nicked it when I went to practice. That was my ball and nobody else was getting their grubby mitts on it.

For all that Ferg whistled me up into the first team at Congs, for the first few games all I did was bowl two or three overs and

spend the rest of the innings fielding, wondering when I was going to get another bowl. After a few games, I started to find this frustrating. 'Ferg,' I said, 'why do you want me here playing a fifty-over game if I'm only going to bowl a few overs?' The answer was that he was easing me in, allowing me to get a feel for first-team cricket before too much was expected of my bowling. He didn't want to rush me because this was, after all, a very decent standard of club cricket, probably the best in Yorkshire (and therefore, so some locals would have you believe, probably the best in the world).

As the season progressed, I started to bowl a few more overs, but I was given an early idea of the quality I was up against when we played Spen Victoria. That was the game I came across Chris Pickles, the Yorkshire all-rounder who was coming to the end of his county career but spent his weekends terrorising club bowlers. He just used to come in and blast it; most of the grounds weren't very big and he could smash 100 in no time.

I opened the bowling that day and had one of the openers caught at slip with a lovely outswinger (no shoe polish involved this time, just the new ball curving away nicely). Pickles was next in and he wandered out to ask the other opening batsman what was happening. 'Oh, it's just swinging a bit,' his mate said.

I'd heard all about Pickles, so I ran in really hard at him next ball. The ball swung alright, and landed on a length, but he just plonked his front foot down the wicket, hit through the line of the ball and sent it soaring over cow corner, where it landed on top of some faraway nets. I couldn't believe it. I just stood halfway down the wicket, hands on my hips, looking at him with a puzzled expression on my face. He ambled down the wicket, tapped the pitch with his bat, and muttered out of the corner of his mouth: 'Anti-swing device, son. Anti-swing device.'

So I was on a steep learning curve, but I loved the atmosphere and I just wanted to bowl. We had a good team, including former Yorkshire players like Ferg and Neil Hartley, and current ones like Richard Kettleborough, while James Middlebrook came up

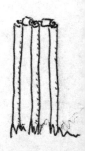

through the ranks with me. We also had some very useful over-seas players, such as VVS Laxman from India and Yousuf Youhana from Pakistan. I'd be bumping into them again later in my career.

Lax was only 19 when he came to us, but it was clear he was a class act. After one game in which he'd scored a few runs and I'd taken a couple of wickets, we were chatting to Ferg in the club-house. 'One day,' Ferg said, 'you two will play against each other in Test match cricket.' We just laughed at him and told him not to be so daft. Lax had only played a handful of games and I was a raggy-arsed 17-year-old who'd just broken into Pudsey Congs first team, so it was a pretty outlandish thing to say.

The sad thing was that Ferg didn't live to see his prediction come true. In January 2000, at the age of 47, he died after suffering from leukaemia. Less than two years later, I played for England in Mohali against an India team that included VVS Laxman.

He was a great man, Ferg, and I miss him terribly. It's impos-sible to overstate his influence on me in those early days at Congs. He really took me under his wing. Whether we were out in the field or chatting in the bar after a game, he always had time for me. With my bowling, he would always emphasise to me the importance of length. 'Length, Matthew, length.' He'd tell me to go to the nets, put a hankie down on a length and see how many times I could hit it in an over. I used to spend hours doing that, going up to the nets at Congs after school and bowling on my own at a set of stumps with a hankie or a lump of wood on a good length. And then, when we were playing a match on Saturday, I would have Ferg standing at mid-off and growling at me. Even now, fifteen years later, when I bowl too short or too full, I can some-times hear Ferg's gruff voice grumbling in my ear: 'Length, Matthew, length.'

But I must have been getting my length right most of the time, because in 1995, after only a couple of seasons in the first team at Congs, Ferg recommended me to Yorkshire. I was still only 18, doing the second year of my A-levels at Grangefield comprehensive, but when schoolwork allowed I was able to take the next steps of my cricketing education in the Yorkshire Second XI.

In general, club cricket with Pudsey Pongos prepared me pretty well for life on the county Second XI circuit. There were always new lessons to be learned, but I don't remember feeling particularly out of my depth at any point, at least not from a cricketing point of view. But one thing that is drastically different about playing three-day matches, and spending a lot of time on the road as a result, is that you spend a hell of a lot of time with your teammates.

This is a group of young blokes, many of whom are easily bored and need to find things to occupy their underdeveloped brains, a situation that inevitably results in a lot of practical jokes. For quite some time in the Yorkshire second team, I felt well out of my depth in terms of the pranks. And to make matters worse, the prankster-in-chief was the coach himself.

Doug Padgett was a coach from the old school, a former Yorkshire batsman who had been the club's coach for donkey's years and usually travelled with the second team. He was a good bloke, but he had a time-honoured way of making a new lad feel welcome.

Take the piss out of him whenever possible.

This is the man who would welcome a lad making his debut by sending him round to take the day's lunch order. 'Here, Twatook,' he would say (he called all the younger lads Twatook). 'Do the lunches for us, will you? Go round and see how many of the lads want steak and how many want salmon, then nip to the kitchen and tell the chef.' So the new lad would eagerly set about his task, taking all eleven orders, only to find when he got to the kitchen that the only option available for lunch was lasagne, something that Padge and the other ten players were only too well aware of.

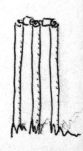

Another trick of Padge's was to ask a new lad to go to his car and find out the Test score from the radio. James Middlebrook was one who stumbled into this trap. 'Midders, Twatook, nip to your car and find out the Test score for us, will you? There's a good lad.' So off Midders trooped to his car and sat there for ages, frantically tuning and re-tuning the radio in an attempt to find Test Match Special. He returned slightly crestfallen, having failed in his mission.

'Sorry, Padge, the Test match doesn't seem to be on the radio today.'

'No, Twatook, it wouldn't be. They don't play Test cricket on a Wednesday.'

A lesson swiftly learned for Midders, who would think twice before his esteemed coach sent him off on any errands again. I'd say I felt sorry for him, but most of us suffered in a similar way, some worse than others.

Midders got away lightly compared to the poor young whippersnapper who had travelled with Padge on an away trip to Glamorgan a few years earlier. This was before my time, but the tale was often told of an unnamed player – let's just call him Twatook – who sat in Padge's car for the long drive down to Wales along with a couple of his new team-mates.

As they travelled down the M5 and started to approach the Welsh border, Padge turned to the young lad sitting quietly in the back.

'You have got your passport with you, haven't you, Twatook? We're about to go into Wales.'

'Erm, erm, erm, no Padge, I don't think I have,' came the timid reply.

'Oh Christ, didn't anybody tell you? We're going to Wales. It's a different country. What are we going to do when we get to the border? We're going to have to hide you.'

So Padge pulled his car over, opened the boot, moved several cricket bags to the back seat and told his victim to lie down in the boot until they had crossed the border. Young Twatook climbed in, snuggled down and Padge slammed the boot lid shut. He drove off into Wales, leaving his captive in the boot to think about the foolishness of forgetting his passport. Once the border had been safely negotiated – armed checkpoints and all – the hostage was released, poor lad. I'm sure Padge felt that it was all good character-building stuff.

Where Padge had led, there were plenty of disciples ready to follow, which has made the Headingley dressing-room a dangerous place to be at times over the last few years. Probably the biggest irritant in the Yorkshire team in recent years – myself aside – has been Anthony McGrath.

The problem with Mags is that he is easily bored and he likes to fill his time by pissing off his team-mates. A few years ago, one of his little pet projects was to put his team-mates' cars up for sale in *Auto Trader* magazine, always at a bargain price carefully calculated by Mags himself. The advert for the car would usually say something along the lines of:

'Owner forced to move abroad. Price reduced for quick sale. Please call ...'

and then include the player's mobile phone number. Inevitably, for such a bargain, these adverts attracted plenty of interest from potential buyers, prompting an endless stream of phone calls to the victim's mobile. Time after time, he would have to say, 'I'm sorry for the misunderstanding, but it's not for sale.' Which could be quite amusing on the first two or three occasions. But when it came to the 25th call in the space of an hour, it could start to become more than a little irritating.

Bogus adverts aside, Mags has often been implicated in one of the great scandals that has swirled around the Yorkshire team for several seasons now. This is the ongoing mystery of Jack the Snipper, a long-running case that has yet to be cracked and has

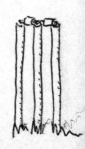

baffled some of the finest criminal investigators in Yorkshire and beyond.

The culprit in this case is known to be someone with access to the Yorkshire dressing-room. He (or she?) waits until the dressing-room is deserted, then quickly seizes his (or her?) moment, moving in with a pair of scissors and snipping the toes off a sock belonging to the intended victim. When the victim goes to pull his sock on after the game, he pulls it up to his knee and realises, to his horror, that he has become the latest victim of **JACK (OR JACQUELINE?) THE SNIPPER**.

Understandably, nobody has ever owned up to these crimes, so the mystery remains unsolved. Police now suspect that the culprit may have multiple identities.

Not the most original of practical jokes, perhaps, but most of the Yorkshire players have seen it as a mildly amusing, relatively harmless gag if they happened to be a victim. But one season the Snipper targeted David Byas so many times that he no longer saw the funny side. Gadge, as he was known (for his extraordinary Inspector Gadget-like extending arms in the slips), was our captain at the time and, after his socks had been snipped for the umpteenth time, he decided the time had come to put an end to the tomfoolery.

In the build-up to one Sunday League game at Headingley, Gadge told us that we all had to be at the ground by 10 o'clock in the morning, even though the match wasn't due to begin until 1.30 in the afternoon. It seemed a strange request, but Gadge was keen on punctuality, so everyone dutifully turned up at the appointed time. At which point the skipper took us all out to the middle of the ground at Headingley and asked us to sit in a big circle. He sat down with us and then told us why we were all sitting there looking as though we were about to play Pass the Parcel. 'Right, you lot,' he said, 'nobody is moving from this circle until I find out which pillock has been snipping my f***ing socks. I just want to know who it is, then we can have a quick chat, move on and all go for some lunch.' Nobody said a word. For a good few minutes there was complete and utter silence.

'Come on,' said Gadge, after a while. 'I'm not joking here. We're going to get to the bottom of this nonsense. Whoever has been snipping my socks is sitting in this circle and I want to know who it is.'

Still nobody said anything. There was another long, uncomfortable silence. After we'd been there for about half an hour, Gadge became more insistent – still reasonably calm, but the tone of his voice raised slightly. 'Listen,' he said. 'If nobody has got the balls to own up to doing these stupid stunts, it's a piss-poor effort. All you need to do is be big enough to own up, then we can move on.'

And still nobody said anything. We had probably been there for around an hour when Gadge started to get angry. 'For f***'s sake,' he said, 'will somebody **PLEASE** tell me who has been snipping my f***ing socks?'

Once again, there was only silence. And I kid you not, we were sitting out on that field, in that circle, for three hours. **THREE WHOLE HOURS!** Eventually, at one o'clock, the opposition captain arrived out in the middle, asking if we were ready to toss up, and Gadge, as captain, had no option but to get up and leave us. So Jack the Snipper had slipped off the leash again and he remains at large to this very day. If you ever find yourself having to spend a day in or around the Yorkshire dressing-room, it may be worth your while packing a spare pair of socks.

The same season as that unfortunate incident, there was an outbreak of a similar – but unrelated – crime in the Yorkshire second team. At the time, I was in and out of the first and second teams, so I saw some of the events first hand and have called on extremely reliable witnesses to fill me in on the bits I missed. Again, this spate of crimes involved some tampering with the kit of a

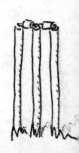

senior member of the dressing-room, but this time socks were not involved. This time the crime was theft and the stolen items were underpants belonging to Steve Oldham, Esso, the second team coach.

Pinching someone's underpants might, again, seem like a fairly low-level jape, causing brief hilarity in the dressing-room, and mild irritation to the victim. But if you're playing away from home for a four-day match and you have four pairs of undies stolen, it can be more than a little frustrating. It's diffi-cult to replace the pants, for a start, because you have to be at a cricket match all day while the shops are open, and a week without undies is, I imagine, not much fun. And if, like Esso, this happens to you for seven four-day matches in succession, that's twenty-eight pairs of underpants that have gone missing. Boxer shorts, Y-fronts, briefs; you name them, Esso lost the lot.

As you'd expect, Esso grew more and more frustrated as his stock of underpants became gradually depleted during the season. But he tried hard to keep his cool, to make it seem as though the thefts weren't getting to him, to deny the prankster the satisfac-tion of seeing him upset.

That pretence of calm became harder to maintain once his pants started to reappear in increasingly unusual ways. The first pair was returned during a game at Bradford Park Avenue. Esso was sitting watching the game, when he casually glanced up at the flag-pole and noticed a pair of his Y-fronts billowing in the breeze where the Yorkshire flag should have been. Nobody would own up to hoist-ing the offending item, so Esso made us all run around the ground for an hour in the pouring rain at the end of the day's play.

The next second team game was at York and we travelled to the ground as usual in three or four cars. I was in one of the middle cars and Esso was in one of the cars further back. When we turned off the A64 for the last leg of the journey, we saw the road sign saying 'Welcome to York', but hung over the corner of the sign

was another pair of Esso's undies. I'm not sure whether he stopped his car to retrieve them or not, but at the end of the game at York we found ourselves running round the outfield again as punishment.

Perhaps the thief was starting to take pity on Esso by now, because the underpants were being returned to him on a regular basis. Never in a straightforward way, but at least he was gaining pants rather than losing them. I wasn't around to see the next pair returned, but I heard that they were discovered during the second team's next home game at Bingley, where the grounds-man had a dog. At some point during that game, the grounds-man's dog was spotted running onto the field, wearing what looked very much like a pair of men's briefs. I missed out on the post-match laps of the boundary that time, but by this stage Yorkshire's second team must have been the fittest side on the circuit.

It was now getting towards the end of the season and, whether or not the thief was running out of ideas, he was running out of time to return the rest of his loot. Our final home game of the season was at Castleford and, when Esso drove into the ground, he was finally put out of his misery. Strung around the railings of the car park, like bunting at a school fair, were the remaining twenty-one pairs of underpants, good as new, ready to be reclaimed by their rightful owner, and Esso's torment was at an end. Isn't it nice when a crime story has a happy ending?

I don't want to name names here in case anyone's lawyer gets onto me, but there were strong suspicions that Alex Morris, our gangly all-rounder from Barnsley, may have been involved in these pranks. And Gareth Batty, the off-spinner, was also considered not to be beyond suspicion. But once again, the crime remained unsolved. For some reason, Alex left Yorkshire a couple of years later and moved to the other end of the country to play for Hampshire. Similarly, Batts soon departed to play for Surrey. I've never found out whether their departures were related to the case of Esso's undies.

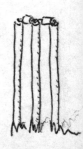

Once I had finished my A-levels in 1995, I spent most of the summers of 1996 and 1997 playing for Yorkshire's Second XI. I made my first-class debut in July 1996, against South Africa A, but didn't get a run of games in the first team until a couple of years later. In the meantime, I was able to go back on a weekend and play for Pudsey Congs with Ferg and my mates. And that would invariably be followed by a good few beers in the clubhouse on a Saturday night, which I was quickly learning was all part of the fun.

By this time, a promising ginger-haired wicketkeeper called Matthew Duce had made his way into the first team at Congs. For me, as an outswing bowler, it is always important to have a decent wicketkeeper in your side to hang onto all those nicks, so Ducey was good for me because he had a safe pair of hands. And the fact that he had an attractive sister who would come to watch us was an added bonus.

Sarah was a similar age to me, she was single at the time, and this gave Ferg an idea. One Saturday, when we were playing away to East Bierley, I was sitting watching the game while we batted, and Ferg said to me: 'I bet you couldn't get a date with Ducey's sister, Hoggy. No chance at all. In fact, I'll bet you a fiver that you can't.'

Unbeknown to Ferg, in the previous couple of weeks Sarah and I had already had a couple of liaisons that we had managed to keep a secret. But I wasn't about to tell Ferg that, so the next week I turned up and was able to announce, to his astonishment, that I had indeed managed to get a date with the supposedly impossible Miss Duce, and I would be going out with her that evening. What a result! A date with an attractive girl and a fiver from Ferg already in my pocket to buy her a couple of bags of crisps. That must've been the easiest money I've ever earned.

Sarah and I soon became good mates and, for a girl, she wasn't a bad 'un at all. I must have been keen, too, because I even started

taking her along when I went to meet Ferg in the pub (yes, I knew how to show a girl a good time). I used to go to his local, the Busfeild [*sic*] Arms in East Morton, he would have a pint of Tetley's, I'd have a pint of Guinness and we would talk about cricket, the universe and everything else besides.

Even once I was on the books at Yorkshire, if I ever needed a few words of wisdom I would go back to Ferg's pub to chat to him, and Sarah would usually come with me. Halfway through the 1998 season, I was becoming fed up with the lack of first-team cricket I was getting at Yorkshire. I'd been doing well in the second team, but there were a lot of pace bowlers around at the time. There was Darren Gough and Peter Hartley opening the bowling, then Chris Silverwood, Craig White, Paul Hutchison, Ryan Sidebottom, Gavin Hamilton and Alex Wharf. It was an amazing crop of seam bowlers.

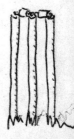

In one second-team game at Harrogate, I took seven wickets against Worcestershire and they expressed an interest in signing me. I asked Ferg for advice and he suggested that I should go down to Worcester with Sarah, have a look around the place and see what we thought. We went down there for a weekend, stayed in a hotel and had a chat to Bill Athey, who was Worcestershire's second-team coach. He had played in that game at Harrogate and kindly missed a straight one that I bowled to him. We quite liked the look of Worcester, but I went back to Yorkshire and told them my situation, and they persuaded me that I still had a good chance of playing in the first team. We mulled it over and eventually I decided to back myself to succeed at Yorkshire.

So Sarah and I were very much an item by now and before long I was invited for a game of golf with her dad, Colin. We went to play at Gotts Park in Leeds and it soon became apparent to me that I was dealing with a family who weren't backwards in coming forwards when Colin told me that he had had a vasectomy. Why did he need to tell me that? I'd only just met the bloke, and I barely knew what a vasectomy was, but Colin clearly decided that it was something I needed to know. There must have been a long and awkward silence while I worked out what I was supposed to say in response. In the end I probably just grunted.

Things didn't get any better once the golf started. On one of the early holes, he played his tee shot, then wandered off to the right and rested his three-wood against his golf bag. I told him he'd be well advised not to stand there, because I never really knew where I was going to hit the thing. So he stepped back a couple of paces, and it was a good job he did. From my tee shot, I whacked the biggest slice imaginable. The ball flew off at 45 degrees and smashed straight into Colin's three wood. It was a freakish shot, it hit bang smack in the middle of his carbon shaft and the club snapped clean in two.

Not the best of impressions to make on my prospective father-in-law.

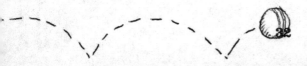

But at least Colin seemed to like me, which was something that certainly couldn't be said of Sarah's mum, Carole, in those days. She had found out about the start of our relationship while she and Colin were away on holiday in France. Sarah hadn't gone with her, so Carole phoned up while she was away to check that all was well.

'How are things at home?' she asked Sarah. 'Any news?'

'Not much really, Mum,' said Sarah. 'Oh, except I've got a new boyfriend.'

'Oh, that's nice. Anyone I know?'

'Well, yes, you know of him.'

'Is he from the cricket club?'

'Yes, he is.' There was a short pause while Carole worked out the likely candidates.

'And will I like him?' she asked.

'Erm, not sure, Mum. I think you will.'

'Oh, Sarah, please don't tell me it's that Matthew Hoggard. That boy is so rude. And he's always drunk.'

'Er, yes, I'm afraid it is him. Sorry, Mum.'

So even from that early stage, Sarah was feeling the need to apologise for me. But I'm glad to say that the relationship with my in-laws has progressed considerably since those first days. We get on like a house on fire now and I couldn't wish for better in-laws. I still regularly play golf with Colin – the Badger, as he has come to be known, because he's as mad as a badger about his cricket, buying a season ticket for Yorkshire and sitting in the same seat at Headingly all summer. I also still play cricket with Ducey, Sarah's brother, when I can. As for Carole, I gradually managed to persuade her that I wasn't *always* drunk and that I wasn't quite as rude as she had first thought. I've got absolutely no idea what gave her those impressions in the first place, no idea at all. She eventually realised what a fine, upstanding, polite, charming, sober, intelligent individual I was. But it's a good job that Sarah didn't listen to her mother's advice on everything, or I don't think our relationship would have lasted too long.

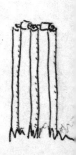

FIVE GREAT THINGS ABOUT BEING A CRICKETER

WORKING CONDITIONS

You don't have to work in the rain, in the dark, or in the winter: when it gets cold, we just go to a warmer part of the world and play there instead.

REGULAR BREAKS

You get breaks for lunch *and* tea built into your working day. And breaks for drinks every hour or so as well. Imagine trying to take that many coffee breaks in a normal working day.

LATE STARTS

Our work doesn't really start until 11 o'clock: okay, we usually have to be at the ground for 9 o'clock, but we don't really have to be functioning fully until play starts at 11 o'clock.

THE GREAT OUTDOORS

We get to spend all day outside rather than being stuck in an office: a bad day on the cricket field is better than a good day in the office.

SKIVING

Half the time when we're at work, we don't actually have to do anything: when your team is batting, you can either sit and chat with your mates or, if necessary, go to sleep on the job. Nice work if you can get it, eh?

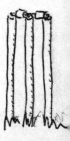

Sarah's Guide to

	MATTHEW	SARAH
MON	Tidy bedroom	
TUES		
WEDS		Sort Matthew's diary
THURS	Cut grass	
FRI		
SAT		
		Chris & Sarah pm
SUN	Cook dinner	

Hmmm, not one of Matthew's strengths. The real danger area is down his side of our bed, which is just one BIG PILE OF STUFF. Loads of books, pairs of jeans, paperwork (often unopened). Not a pretty sight.

Toy air guns BANNED!
(Matthew, not Ernie!)

He's FANATICAL about his grass. He'll happily spend hours on his little tractor getting the stripes right on the lawn. I can tell by the look on his face if it's been a good cut or not!

Matthew's very keen on Trivial Pursuit or Scrabble after a meal, whether with friends or just the two of us. He's ridiculously competitive. He used to have a right old sulk if he lost, although he's getting better at hiding his disappointment in his old age.

36

Hoggy Around the House

ERNIE	DOGS
	Biscuits
Daddy Day!	
	Bath
Go to Fun Barn	
Nursery	
	LONG walk

Record Ross Kemp on Gangs NO!!

Matthew is absolutely brill with Ernie: changing nappies, feeding meals, taking him swimming. When I come home, they'll both probably be filthy and Ernie will be wearing a strange outfit. But they'll both have had the time of their lives.

Given the choice, my beloved husband would live his whole life wearing old tracksuit bottoms and a scruffy t-shirt or dodgy jumper. Sometimes he'll go out in public like that, with his slippers on, to collect a takeaway or pick Ernie up from nursery. I wonder if they think he's a tramp?

Oh yes, the lad can throw a good roast dinner together. And he's always coming up with new concoctions (some of which I think he's going to reveal later in the book) Be careful, though, because they don't always work.

Matthew, chuck old clothes away – especially GREEN AND MAROON JUMPER!

PUZZLES

I've no doubt that 999,999,999 of my 1,000,000,000 readers will be completely engrossed in the book by now and desperate to get to the next chapter. But just in case you're the odd one out and feel in need of a break, here are a few puzzles to keep you amused. If you like SuDoku, sorry, I couldn't draw one of those ...

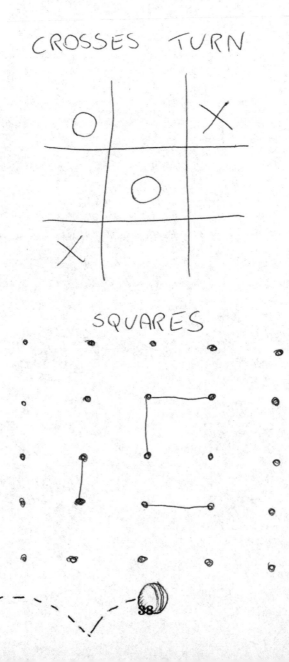

CROSSES TURN

SQUARES

YOUR TURN

H E _ D _ _ G _ E _

MY HOME GROUND

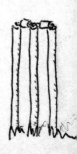

39

3

Wild and Free

I can remember coming of age clearly, because turning 18 hit me with a thud. The precise moment that the thud occurred was during my 18th birthday party at Pudsey Congs clubhouse (where else?). I was standing on a chair, getting carried away dancing to *Cotton-Eyed Joe*, and I smashed my head on the fire exit sign. Not quite behaving like a proper grown-up yet, then.

Unsurprisingly, it was Ferg who decided that the time had come for me to broaden my horizons beyond the playing fields of Yorkshire. I'd played my first few games for the county Second XI in the summer of 1995, and not done too badly, but I was still extremely raw, both as a bowler and as a lad.

So Ferg got in touch with Richard Lumb, his old Yorkshire teammate, who had moved out to South Africa and was involved with the Pirates club in Johannesburg. 'Hoggy, it would do you good to go abroad,' Ferg said. 'I've sorted you out a club in South Africa, You'll have a great time. See you in six months.' And that was pretty much that.

I spent two winters with the Pirates, then returned to South Africa a couple of years later in 1998, a little less raw, for the first of two seasons playing first-class cricket with Free State in

Bloemfontein. Both of them were fantastic experiences which, in different ways, helped me to find my way in the world.

My first spell in Johannesburg, shortly after I'd done my A-levels in 1995, was the first time I'd lived away from home. It was also the first time I'd been in an aeroplane. We'd been on umpteen family camping holidays to France when I was younger, but we'd always driven in the car and I'd never been up in the skies. My mum and dad drove me down to Heathrow, and by the time we got to London, I think my fears had gradually given way to excitement. Never mind the six months away from home, I thought, I'm actually going to go up in an aeroplane! *Nneeeeeooowwwm-mmm!*

When I landed at Johannesburg airport, I must have come across like a little boy lost. For what seemed like ages I was looking for Richard Lumb and he was looking for me, both of us without success. He was going round asking anybody with a cricket bag – and there were quite a few – if they were Matthew Hoggard; I was going round looking for a tall bloke with grey hair, and there seemed to be plenty of them as well. Eventually, we found each other and got into his car. We got lost on the drive away from the airport, but he finally managed to take us to the famous Wanderers club, where he set the tone for my trip by buying me lunch and a beer or two.

And that was to become my staple diet for much of my stay in South Africa. Not so much the lunch; just the beer.

I don't think I'd been warned, by Ferg or anyone else, just how much the South Africans like their beer. They must be the thirstiest nation on earth. Given the chance, they'd have beer for breakfast, and plenty of them do.

Before I'd even played a game with my new team-mates at the Pirates, they took me out to welcome me to the club. We went to the bar at the Randburg Waterfront, a lake just outside Johannesburg with loads of bars and restaurants around it. The evening started with a few convivial drinks, which helped me to relax as I

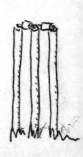

was introduced to these strange people who, like it or lump it, were to become my new friends.

After we'd been in the bar for a couple of hours, I felt myself being shepherded towards the stage. When I was up there, everyone started singing, and I was given a half-pint glass full of the most disgusting-looking green drink. I had no idea what was in it, but something in it had curdled. I later found out that they had gone along the top shelf of spirits and topped up the glass with Coke. Yum yum.

The whole pub was singing at me to down it, so what else could I do? I remember drinking it, but I don't recall much after that. I just remember waking up in the morning feeling very, very ill. But that had been my initiation ceremony at my new club. Welcome to the Pirates.

The problem was that just about every week seemed to be an initiation. The first game I played was for the club's second team, so they could have a look at what I was capable of (and perhaps to check that I was still able to bowl a ball in a straight line after my ordeal at the Waterfront). That first game was away from home against Wits Technical College and, in one of those strange coincidences that cricket often throws up, also making his debut for Pirates that day was Gerard Brophy, who a couple of years later would be my captain at Free State and a few years after that came to keep wicket for Yorkshire.

I was quite surprised to find that it was really cold that day. I hadn't initially planned to pack my cricket jumpers, I just expected it to be baking hot all the time, but I was glad I'd shoved them in at the last minute because it was bloody freezing. Anyway, both Gerard and I did the business on our debuts: he got 100 and I took four wickets.

So the cricket had gone well, but what really got to me was the fines system in the clubhouse afterwards. This was basically an excuse (yet *another* excuse) for making people drink vast quantities of beer, as decided by the fines-master of the day. Fines would

be handed down for stupid comments made during the day, for embarrassing bits of fielding or for any other random transgression that could be deemed punishable by beer. This wasn't something I'd encountered back at Pudsey Congs. Depending on who the fines-master was for that particular game, the punishment for a brainless comment would probably be to down a bottle of Castle. And that stupid shot you played? Oh yes, you'd better down another bottle for that as well. Needless to say, there was no mercy shown to the newcomers.

The worst offender for each game would be sentenced to death, which meant downing a beer every five minutes. The fines-master would have a watch, and every five minutes a cry of 'Cuckoo, cuckoo!' would ring out, signifying that the victim had to stand up and sink another bottle of beer. This would continue for as long as the fines session lasted, sometimes well over an hour. And to thank us for our sterling contributions in our first game for the Pirates, both Gerard and I were sentenced to death that day. So that was Initiation Mark II and another grim hangover the next morning. And there would be plenty more of those to follow.

Throughout my first year in Jo'burg, I stayed with the club chairman, Barry Skjoldhammer (pronounced Shult-hammer) and his family, his wife Nicky, their daughter Kim who was 11, and her brother David, who was 9. I'm not sure they knew what they were letting themselves in for when they agreed to take me in, but they were absolutely fantastic to me and treated me like one of their own. They had a nice house, a games room with a pool table, their own bar and a nice garden with a swimming pool. Life was good. They even took pity on me one morning after I'd come in from a night out at 5.30 a.m. The front door had been bolted and I couldn't get into the house, so I kicked Sheba, the family dog, out of her bed on the veranda and curled up there for an hour before everyone else woke up. I wasn't sure what Nicky would say when she found me lying there at 6.30 a.m., but she actually told me off for not waking them up to let me in.

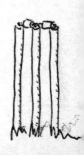

After about three months, the chance came up for me to move out and go to stay in a flat with Alvin Kallicharran, who was also playing club cricket out there. By now, the Skjoldhammers knew that I was a bit wet behind the ears because they said that they wanted me to stay with them so they could keep an eye on me. And no way did I want to go: I got cooked for, I got lifts everywhere, there were kids to play with and they were lovely people. It was great. Even now, I look on the Skjoldhammers as my second family.

It wasn't just at my new home that I was made to feel welcome. Although it may seem as though they were setting out to kill me with alcohol (I survived more than one death sentence), I couldn't have been happier with the Pirates.

For a start, we had a very decent team. When they weren't playing for Transvaal, we had Ken Rutherford, the former New Zealand captain, Mark Rushmere and Steven Jack, who both played for South Africa, and a few guys, like Paul Smith, my fellow opening bowler, who had played for Transvaal.

I also managed to take a few wickets, which helped me to be accepted quickly. It didn't take me long to adjust my bowling because conditions suited me nicely. We were at altitude in Jo'burg, where the ball tends to swing more in the thinner air, and I was fairly nippy in those days and generally caused a few problems.

It was quite a different club from Pudsey Congs. Back home, I'd been used to there being lots of families around on a weekend. Cricket matches were a family day out on a Saturday and there would always be wives and kids in the clubhouse after the game. Pirates was a bit more spit and sawdust. The wives might come to watch for a while, but the club was mainly frequented by men. For me, that was just part of the learning about a different cricketing and social culture.

There was always a great atmosphere at the club. We used to play our games over two days at a weekend and, as a bowler, there was nothing better than getting your overs out of the way on a Saturday, then turning up on a Sunday morning to watch the batsmen do the hard work, especially as play started at 9 a.m. on the second day.

The Pirates' ground was in a bowl, so we used to sit up on the banking and start up a *scottle braai*, a gas barbecue with a flat pan on top, and cook up breakfast for everyone. We'd take it in turns to get the bacon, the eggs, the sausages, and fill our faces with sandwiches while the batsmen went out to do their stuff. I would lose count of the number of times that someone would have just got a sandwich in their hand and a wicket would fall, prompting a distressed cry of: 'Shit, I was looking forward to that sandwich. Can someone hold onto it for a while?'

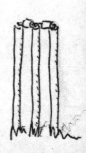

I wasn't paid to play for Pirates and I lived rent-free with the Skjoldhammers, but I did a few odd jobs to pay for my beer money. I helped out at Barry's Labelpak business, for example, putting together packs of flat-packed furniture, I coached the Pirates kids on a Saturday morning and also did a bit of coaching at Rosemount Primary School during the week. At the school, I remember clipping one irritating lad round the back of the head when he wouldn't do as I told him. I then got a bit worried when he said: 'I'm going to go and tell the headmaster you did that.'

Fortunately, the headmaster was Paul Smith, the Pirates' opening bowler. When the young lad went into the headmaster's office, he said: 'Mr Smith, Mr Hoggard just hit me round the back of the head.' So Smithy hit him round the back of the head himself and said: 'Well, you must have deserved it then. Now get back to your lesson straight away.' Good job that wasn't a few years later. I'd probably have got a lawsuit for doing that nowadays.

The best job I had in Jo'burg was being a barman at the Wanderers' ground for the big games there. The Pirates had a box and, naturally, they asked me to man the bar. I can't say it was the most taxing of jobs. I didn't even have to take cash because there was always some sort of raffle ticket system in operation. I just had to open a few bottles of beer, pour the occasional glass of wine and watch a lot of cricket. And it just so happened that England were touring South Africa that year, so I got to spend a full five days at the second Test when Mike Atherton and Jack Russell staged their famous rearguard action. They certainly worked a lot harder out there than I did up in the bar.

But the important thing about my jobs was that they gave me enough beer money to take advantage of the opportunities for socialising provided by my thoughtful Pirates team-mates. There were plenty of them. Sometimes, I would go out the night before a game with the Smith brothers, Paul and Bruce, and we would put our cricket kit in the car before we went out. That way, we could stay out until the early hours, then drive to wherever we were playing, get a few hours' kip in the car and wait for our team-mates to wake us up when they arrived. One important part of the procedure was that, before you went to sleep, you had to make sure that your car was under a tree and facing west, so you wouldn't get burned by the sun when it came up in the morning.

Drink-driving was just not an issue in South Africa in those days. There would be times when we would go on a night out and, while we were driving from one bar to another, everyone would jump out of the car at a red traffic light, run around the car until the lights turned to green, then the one standing nearest the driver's door had to jump back in and start driving. Everyone else had to squeeze in as well if they could and, if they didn't, they were left behind. There would be people jumping through windows, hanging onto the roof. We obviously thought it was funny at the time, but it seems like absolute bloody madness now.

Another time when I was out with Bruce Smith, we'd ended up in the Cat's Pyjamas (nice name), a 24-hour drinking place. For some reason, Bruce suggested we go to the Emmarentia Dam, which was a short drive away. He dared me to swim the 30 metres or so across it, run round a lamppost at the other side, and swim back again. In the clear-sighted wisdom created by God-knows-how-many bottles of Castle lager, I said I'd do it, as long as he did it with me.

We parked up by the dam on an empty side street, took our clothes off in the car and walked to the dam, stark bollock naked. We started swimming across the dam and I was going fairly well, thinking: 'Yep, this isn't so bad, I'll manage it no problem.' Then it suddenly started thundering and lightning, which made me think we ought to get a move on. We swam across to the other side of the dam, ran round the lamppost and had swum halfway back across the other way when lightning struck the dam. I'll never forget that feeling when the shock got through to me, sending tingles throughout my body. Even in my less-than-sober state, I was more than a bit worried. 'Do you feel all right?' Bruce asked me. 'Erm, yes, I think so,' I lied back.

We were even more worried when we approached the shore and saw a police van parked up near our car. The policemen were wandering around, shining a light into the car and checking the surrounding areas. We stayed in the water[†] and hid in the reeds at the edge of the dam. 'If I get caught here, stark bollock naked,' I thought, 'I really am in trouble.' The police seemed to be there for ages and we ducked down every time they shone their torches towards the water. Thankfully they went eventually without spotting us and we scuttled off home to bed, feeling a lot more sober than we had done an hour or two before.

I suppose that these days were my first real taste of freedom, the slightly wild days that everyone needs to get out of their systems. No real responsibilities, no ties, just a fantastic opportunity to make the most of. Some people get that when they go travelling or to university; I was being educated in a rather different sense, concentrating my studies on taking wickets and downing beer.

I even ended up smoking cannabis once or twice, something I'd never even encountered back in Pudsey. And I'll never forget the

---

[†]**HOGFACT:** There are more atoms in a teaspoon of water than there are teaspoons of water in the Atlantic Ocean. I know, I've counted them.

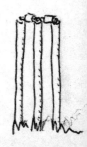

first time I tried it, with a bloke called Dean who I played indoor cricket with. We'd been out drinking and playing pool, and Dean then drove us in his VW Beetle to the top of a multi-storey car park that had amazing views over the whole of Jo'burg. He then took his weed out and rolled us a joint. In South Africa, the cannabis is so cheap that they don't tend to mix it with tobacco, they just smoke the stuff on its own, which makes it pretty powerful, especially if you've never touched the stuff before. Dean had certainly touched the stuff before; I hadn't.

Unsurprisingly, it hit me in a big way. To start with, I got the giggles, uncontrollably. Whatever Dean said, it made me double up with laughter. We then went on to a 24-hour kebab and burger joint to satisfy our munchies. I remember ordering my kebab, sitting down for a while and then walking up to collect my food. All of a sudden, I started to feel really ill. I was going to pass out and I started to panic, thinking of all the stories you see on the news of people who die the first time that they take drugs. And I distinctly remember thinking:

'I'm going to die, I'm going to die! I don't want to die, I'm too young to die! What will my mum and dad say if I die like this, slumped in a kebab shop after taking drugs?'

As far as I know, I didn't die on that occasion. I was woken up shortly afterwards by a big fat bloke handing me my kebab. But it shows how naïve and inexperienced I was that I thought I might be killed by smoking cannabis for the first time.

And so my education continued. I'd better say at this point that, while all these shenanigans were going on away from the cricket field, I was still doing my stuff for the Pirates on a weekend. Both seasons that I was there I ended up as the club's bowler of the season, something that still makes me proud when I think of it. If you're turning up to a place where nobody knows you from Adam, the best possible way to make yourself popular is to prove you're worth your salt as a cricketer.

But more importantly, I really did learn a lot more than just how to live the high life in Jo'burg. Those stories are just the silly bits that stick in my memory the best. But my eyes were opened in a much broader sense by having to make friends in a foreign country, by learning the culture, working out what makes different people tick and how to fit in with them yourself. And I was doing this all on my own. I might not have had much in the way of responsibilities in Jo'burg, but the experience made me much more capable of standing on my own two feet in the future. It's an experience that gave me a lot of confidence and one for which I shall always be extremely grateful. So thanks again, Ferg, another masterstroke.

If those two years in Jo'burg helped to broaden my views of the world in general, it was during the two seasons I spent playing for Free State in Bloemfontein that I learnt some of my most enduring cricketing lessons. I was much more sensible there. The focus was well and truly on the cricket.

Apart from the fact that I was playing in the first-class game rather than club cricket, the pitches were much more challenging for a seam bowler. Whereas in Jo'burg I'd been bowling at altitude, swinging the ball around on pitches that were often green mambas, in Free State there was no altitude and the tracks resembled the M1. They were flat, flat, flat, so you had to do a bit more than run in and turn your arm over if you were going to get a decent batsman out.

Ironically, it was bowling on a seam-friendly wicket at Headingley that had got me an invitation to Bloem in the first place, which was a complete and utter fluke. In August 1998, seventeen months or so after I'd finished my second season with the Pirates, South Africa had just lost a Test series in England and were having nets at Headingley before the start of a one-day series with England and Sri Lanka. By this time I was 21 and I

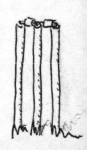

wasn't quite a regular in the Yorkshire side, but I was getting there.

When the South Africans were in town, I was just coming back from injury and it was suggested that I go and bowl at them in the nets at Headingley. As they were preparing for a one-day series, I was bowling with a white ball and the practice pitches at Head-ingley were sporting, to say the least. It was swinging and seam-ing all over the place. I steamed in and I must have bowled out every South African batsman, more than once in some cases. Shaun Pollock, Jonty Rhodes, Hansie Cronje: it was quite a list of conquests. They made me look like the best bowler in the world. It was extremely generous of them.

South Africa's bowling coach on that tour was Corrie van Zyl, who was also a coach at Free State. After I'd finished bowling, he wandered up to me and casually enquired whether I had any plans for the winter. I didn't, as it happened, so he asked if I fancied going out to Bloemfontein to act as cover for Free State's bowlers. Given the time I'd had out in South Africa before, this was an opportunity that I wasn't going to pass up. A couple of months later, I was on my way back there.

I had to bide my time once I'd arrived, though, because the Free State management were reluctant to pick an overseas player ahead of the established locals, particularly in the SuperSport Series, the four-day competition. But I was bowling well in the nets, I turned in some decent figures in one-day cricket and took plenty of wick-ets in club cricket for the Peshwas. Above all, on those hard, flat pitches, I was learning the value of bowling maidens, boring a bats-man out and making him give his wicket away.

I wasn't given a real run in the four-day stuff until February, but in my second game, against Eastern Province in Bloem, I got five for 60 in the first innings and two for 19 from twenty-one overs in the second innings. They couldn't really drop me after that.

I was lucky at Free State to play with some very handy crick-eters and, when we were at full strength, we had a pretty powerful side. If they weren't away on international duty, we had Gerry Liebenberg as captain, Hansie Cronje, Nicky Boje and, best of all for me, we had Allan Donald.

Just to turn up at the Free State nets and watch AD go about his work was an inspiration. At the time, there was no bigger super-star in South African cricket, but he would have as much time for a young lad at the Bloemfontein nets as he would for Hansie Cronje. A nicer, more modest and down-to-earth bloke you couldn't ever wish to meet. Within a few weeks of me being there, AD had roped me in as a babysitter for Hannah and Oliver, his kids, while he and Tina went out for the evening. We've been firm friends ever since.

He was also a real help with my bowling. When I arrived in Bloem, I was having a few problems with my run-up and bowling lots of no-balls. To my amazement, AD took me to one side and took a load of time to help me get it right. He moved markers, watched my take-off and landing, and helped me to work out how I could find my rhythm. With his help, I soon got myself sorted.

He also gave me a few tips on reverse-swing, which I didn't know much about in those days. I was playing in one game at Goodyear Park when AD was just watching, playing with his kids on the boundary and having a drink with the groundsman in the family enclosure. I was bowling at the time but, in the overs in between, I was fielding on the third-man boundary and I signalled to AD to come over for a chat. He came down and I said to him: 'Al, I need to know something. It's reversing out there, and I know how to reverse it *in* to the batsman, but how can I get it to go *away*?'

'You know how you try to bowl inswingers with a normal ball, pushing it in with your fingers and your wrist?' he said. 'Well, just turn the ball over so the shine's on the other side and try to do that. You watch, it'll swing the other way.'

So halfway through my next over, after I'd bowled a couple of inswingers, I did exactly as he'd said. Would you believe it, the ball swung the other way, the batsman got a big nick and was caught

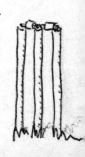

behind. The first bloody ball I'd tried it! I yelled in celebration, turned round and pointed with both hands at AD in the family enclosure, where he gave me the thumbs-up back.

In one-day cricket, he used to bowl as first change while I shared the new ball with Herman Bakkes, another right-arm swing bowler. But in one particular one-day match, not long after I'd arrived there, we were playing at home against KwaZulu-Natal. They had a dangerous pinch-hitter called Keith Forde who opened the innings and Gerry Liebenberg said that we wanted our best bowlers bowling at him, which meant AD taking the new ball instead of me. Fairly understandable, I suppose, but I was still a bit pissed off at the lack of confidence shown in me.

Anyway, within the first couple of overs, Herman got Forde out, clean bowled, and Gerry said, 'Get loose, Hoggy. You're on at AD's end next over.' So I warmed up quickly and, with my third ball, I trapped their number three, Mark Bruyns, lbw plumb in front. As we celebrated the wicket, Gerry came up to me and said: 'Hoggy, I know you've just taken a wicket, but they've got Jonty Rhodes coming in next. We want our best bowlers bowling at him, so you're coming off at the end of this over and I'm bringing AD back on.'

Now that really did piss me off. I went back to my mark in a huff and steamed in at Jonty. His first ball was outside off stump and he left it. The next one nipped back into him and ripped out his middle stump for a duck.[†] I sprinted down the pitch, arms in the air, and went straight to Gerry, who was keeping wicket, and shouted: **'JONTY F***ING WHO?'** I think Jonty heard me on his way off and, a couple of years later, I did offer a belated apology and explained why I'd reacted like a nutter. I was a teensy-weensy bit wound up at the time. I think I'd made my point to Gerry in

---

†**HOGFACT:** In Minnesota it is illegal to cross state lines with a duck on your head. Well, why wouldn't it be?

the best possible way and I was allowed to complete my spell, so on that occasion at least AD had to wait his turn.

No doubt about it though, AD will go down as one of the real good guys of the game. The same probably can't be said of Hansie Cronje, although I have to say I was as shocked as anyone when all the stuff about his match-fixing was revealed. I got to know him fairly well, or so I thought (as did many other people). When you share a dressing-room with someone, you tend to think that you know someone pretty well, but that certainly wasn't true in Hansie's case.

He was captain of South Africa while I was at Free State and you could see why everyone thought so highly of him as a skipper. He was a really positive character, building everybody up so they felt good about themselves. Funnily enough he was also big on discipline, drilling it into everyone that you should always arrive early, whether it's for a practice or a game, to make sure that you're in the best possible frame of mind. I liked the guy and I was absolutely flabbergasted when the news broke of his wrongdoing. I would never have guessed it of him.

I mentioned a little earlier that, off the field, my time in Bloemfontein was spent much more sensibly than those slightly wilder days in Jo'burg. That was partly because I was a couple of years older, partly because the cricket was more serious and partly because Sarah came out to stay with me in Bloem, so I had someone to keep me company in the evening.

Having said all that, our time in Bloem was not without its incidents, often involving cars rather than alcohol (and not the two mixed together this time). One such escapade occurred in my second season with Free State, in 1999–2000, at the same time as England were playing a Test series in South Africa. I was driving with Sarah down from Bloemfontein for a few days' break in Cape Town, which is about a ten-hour drive. At least, it *should* be a ten-hour drive, but I got badly lost, so it mushroomed into the small matter of a thirteen-hour drive.

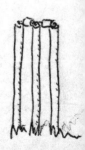

To try and make up for lost time, I ended up in a bit of a hurry, and whenever I got the chance to put my foot down I put it **ALL THE WAY** down. We had a motor that could shift, because we were in a BMW belonging to Andy Moles, the Free State coach. For most of the journey, Sarah was fast asleep alongside me because we'd been out with Molar the night before and she was suffering. Or maybe it was the quality of the conversation that was sending her to sleep. Occasionally, she'd open her eyes and say: 'Slow down, will you, Matthew? You've got to keep an eye out for the speed cops.' So I would slow down while her eyes were still open, then speed up again when she went back to sleep.

Sarah must have been dead to the world when I came to one massive straight road, like a huge wide Roman road, on which there was no other traffic whatsoever for miles and miles and miles. I put my foot down and had reached about 180 kph (about 110 mph) when a policeman stepped out from behind a bush with a card-board sign saying: 'Stop!' Sounds like a cartoon, I know, but it felt real enough at the time. I slammed on the brakes and managed to come to a halt – about half a mile down the road – and reversed all the way back to say hello to the nice policeman.

Once he'd established that I wasn't a local, he said: 'Have you got your passport on you?'

I said no, even though my passport was with my kit in the boot of the car.

'Have you got any other ID?' he said.

I gave him my international driver's licence.

'What are you doing over here?' he asked, and I told him that I was playing cricket. He thought for a moment or two, while he wrote out a speeding ticket, and then said:

'Hey, you're not here playing for England, are you?'

'Yep, I sure am,' I lied again.

The policeman paused for thought again, then started smiling. 'Oh, I don't think you need to worry about that ticket, then. You can tear it up, on one condition.'

'What's that?'

'You give me your autograph.'

So I gave him my autograph, shook his hand and got back in the car. I just counted myself lucky that he didn't know enough about the England team – or the Free State team, come to think of it – to realise that I was telling him a fib. I hate to think of him sitting down to watch the Test match, telling his mates he'd got one of the England players' signatures, then discovering that he'd actually been diddled and the bloke whose autograph he had was playing a game in front of two men and a baboon down in Cape Town.

I imagine he'd have been pretty peeved, but I hope he didn't rip the ticket up and throw it straight in the bin, because a few months later I made my Test debut. My autograph might actually have been worth having then ...

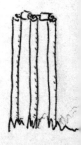

TOP 5 ANGRIEST BATSMEN

I have a morbid fascination for watching an angry batsman when he gets back to the dressing-room, throwing his bat and gloves and having a paddy. I suppose it's a bit like watching car-crash television, only very close up. At Yorkshire we used to have spread bets about how many times Michael Bevan would say 'f***' in his first minute back in the dressing-room. The spread was normally between 40 and 50. Here are five of the angriest:

MICHAEL BEVAN

I once saw him come into the changing-room after a bad decision and sit underneath a shower fully clothed, still wearing all his batting gear, pads and all.

MARK RAMPRAKASH

In India in 2001 there looked to be a serious danger that Ramps might punch a dressing-room attendant who was a bit *too* attentive shortly after he had been given out.

NASSER HUSSAIN

Once gave me a bollocking for not getting him a drink out of the fridge in Pakistan. He was sitting right next to the fridge, I was at the other side of the room.

DARREN LEHMANN

Boof had just been run out by a bad call from Gavin Hamilton at Scarborough. I was at the other side of the ground and I could hear Boof in the dressing-room shouting: 'Stupid f***ing Scottish prick!' If I could hear it, Gav, still out in the middle, would certainly have been aware of Boof's feelings.

ANTHONY McGRATH

When we were playing in the Yorkshire second team, I was sitting in the dressing-room when Mags came back after playing a stupid shot. He started throwing his kit around, f-ing and blinding, and everyone else cleared out of the dressing-room. When everybody had cleared off, and there was only me and him left, he smiled at me and said: 'I thought I should do that to make it look as though I'm bothered.'

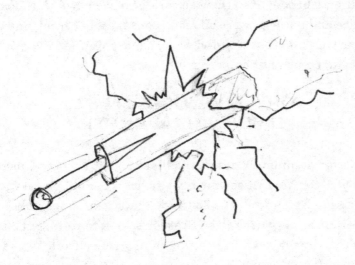

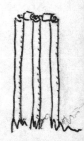

4
England Calling

I had just got out of the shower and was brushing my teeth when the call came through from David Graveney. It was June 2000 and we were living in our first house together at the time, on Moorland Avenue in Baildon, and Sarah came rushing into our little en-suite bathroom from the bedroom. She had a look of shock on her face and her eyes were about to pop out of her head. She was holding the phone out to me with one hand, pointing to it with her other and mouthing the words:

'OH ... MY ... GOD ... IT'S ... DAVID ... GRAVENEY!'

This came completely out of the blue for me. I'd been bowling quite well for Yorkshire, but I really hadn't thought yet about playing for England. I was 23 (and a half), not long back from my second season with Free State in Bloemfontein, but I still hadn't really played a full season of county cricket. We had a load of talented bowlers at Yorkshire at the time and, to my mind, I had my hands full just hanging onto my place at the club.

But who was I to argue with David Graveney, the chairman of selectors? I took the phone from Sarah and Grav said: 'You're coming down to Lord's for the second Test against West Indies. It's not just one of those things where we've picked you for the experience, so be prepared to play.'

'Erm, right, OK. Thanks very much. Thanks for letting me know. Much appreciated.' I don't think I've ever been so polite to anyone in my life. I went back into the bedroom, told Sarah and she started jumping around the room. Then we rang our parents and everyone else we could think of to tell them. Ringing my dad was particularly special. Playing at Lord's for England was a long way from our games messing about at Post Hill with a big tree for wickets.

As far as I knew, the stumps in Test cricket would not be a sapling six feet high and three feet wide and you wouldn't be given out for hitting Curtly Ambrose for a six over some trees (wishful thinking, I know).

I think the game that had probably put me into the selectors' minds was a televised Benson & Hedges Cup one-day game a few weeks earlier against Surrey at Headingley. I had a shaved, bald bonce at the time, which probably helped to get me noticed, as it would have been the first time a lot of people had seen me in action. But I didn't bowl too badly either. The ball was swinging round corners and I got out Mark Butcher, Graham Thorpe, Ali Brown and Adam Hollioake. Not a bad haul.

When it came to the morning of the game itself, we didn't know until shortly before the toss whether I was playing or whether they'd go for Robert Croft, the spin option. I was hoping for clouds, Crofty was hoping for blue skies, and there was actually a bit of both. It was an agonising wait. Crofty kept coming up to me and saying: 'Do you know who's playing yet?'

'No,' I'd say. 'Do you know.'

'No bloody idea yet.'

'How about we say that the first one to get their whites on gets to play?'

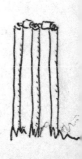

In those situations, as your stomach churns with nerves, there's probably a tiny part of you that thinks: 'God, maybe my life would be a lot easier if they went for Crofty. I might get smashed everywhere if I play and never get picked again.' But it was only about one per cent of my brain that was thinking that. The rest was praying that I would get the nod. And about fifteen minutes before the toss, Alec Stewart, who was captain for that game, came up and told me that I was in.

I vividly remember turning up in the dressing-room for that game as the new boy, never an easy experience. I was quite lucky, because there was Craig White, Darren Gough and Michael Vaughan, all Yorkshire team-mates, but it was still quite a scary place to walk into. In one corner there would be Thorpey, Stewie and Mike Atherton, the older guys, in another there'd be the likes of Andrew Caddick and Graeme Hick. It was quite a cliquey set-up at that time and I can imagine it being a fairly horrible place to walk into if you didn't know anyone. But the Yorkshire lads made it easier for me, especially Goughie, who crossed the boundaries between the different groups.

That was the era before central contracts came in and selection was much less consistent in those days. As a result, I think that players in general were a bit more concerned with looking after themselves. Not in a way that was particularly unpleasant, but in my later years as an England player there was a much more welcoming feel to the dressing room and that came about through consistency of selection. It is much easier to play for the team if you know you're going to be part of the team for the next game. That's not intended as a criticism of particular individuals; insecurity is a perfectly natural reaction when you're not sure of your place in the team. But the whole experience of playing for England was just a massive thrill, especially to be starting out at Lord's, which is always that little bit more special, especially for a wide-eyed lad from Pudsey. I particularly remember opening my big box of prezzies, containing all my different pieces of England kit, and thinking: 'Bloody hell, do I get to keep all this?'

I was glad when we were bowling first because that meant no more waiting around to get on with the damn thing. Caddy and Goughie didn't bowl too well to start with and the Windies were none down when I came on from the Pavilion End in the eleventh over. My first ball was to Sherwin Campbell, who absolutely slapped it, but it went straight to cover. **PHEWEE!** I then managed to make him play and miss a couple of times and my first over in Test cricket was a maiden, which helped me to breathe a big sigh of relief.

I bowled okay in that initial spell, but didn't get any wickets and got a bit of a tap in my last couple of overs. As a first bowl in Test cricket, though, it could have gone worse.

I also took a catch when Campbell top-edged a hook off Dominic Cork to fine leg. I made a right old meal of it, rolling over backwards after I'd caught it. It was swirling in the air[†] for ages and I could feel my heart thumping in my chest like a drum. But I clung on, heard the crowd cheer and thought, 'Yep, I could get used to this.'

In the second innings, the West Indies were bowled out for 54, which wouldn't even have been a good score down at Post Hill with a big tree for stumps. I didn't bowl in the second innings, but I can't say I was too disappointed, because wickets were falling all the time. Piece of cake, Test cricket.

Then, of course, we had a run chase in the fourth innings that didn't quite go according to plan. Chasing 188 to win, we still needed 39 when Nick Knight was the seventh man out and, as number eleven, I had to put my pads on. At that stage, I'm not ashamed to say, I was **ABSOLUTELY POOING MYSELF**.

[†]**HOGFACT:** A cough or sneeze makes the AIR in the human respiratory system move faster than the speed of sound. So if someone sneezes right in front of your face, you've got to be pretty sharp to get out of the way.

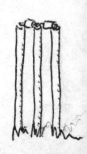

The situation only got worse when Caddy was lbw to Ambrose, leaving us 160 for eight. For anyone on their Test debut, that would be a fairly nerve-wracking situation. For a number eleven batsman potentially going out to face Curtly Ambrose and Courtney Walsh with a Test match in the balance, it just didn't seem fair. I didn't get picked for England to score runs, but that, I thought, was how I was going to be judged. And this was the second match in a five-Test series, with England already 1–0 down, so if we lost at Lord's, the series was as good as gone.

I just sat there in the dressing-room, rigid in my seat with all my body armour on: helmet, chest guard, arm guard, thigh pad, bat between my legs, resting my chin on the top of the handle. I'd actually batted quite well in the first innings, when I got 12 not out, slogged Curtly and survived a few balls that whistled past my lugholes. But that wasn't giving me any more confidence in this situation.

One second I'd be thinking: 'Please, please, please don't let me have to go in.' Then, a couple of moments later, another thought would flash through my mind: 'What happens if we only need four to win and I go out and bash one through the covers to do it?!' No. Calm down, Hoggy, calm down. How about: 'What happens if it's four to win and I miss a straight one?' Far more likely.

For every run that was scored by Corky or Goughie, everybody was on their feet. For every ball that was stopped by a fielder, there was a groan of disappointment. I just stayed silent. Then Corky nudged Walsh through the off-side for four, we had won and everybody was jumping around, screaming and celebrating like mad. So I did the same.

The next Test was at Old Trafford, on a more spin-friendly surface, so Crofty came back into the side and I wasn't required for the rest of the series, but I was picked for the winter tours to Pakistan and Sri Lanka. Much to my surprise, I found Pakistan a most hospitable place to a seam bowler, at least as far as the wickets for practice matches were concerned. On pitches that seemed to have been tailor-made for me, I managed the ridonculous stat of taking 17 wickets in two first-class matches. Mind you, I seem to remember Marcus Trescothick turning his arm over and conning a few people out with his wobbly seamers, so taking wickets can't have been that difficult.

Despite picking up all those wickets, I didn't get a sniff at the Test side because Caddy and Goughie were well established as the first-choice quick bowlers. They were a good opening pair who complemented each other well: one was a lanky git, the other a short arse; one a bit short of self-belief, the other with enough confidence for both of them and the rest of the team put together. They worked well together, but I don't think I've ever seen such a keen rivalry between two players in the same team.

On one tour to the subcontinent, Caddy developed a habit of occasionally coming off the field during the warm-up games. Nothing unusual there; bowlers often do that in the build-up to a Test series to rest a niggle or strain. But during one warm-up match, he came off the field when we hadn't taken too many wickets and the opposition were scoring plenty of runs. Goughie was not amused, and at the end of the day's play he had a go at Caddy. 'I've been sweating my bollocks off out there, busting a f***ing gut while you sit on your arse in the dressing-room. You're not f***ing injured, but if you do that again, I'm going to break your f***ing legs.'

That was not an untypical exchange between them. They were mates, up to a point, and keen for the other one to take a few wickets, as long as they were taking more wickets themselves. I reckon that each of them always kept a precise tally of how many Test wickets the other had taken. How petty can you get? Both of them are good pals of mine, but I would never dream of slipping into a conversation with either of them the fact that Goughie took 229, Caddy got 234 and I got 248. The thought would simply never enter my head.

Anyway, back to my early days with England. After failing to make much headway on the tours to Pakistan and Sri Lanka, I

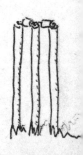

had to wait until the following season for my first Test wicket. I was called up for my second cap against Pakistan at Old Trafford, where I managed to pick up three wickets in each innings. There had been plenty of times in the preceding eleven months, since my debut against West Indies, when I had wondered whether I would ever take a Test wicket, but the all-important first one came when Younis Khan shouldered arms to one of my devilish outswingers that fails to swing. And I'm not absolutely sure that the ball was going on to hit the wickets.

BUT WHO CARES? I'D WAITED ALMOST A YEAR FOR THIS!!!

A few overs later, I had Inzamam-ul-Haq caught, slicing a drive to Ian Ward in the gully. Now that one was definitely out and I was beginning to feel a bit more like a proper Test cricketer.

Unfortunately, I injured my knee shortly afterwards and missed the whole of the 2001 Ashes series. Maybe my body sensed that there was a very good team coming up and decided to give me a break. That ailment also meant that I only played seven matches in the season that Yorkshire won the County Championship for the first time in thirty-three years. I was still working my way back to full fitness with a few one-day games when the title was wrapped up against Glamorgan at Scarborough, but I was fit enough to join in the celebrations. It was a particular triumph for David Byas, our long-suffering captain, and Darren Lehmann, our incomparable over-seas player who was such an influence on my generation at Yorkshire.

The first time I encountered Darren, or 'Boof', as he is univer-sally known, I was a second-teamer turning up to practice at the start of a new season. On days like that, you have a look around to check out for the usual suspects and for any unfamiliar faces. I remember saying to Chris Silverwood: 'Spoons, who's that short, fat bastard over there?'

'That's the new overseas player,' Spoons said.

'It can't be,' I said. 'He's fat.'

But one look at Darren Lehmann with a bat in his hand and we knew immediately what a class act we had on our hands. This is someone who makes the game look ridonculously easy. He could have walked into other any Test team in our era and he should have played much more for Australia. His confidence, his personality and his competitive steeliness worked wonders in the Yorkshire dressing-room.

As captain we had David Byas, who was strict, straightforward and basically had the attitude: 'I'm the captain, you're not and I don't really care if you like me, you'll do as I say.'

Boof, as senior pro and vice captain, was a good foil. He was one of the lads, but if a bollocking needed to be given he wouldn't hesitate to hand it out. He's a laid-back guy, but knows exactly when to flick the switch to go into his match mode. That is a difficult balance for a player to strike; few people can do it successfully, but then few people have been as good as Darren Lehmann.

Yes, he liked a beer or three after a game and he was a bit old-fashioned in that way, but you would never find him giving less than his all in a match. I'll never forget playing in the game after the championship had been clinched at Scarborough in 2001. Two days afterwards, we had a Sunday League game against Nottinghamshire and, in the celebrations of the previous two nights, Boof had certainly not taken a back seat. This was evident from the fact that, before he went out to bat on the Sunday, there was still a pool of champagne left in his upturned helmet from the post-match party we had held in the dressing-room.

When the second wicket fell against Nottinghamshire and his turn had come to bat, he picked up his helmet, swigged the champagne from it, popped it on his head and announced: 'Right, watch this, boys. This could be special.'

He was as good as his word. He proceeded to score 191 off 103 balls, which was one of the most amazing innings I've ever seen. He was playing some incredible shots, down on one knee, hitting

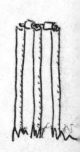

it over the keeper's head, swatting it between fielders with one hand, pretty much doing as he chose. Nobody else could have played an innings like it. It was extraordinary.

A few years later, I shared a bit of a stand with Boof against Sussex at Arundel when the ball was reverse-swinging all over the shop. James Kirtley was curving it wickedly away from me one ball, then back into me next ball, I didn't have a clue which way it was going to go from one ball to the next. So at the non-striker's end, Boof said: 'I think you need a bit of help here, Hog. I'll have a look at how the bowler's holding the ball in his run-up. If I hold the bat in my right hand, it's coming in to you. If I hold my bat in my left hand, it'll go away. If my bat's in between, I haven't got a clue.' And every time he went right or left, he was absolutely spot on. I had a marvellous time, suddenly started looking like a competent batsman, and there were some looks of genuine surprise on the faces of the Sussex fielders.

In that same innings, Mushtaq Ahmed was bowling at the other end from Kirtley. Boof had reached his 100 by this time and he was ready for a bit of fun, so he said: 'Right, Hoggy, where do you want me to put Mushy's next ball?'

I had a look around the ground and said: 'Oh, just plonk it on top of that marquee, will you, Boof?'

The next ball was fullish in length. Boof bent down to sweep, put his bottom hand into it and duly deposited the ball on top of the marquee at mid-wicket, as requested.

'OK, Hog, where shall I put the next one?' he said. 'I think I'll go over mid-on this time.' Sure enough, Mushy's next ball disappeared over mid-on, and I started creasing myself as I wandered down the wicket.

'OK, Boof, what's next?' I asked.

'We're gonna run two into the covers, OK?'

And you can guess what happened next ball. He called it perfectly. If I hadn't seen it with my own eyes, I'm not sure I'd have believed it.

And this was against Mushtaq Ahmed, not some second-rate bowler just called up from the second team. I've seen plenty of other people try a stunt like this and come a cropper, predicting that the next ball would be a bouncer only to have their middle stump ripped out by a yorker. I might even have been guilty of trying it myself on the odd occasion.

But Boof was different. It was a privilege to play alongside him. And a hell of a giggle.

The winter after we won the championship with Yorkshire, I underwent something of a dramatic transformation as an international bowler. Without so much as playing another game for England, I went from being a novice who had only played two Tests to become the leader of England's attack. Compared with Jimmy Ormond (one cap), Richard Johnson and Richard Dawson (both uncapped), I was a grizzled, gnarled veteran with the grand total of six Test wickets. We were supported by a couple of all-rounders in Andrew Flintoff and Craig White, but this was hardly an attack to make Sachin Tendulkar toss and turn at night.

This was the tour that came shortly after the 9/11 terrorist atrocities in the US and Andrew Caddick and Robert Croft had opted not to tour. Alec Stewart and Darren Gough had already decided to take the winter off and Mike Atherton had just retired. As a result, we were huge underdogs, there was very little expected of us, but we scrapped and scrapped for everything, and did fairly well to restrict India to a 1–0 win in the three-Test series. Myself and Freddie both did our bit with the ball, and pride was certainly maintained.

This was also the Test series when Phil Carrick's prediction that VVS Laxman and I, both former team-mates at Pudsey Congs all those years ago, would play each other in a Test match came true.

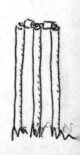

Seven years after he had made it, I was walking onto the outfield at Mohali to warm up for the first Test and I saw Lax having a net with the rest of the Indian lads at the other side of the ground. I looked up to the sky and said: 'Who'd have thought it, Ferg? You were right.'

Taking on the might of India with a group of spotty youths, we needed a strong and stern headmaster to guide us in the right direction. We had just the man in Mr Nasser Hussain, who did a great job in keeping order in the class. Not that I always saw eye-to-eye with him, and there were a few occasions when I thought I might end up getting the cane. At the end of that first Test in Mohali, we had a massive barney. Or rather, he had a massive barney at me.

We'd been pretty much outplayed throughout that game and our batting had collapsed fairly meekly to 235 all out in the second innings, just avoiding an innings defeat. India then needed only five runs to win, so they opened the batting with Iqbal Siddiqui, a tail-end slogger who had batted at number ten in the first innings.

Nasser didn't like them doing this. I think he was fairly insulted. As I was opening the bowling, he told me to bounce Siddiqui and make them think twice about doing this sort of thing again. Even though they only wanted five to win, he wanted to show that we were still scrapping.

So Muggins here thought: 'Bollocks to that, I'm going to try to get him out.' So I pitched the ball up outside off stump. It was quite a good ball, Siddiqui had a go at it and snicked it through the slips for four. Next ball he clipped one through the leg-side and it was game over.

Back in the dressing-room, I got the biggest bollocking of my life. 'If I tell you to bowl a f***ing bouncer, I want you to run in and bowl a f***ing bouncer!' Nasser yelled in my face. 'You don't see f***ing McGrath and f***ing Ambrose coming in and bowling piddly half-volleys on leg stump.' And so it went on. 'F-this, F-that and F-the F***ing other.' All of which basically amounted to me getting an almighty bollocking for failing to defend a **TARGET OF FIVE**.

This happened in front of everybody else in the dressing-room and it made me really upset. When we had to go back out onto the field for the presentation ceremony, I was standing on my own with tears in my eyes. It was my third Test match and I'd just been given the rollicking of my life by the captain when I barely felt that I deserved it. I had people coming up to me and putting their arm round me telling me not to worry about it. But it was a bit late for that.

A couple of hours later, back at the hotel, I was still seething in my room when there was a knock on the door. It was Duncan Fletcher, the coach. I hadn't had much to do with Fletch up to this point, because he tended to keep himself to himself in the dressing-room and only intervene when he felt it necessary. He clearly felt it necessary this time and said: 'Don't take it personally. Nass was just really het up. You didn't deserve it.' Half an hour later there was another knock on the door. Nass walked in and gave me a cuddle, told me that he was sorry and walked out again.

Fair enough. That was Nass. He was a very intense, very fiery character, but deep down he can be a really lovely, compassionate guy. When his emotions got the better of him, he could be a complete and utter twat, but I don't think he ever meant badly. Nass was Nass.

The first time I had encountered his temper had been on that first tour to Pakistan the previous winter. At one of the Test matches, I was one of three or four twelfth men who would take it in turns, session by session, to run errands out onto the field, while the other twelfth men stayed to look after the dressing-room.

On one of the sessions that I was on duty, Nasser had just been dismissed. At the fall of the wicket, I'd done my duty by running down to look after the batsman out in the middle, Mike Atherton, taking him a spare pair of gloves, a drink and some ice. I then

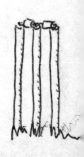

went back up to the dressing-room, sat down in my seat and started sending a text message to my missus. (Those were the days when we were still allowed mobile phones in the dressing-room.)

All of a sudden, across the other side of the room, Nasser erupted: 'I'll get my own f***ing drink then, shall I?' he shouted at me. At this time, he was sitting right next to the fridge and could have reached over to open the door himself to get a drink. I was sitting miles[†] away from the fridge, presuming that I'd done my duties by attending to Athers. But poor old Nass was a bit upset at getting out and I was in the firing line. I heard a couple of the lads sniggering behind me but didn't think it wise to join in. I don't think Nass was in the mood to see the funny side at the time.

So I had plenty of run-ins with Nass because he was a strict disciplinarian as captain and, in those days, I was one of the class clowns. There was one practice day during a one-day series in Zimbabwe when I had taken to making chicken noises all day. I can't remember why, but I'm sure there was a very sensible, grown-up reason for doing so. For some reason, Nass was getting a bit fed-up of the chicken noises, so he bought Chris Silverwood into the dressing-room and said: 'Spoons, your job is to keep that twat over there quiet. If I hear any more bird noises out of him. I'm sending the pair of you back to England.' Spoons and I looked at each other and both started clucking at the top of our voices. Nasser just burst out laughing, shouted, 'Piss off,' and legged it out of the dressing-room. Just as well he saw the funny side, really. I wouldn't have wanted my international career to end for making a few bird noises.

His stricter side was more evident out in the middle. Whenever I bowled a bad ball, I'd turn round to walk back to my mark

---

[†]**HOGFACT:** The average housewife walks ten MILES a day around the house. I wonder how much of that is walking to the telephone and back to natter to her mother or her friends?

and see him kicking the dirt at mid-off, which I'm not sure was the most constructive of responses. But Nass did a hell of a lot of good for English cricket while he was captain. He is an immensely passionate person and that rubbed off on a lot of people. His relationship with Fletch was the catalyst for our recovery. They started the consistency of selection that helped to create such a healthy dressing-room environment. Once the older brigade had gone, you wouldn't just go out with your mates in the same groups for a meal in the evening. Anybody could go out with anybody else.

I think that tour to India, with such a young team, gave Nass and Fletch the opportunity to really stamp their mark on the England team and its culture. And in the longer term we were much better for it.

For the tour that followed to New Zealand in early 2002, we had a couple of older heads back on board and drew the Test series 1–1. The first Test in Christchurch was one of the most bizarre in history, played on a drop-in pitch that seamed about all over the place to start with and then became flatter as the game went on. Nass made a magnificent hundred out of 228, then I got seven for 63 as we skittled them for 147. Nice to have a slightly friendlier pitch to bowl on after slogging away on those dead tracks in India.

We then set New Zealand 550 to win after Thorpey had made a double-century and Fred hit his first hundred, so our victory was just a matter of time. Or so you would have thought.

By now, the pitch was as flat as a fart and Nathan Astle started to chance his arm. The result was that he scored the fastest double-hundred in Test history, hitting sixes left, right and centre. It was a freakish innings. The ball kept going just over someone's head, or landing just out of somebody else's reach, but he certainly made the most of his luck.

Chris Cairns had been injured and came in at number eleven – he only came in because they had an outside chance of victory – and when they whittled the target down to fewer than 100 to win, we were feeling seriously jittery. I don't think we'd have been allowed

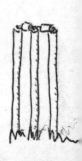

back to England if we had conceded 550 to lose a Test. Come to think of it, I'm not sure we would have wanted to return. So just when I was wondering whether I would be spending the rest of my life shearing sheep in New Zealand, I managed to get Astle out, caught behind by James Foster off a slower ball. There was a photo in the papers the next day of me celebrating and all the veins looked like they were going to pop out of my neck. We were that relieved.

We may have only drawn the series but I took seventeen wickets in the three Tests and was starting to feel like this Test cricket lark might not be quite so bad after all. As ever with this game, though, you can never make yourself too comfortable. The saying that you are only as good as your last game is one of sport's biggest clichés, but as an international cricketer it's something you're of aware of all the time. You could play like a king one game, but then as soon as you mess up in the next match the first game may as well have never happened. Get ahead of yourself and the game will catch you up and bite you on the bum.

In the first Test of the 2002 English season, against Sri Lanka at Lord's a couple of months later, I really struggled. I took a couple of wickets, but I went for more than four an over and I was some way short of my best. To make matters worse, before the second Test at Edgbaston I played a Benson & Hedges Cup game for Yorkshire against Essex and got knocked around by Nasser Hussain, of all people, who hit a hundred. Great timing to come up against the England skipper when I was scraping the barrel for anything resembling form.

When I turned up at Edgbaston, my confidence levels were fairly low and Duncan Fletcher knew it. Whether Nass had had a word in his ear or not, I don't know. In the old changing-rooms at Edgbaston there was a small coach's office off to one side, and Fletch called me in. 'Uh-oh,' I thought. 'This could be bad news.'

'Sit down, Hoggy,' said Fletch. So I did, and held my breath. 'I just wanted to ask you whether you want to play in this Test match,' he said.

'Hell, yes, of course I do, Fletch.'

'Do you think you are confident enough to play?'

Difficult question to answer. I wasn't feeling on top of my game and there had been a bit of debate about whether I should hang onto my place. But if you tried to pick and choose your games at international level, waiting until you felt on top form, you'd be no use to anyone.

'I know I haven't been at my best in the last couple of weeks, Fletch, but I'm desperate to make it up in this game and, yes, I'll back myself to do so. I definitely want to play.'

I was lucky at this point that I'd had a good winter in India and New Zealand and this was the time that Fletch was really trying to impose some consistency in the selection. He showed faith in me, gave me another chance and I was extremely chuffed to be able to repay that faith. I took a couple of top-order wickets in the first innings, got 17 not out with the bat, helping Thorpey to add 91 for the last wicket, and then picked up a five-fer in the second innings. We won by an innings and I was named Man of the Match.

I was ecstatically happy after that game, pleased that I'd justi-fied Fletch's confidence in me and proud that I'd shown the balls to stand up and fight my corner. We had a team meal after the game and then went out to the Living Room in Birmingham. As David Brent would say, 'El Vino did flow.'

That evening, I was due at my friend Tony Finch's house on the outskirts of Birmingham for a barbecue. Sarah had gone there to wait for me and Allan Donald was there with Tina, his wife, and their kids. By the time I rocked up in a taxi rather late in the evening, I could barely speak. To get myself to Finchy's house, I had to ring him up and pass the phone to the taxi driver because I was in no state to pass on directions.

We finally got there and I continued to have a thoroughly marvellous time until it was time to for Sarah and me to go home in a taxi with AD and family. The only memory I have of that

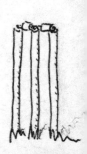

journey home is of Hannah, AD's oldest, saying: 'Daddy, why has Matthew got his head out of the window?'

AD said, 'I don't think he's feeling too well, Hannah.'

So I was back on track and I then had a decent enough series against India, with the exception of Headingley, where the ball swung all over the place, they got 600-plus and, try as I might, I just couldn't make Rahul Dravid play. It swung and he left it, time and again.

I had a chat with Fletch about what was going wrong and he suggested that I go wider on the crease, but I wasn't sure that he was right on this one. At very least, I wanted to try it out for myself, so between Tests I did a bit of work on my bowling with Steve Oldham, the Yorkshire bowling coach whom I respect. I practised quite a bit and, when I got to the Oval for the next Test, I told Fletch that I thought I'd solved my problems. When he watched me bowling, he said: 'You're just going wider on the crease. That's exactly what I told you to do a week ago. Why didn't you listen to me then?'

That was absolutely fair enough, but I had just wanted to try it out for myself and, before I made a major change in a Test match, to be comfortable and happy in myself that I was doing the right thing. I suppose what it really came down to is that I can be a stubborn sod at times, and Fletch is very stubborn as well, so there were a few occasions when immovable object met immovable object and friction was created as a result.

I played in all seven Tests that summer and I was the leading wicket-taker against both Sri Lanka and India, so I must have done a few things right along the way. And at the end of the season, before we set off for my first Ashes series in Australia, I was awarded a central contract by the ECB. This meant better pay and a workload managed by the England coach. For the first time in my career, my job description was primarily to be an England player, rather than a Yorkshire player who might occasionally play for England. I won't say that this meant I felt like part of the furniture or settled in the side, but it was at least a bit of evidence that the management had some confidence in my ability. Either that or they just wanted to make sure they could keep a closer eye on me. Whatever the reason, my main bosses were now at Lord's rather than Headingley, and I didn't even have to move to London. But it was beginning to look as though I might be a proper England player after all.

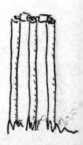

'*Daddy, Daddy, please can I do some words for your book?*'

'Not just yet, Ernie. The nice people want to know all about all the things that Daddy likes to eat that make him big and strong.'

'*But even the dogs have done some words, Daddy.*'

'Maybe later, Ernie, if you're a good boy ...'

REVEALED OVERLEAF ...

The amazing drinking exploits of
Andrew Flintoff ...

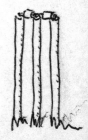

Sorry, I was there, but I don't remember a single thing.

5
Meat and Three Veg

This might sound a bit odd, but when I was younger I used to eat a lot of nettles. It was a bit of a party trick that I would perform from time to time to impress my school friends. I can't remember exactly when or where I discovered it – some misspent afternoon or other when I should have been tidying my bedroom or doing my homework – but I must have read somewhere that if you hold the bottom of a nettle leaf when you pick it, then fold it carefully inwards, you don't get stung. If you then put it in your mouth and chew it, you don't feel a thing. And it tastes like, well, nettles I suppose. (Don't try this at home, kids, unless you have a fully qualified nettle-handler in attendance, such as me.)

As you might expect, not many 8-year-olds in Pudsey were aware of this advanced piece of Nettleology, so they never believed that I would dare to pick up nettles with my bare hands and eat them. So my party piece never failed to impress. No pocket money changed hands, I must stress; my nettle-eating was never a commercial venture. I did it purely to gain friends and influence among the short-trousered community in Pudsey.

Funnily enough, I recently read on the internet that eating nettles actually makes your hair brighter, thicker and shinier. It

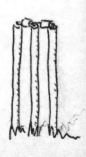

also, apparently, makes your skin clearer, healthier and more radiant. Aha, I thought:

So that's why i'm so bloody gorgeous.

Anyway, I only mention my nettle-eating antics because, as I've grown older, my eating habits have continued to be a bit weird. Don't get me wrong, I'm not a fussy eater. On the contrary, there is hardly anything I don't like. It's just that I tend to be something of a mood eater: I eat when I feel like eating and, if I'm not in the mood, nothing will persuade me to put my snout into the trough. Sometimes I can go a whole day without eating until the evening. At other times I won't be able to stop snacking all day long.

As far as my cricket is concerned, this mood-eating tendency did not made me especially popular with the nutritionists who worked with the England team, making sure that we were following the right sort of diets. Since the introduction of ECB central contracts a few years ago, we have become the first generation of cricketers who are officially supposed to watch what we eat. Not only are we supposed to be cricketers these days, but we're expected to be finely honed athletes as well. In theory, at least.

Unfortunately, my mood-eating habits meant that I usually didn't conform to the nutritionists' idea of what makes for a healthy eating schedule. And their biggest bugbear was my preference for avoiding breakfast.

Generally speaking, I just don't do breakfast, because I don't like eating as soon as I've woken up. I am, in fact, a **GRUMPY GRUNTING GIT** in the mornings and if I eat anything shortly after waking up it makes me feel physically sick. Which, in turn, only makes me even more grumpy.

Now, I'm well aware that breakfast is supposed to be The Most Important Meal Of The Day. My mum told me that when I was a little lad and the nutritionists have told me umpteen times since.

I know that it's supposed to set you up for the day, get your brain and body going, regulate your appetite, blah, blah, blah, blah, blah.

But it just doesn't happen that way for me. And believe me, I've tried it plenty of times, and it always makes me feel grim. That might make me strange, it might mean that I don't fit in with a nutritionist's carefully conceived dietary programme, it might not be the right thing for a professional sportsman to do,

BUT I JUST CAN'T SODDING WELL DO IT! I CAN'T, I CAN'T, I CAN'T!

All England players are required to have a chat with a nutritionist on regular visits to the National Cricket Centre at Loughborough. Over the course of a day on Loughborough Univerity campus, you are put through something of a cricketer's MOT. You have appointments with a representative of every branch of medical science known to man: the physiotherapist, the doctor, the podiatrist and the psychologist. There are fitness tests, eye tests, blood tests, skin tests, jockstrap fitting, underarm hair tests to ensure that your armpits aren't too bushy. (One or more of the above may be fictional.)

Then, if there's any time left, you'll have a chat with Mr Nutritionist, my favourite appointment of the day. My conversation with Mr Nutritionist would usually go something like this:

Mr N: Hello, Matthew, how are you today?
Me (if it's the afternoon): Oh, not so bad, thanks.

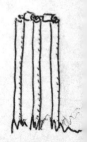

Or

Me (if it's the morning): Grunt.

Mr N: How have you been feeling recently?

Me: Generally pretty good, thanks.

Mr N: Have you been feeling tired or lethargic at all?

Me: Yes, I often feel tired at night, so I go to bed for a few hours. That usually does the trick.

Mr N: And have you been eating healthily?

Me: Most of the time, yes, but I have had fish and chips a few times. Sorry about that.

Mr N: Oh, don't worry, we'll let you off a couple of transgressions. And what about breakfast?

Me: No, I usually have fish and chips for lunch or dinner.

Mr N: I mean, have you been eating breakfast?

Me: Ermmm, ummm, not every day, no.

Mr N: Have you tried any of the suggestions that I made last time, such as a yoghurt?

Me: Yes, it made me feel sick.

Mr N: Cereals?†

Me: Yes, it made me feel sick.

Mr N: Fruit salad?

Me: Yes, it made me feel sick.

Mr N: Milkshake?

Me: Yes, it made me feel sick.

Mr N: Banana?

Me (lying, just to give him something to tick on his chart): Yes, I've tried that a few times, and it wasn't too bad. I'll try to do it every day from now on.

---

†**HOGFACT:** Ireland boasts the highest per capita consumption of CEREAL in the world. And I'd always been under the impression that they had Guinness for their breakfast.

Mr N (ticking box on his chart): Excellent. See you next time,
  Matthew.
Me: Cheerio.

The big problem with me not having any breakfast is that, if I am
playing cricket – and especially if I am bowling – it means that I
may not have a proper meal all day.

From a nutritionist's point of view, I can understand why that
would seem wrong if I've got to get through twenty-five overs in
three sessions. But as soon as we start our warm-ups at the ground
I'll be getting energy from sports drinks. Then there are the energy
gels and booster bars that will keep me going during the day. You'll
have seen on television the Red Bull cart that comes out to keep
us fully fuelled during a day's play: that contains water, bananas,
energy drinks and all sorts of lotions and potions to stop us from
flagging.

But when it comes to the lunch break, if it's hot and I've been
bowling, I'm unlikely to feel like eating any lunch. We only get 40
minutes' break and, if I've been busting a gut out in the middle, I
don't usually feel like filling my guts back in the pavilion. Other
bowlers are not necessarily the same. Andrew Flintoff and Steve
Harmison can scoff loads at lunchtime, whether they're due to be
bowling after the interval or not. Even if we were playing at Lord's,
where the lunches are fantastic, I would probably get a plateful of
food, but just pick at it around the edges, have four or five mouth-
fuls and leave the rest. Fred and Harmy, meanwhile, would be tuck-
ing into their bangers and mash and looking at me as though I
was a disgrace to the Fast Bowlers' Union.

When we've been bowling in the searing heat, maybe against Sri
Lanka in Galle, I'll force down a meal replacement drink at lunch
or tea, plus half an energy bar if I can stomach it. Then, at the end
of play, I'll have a protein shake to help the body repair and recover.
That gets into your body quickly, it's like drinking a pint of Guinness (except a little lower down the fun scale), but it doesn't satisfy

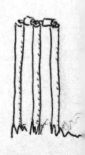

your hunger. So in the evening I'll go out and eat like an absolute horse. By this time I'll be starving. I'll fill myself up with a three-course meal, and that will be enough to see me through the next day.

I'm not saying that my way is the right way to do it. Clearly, my way wouldn't work for everyone. It's just that we're all different – some more different than others, you might say – and my unconventional habits have not served me too badly throughout my career.

Some people might think that if I'd eaten in accordance with the nutritionists' advice all the time I might have hung onto my England place longer than I did. But I was following exactly the same eating patterns at the height of my career, when everyone was praising me for my stamina, bowling in the heat and taking hatfuls of wickets in places like Nagpur and Adelaide. I've always been someone who runs in as hard in the last session as the first, no matter how much I've had to eat. So if anyone turned round to me and said that my performance was suffering because I hadn't eaten properly, that would be

A BARROWLOAD OF BOLLOCKS

There are other days during a Test match, of course, when I don't have to bowl at all. And if we are on a batting day, eating is a different matter altogether. For the bowlers in the England team, those days have been known as FYB days: Fill Yer Boots. On a batting day at Lord's, with little prospect of being summoned to the crease to bat and ample opportunity to fill our faces, more than a few bowlers have thought to themselves: 'This isn't a bad way to earn a living.' We might even rouse ourselves to watch a bit of the cricket, if it was interesting enough. Always providing the batsmen play their part, that is, by filling *their* boots out in the middle and ensuring our leisure time, something that could not necessarily be guaranteed.

I don't want people to come away from reading this with the notion that I want nutritionists to be wiped off the face of the earth. They speak a lot of sense and it's absolutely right that they are employed to advise professional sportsmen. But if you're sensible and your mum has fed you the right stuff when you were younger, you really shouldn't need anyone to tell you what you ought to be eating. I suppose it's nice to know the reasons *why* certain things are good for you from a scientific viewpoint, but a lot of what they tell us is just plain old common sense.

I remember the first time I was given dietary advice, when I was playing club cricket for the Pirates in Johannesburg, which was before I'd made it into Yorkshire's first team. I was only 18 at the time, but I flew down to Cape Town a couple of times to visit the High Performance Centre run by Neil Burns, the former Essex, Leicestershire and Somerset wicketkeeper. We were shown a list of things that the dieticians had decided we aspiring young crick-eters really should be eating. I looked at the list of good stuff and thought: 'Hmmm, isn't that the sort of stuff that people generally eat anyway?' Pasta, vegetables, chicken? We're hardly talking rocket science here.

Perhaps I'm lucky in that I've never really had to worry too much about my food because a balanced diet has always come fairly natu-rally. Most of the time, I'm a meat and two veg type of bloke. Quite often, in fact, it will be meat and three veg, or even four. My favourite dishes to cook are steak and stuffed loin of pork, usually with spuds and a big pile of veg on the side; nothing too toxic there. I know from speaking to blokes like Martin Corry that, as part of their prescribed diet, rugby players have to do all sorts of weird things, like eating broccoli for breakfast. Come to think of it, maybe that's why I gave up playing rugby. But cricketers really just have to be sensible.

As long as we were coming up to scratch in fitness tests, the England management always trusted us with what we were eating. I can't recall Duncan Fletcher or Peter Moores ever tapping me

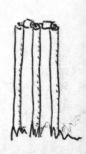

on the shoulder in a restaurant and saying: 'Hoggy, I really think you ought to give the steak a miss tonight. How about some grilled chicken?' If they had done, I'd have told them where to get off. Most people who get as far as the England dressing-room are grownups, and they are treated accordingly. Maybe if a young player is on tour in Sri Lanka for the first time and feels dizzy at the end of a sweltering session, the management would look into what he's been eating. But these days players have usually been on tours to hotter countries when they were younger and they will have been educated then. It's not often that an England player needs his arse wiping. And if he did, he probably wouldn't last too long at the highest level.

I suppose the one time that our diet really has to be controlled is on tours to the subcontinent, when you are constantly trying not to be struck down by the dreaded Delhi Belly.

I know we have to be careful what we eat over there – it is actually in our ECB contracts that we are not allowed to eat shellfish – but by the time we are a few weeks into the tour, we run a serious risk of overdosing on egg, beans and chips.

When you are on tour in India, you just have to accept that at some point on the trip your guts are going to be turned inside out. Within the first week there are usually at least two or three of the lads disappearing off to the toilet at regular intervals. And believe me, it is not a pleasant experience. If you're lucky, the bug will stay with you for a day or so, during which you'll probably have to nip off to the toilet every five minutes. Which makes it quite difficult to get much practising done. And on a match day, even if you've been named as thirteenth man, you never think, 'Time to put my feet up and carry a few drinks.' There's always a fair chance of a couple of last-minute withdrawals that will mean you end up playing.

On my last visit to India in 2006, I had an especially severe case of Delhi Belly. I'll spare you the gory details, but suffice to say that, a couple of days after we arrived on tour, I woke up on the bathroom floor, completely disorientated.

WHERE THE HELL AM I??!!??

I kept looking around, trying to work out where I was. It was a bizarre feeling. As I started to come round, I quickly sussed out that I wasn't at home. I was also pretty sure that I wasn't on holiday. So I knew that I must be somewhere to do with cricket. 'Right,' I thought to myself, 'where have I just come on a cricket tour? Oh yes, that's it, I'm in India. That explains a lot.'

At which point I looked down and noticed the large pool of sick on the floor and a bit of something that had come out of the other end as well. Oops sorry, I forgot to spare you the details.

In the hope of avoiding these pitfalls, on match days and training days in Pakistan and India you are provided with a menu that is almost unimaginably bland. Every day that we were playing or training, we would have a buffet with exactly the same options (or lack of options), which are now indelibly imprinted on my mind.

I'll run you through the uninspiring stroll down the buffet table: the first pot at the table would contain rice. The second tray would have some sort of potato, either baked or, if we were really lucky, mashed. The next dish, without fail, would be grilled chicken. Then would come a very mild chicken tikka, followed by a bowlful of dhal. And finally, there would be a plate-load of beans.

And that was our menu, for the whole tour, every single match day or training day. Sometimes, in an attempt to make the choice seem more interesting, they would switch the trays the other way around, so that the beans came first, the dhal came second, then the chicken tikka ... You get the picture. I think that was their idea of a varied diet.

Occasionally, just occasionally, we would be treated to the dizzying excitement of a bowl of soup. And if we were **REALLY, REALLY** lucky, the flavour of the soup might change, from vegetable soup to chicken. Yippee!! And that really was the height of culinary

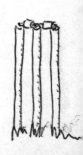

excitement. Even on batting days, I struggled to fill my boots or my belly on those tours.

Later in my career, some real progress was made when some bright spark had the idea of taking a toastie maker into the dressing-room. That was an incredibly popular move, which revolutionised our diets on tour. Once the toastie maker had been introduced, lunch orders in India were a straightforward matter.

Enter the dressing-room attendant, ever willing to please: 'What are we having for lunch today, chaps? Mr Flintoff?'

'A couple of toasties, thanks.'

'Mr Harmison?'

'A couple of toasties, thanks.'

'Mr Vaughan?'

'A couple of toasties, thanks.'

(*Some time later*)

'Er, that'll be twenty-two toasties, thanks very much.'

'And for tea?'

'Oh, the same again will do nicely, cheers.'

Nowadays, everywhere that the England cricket team goes, the faithful toastie maker goes with them.

Of course, it's not that often that we have to be so careful about what we eat. When we're on home soil, an England cricketer is just as likely to give in to temptation and enjoy the occasional pig-out as anybody else. I don't know anybody, male or female, who doesn't look forward to having a complete and utter blow-out on something disgustingly unhealthy every now and then, and I'm certainly no exception. Curries (something with a bit of kick, like a Madras), Chinese (anything on the menu), full English breakfast (as long as it's not first thing in the morning).

Love 'em all

Incidentally, why is it that so many of the nicest things to eat are bad for you? Why can't fish and chips be a supremely healthy meal? Why can't Chinese takeaways be a life-enhancing source of vitamins and minerals? Who decides these things?

If I'm playing for Yorkshire in Scarborough, there's no way that I'm going to survive for four days without guzzling some fish and chips, ideally eaten out of the wrapper, sitting on a bench in the sunshine and looking out to sea. Never mind that fish and chips is a little bit lardy; that is something that just has to be done. Whether it's on the nutritionist's list of 'Things You Shouldn't Eat' or not.

I'm sure that if you were strict enough and dedicated enough to becoming a super-duper athlete, you would avoid these things, you'd follow the nutritionist's advice to the letter and you'd be in tip-top shape, happy and healthy, singing and dancing. But would you be bored as hell? And would it really make much difference to how you performed on a cricket field? Would it bollocks!

As far as I'm concerned, you'd be sacrificing an awful lot for very little. I appreciate that it may be different for footballers and rugby players. Their sports require a different level of athleticism. But I don't really see the point of being anal about your diet. And I don't know many people in cricket who are.

Where Sarah and I live, in Baildon, we're very lucky because, although it's not a particularly big place, there are loads of choices for a decent takeaway feed. Four or five curry houses, three Chinese restaurants, a couple of chippies and a very fine café at our local Morrison's supermarket.

Not so long ago, I was walking through Baildon with my friend, Chris Stoner, and I bumped into one of the waiters from the Rupali curry house. He said hello, and we stopped for a quick chat. We then wandered a little further along and, on the other side of the road, I saw a bloke from the Chinese takeaway. 'All right Hoggy!' he shouted. A few hundred yards further along, we walked past the fish 'n' chip shop and one of the lads called out from there: 'Ayup Hoggy, y'all right, pal?'

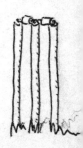

Chris turned to me and said: 'Bloody hell, does *every* takeaway establishment in this place know who you are?'

Apart from a fondness for takeaways, when I'm in a certain eating mood I can lurch from snack to snack all day long. If I'm hanging around the house for the day, our kitchen cupboards tend to get raided on a regular basis. Crisps are a particular weakness: Cheese and Onion, any flavour of Wheat Crunchies and especially Monster Munch, either Pickled Onion or Flaming Hot. Yum yummy yum. I was most peed off a couple of years ago when they stopped making Roast Chicken flavoured Monster Munch: they were my favourite. If you people at Walker's are reading this,

PLEASE PLEASE PLEASE BRING BACK ROAST CHICKEN MONSTER MUNCH!

I am fairly sure that my custom alone will make it worth your while. And if you need some extra persuasion, the next time I'm playing cricket on the telly I could give you some free advertising by pulling a packet out of my pocket while I'm walking back to my mark and munching on a few crisps before I run up to bowl. Please contact my agent if you're interested.

When I'm in snacking mode, I also like to make concoctions from whatever happens to be available in the kitchen at the time. One of my favourite culinary inventions is the glorious **JAM AND CORNFLAKE SANDWICH!** I'm so keen on these that I'm think-ing of patenting the recipe. Ordinary jam sandwiches are okay, but they just don't have enough texture. Shove in a handful of corn-flakes and they've got that little bit extra crunch to them. You really should try one some time, they're great.

One of the many great things about being a professional crick-eter is that you can enjoy these occasional feeding frenzies, but you will always be doing enough exercise to make sure that you don't get fat. If you're managing your lifestyle as you should, you'll be doing some pretty strenuous exercise most days. If you're on the road, staying in hotels for much of the time, the temptation to overindulge is always going to be there, but the chances are that you'll be running around like a silly bugger at nine o'clock the next morning, so there should be ample opportunity to burn[†] off whatever you've eaten. I suppose it's true that there are a few chubby cricketers around. But maybe they're just big-boned.

I've always had a fairly good idea of my optimum fighting weight, which is about 95 kg, just under 15 st. That's not a weight that the fitness experts have recommended – we've never had that sort of thing dictated to us – it's just the number that has generally popped up when I've stood on the scales. Other than our sessions at Loughborough, we don't get weighed as a matter of course during the English season. It's a different matter when you're on tour somewhere hot. You'll be sweating buckets then, so you weigh in at the end of every session to see how much you've lost.

There have only been a couple of times over the course of my career that I've put on a few kilos, and that was out of season, when I've not been training as hard and there has been more time to reach for the crisp cupboard. The last time was before I went away with England to Sri Lanka in late 2007. Since the end of the season, I had gone up to 97 or 98 kg and I decided that, in order to lose the weight before we went on tour, I'd go on a bit of a crash diet for a couple of weeks, similar to the Atkins plan. That meant that I could keep eating loads (which, I'll admit, was the main attraction), but I had to cut out the carbohydrates.

I had to be careful with my exercise while I was doing this. I didn't do any intensive training, because you need the carbs for energy and, if you were to do anything explosive without those in you, your muscles would get attacked. So I restricted myself to

---

[†]**HOGFACT:** It has been estimated that an opera singer BURNS an average of more than two calories per minute during a performance. So why are they all so fat then?

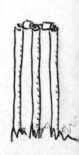

light fat-burning exercise, like nice long walks with the dogs. I didn't tell the ECB nutritionists about it at the time, because I'm not sure they would have approved. I told Sarah and she thought it was a good idea. And it did the trick for me. I turned up feeling fit as a fiddle and better for being a few kilos lighter.

The evening meals on this diet were not a problem at all. I love potatoes and rice and I missed those, but I just had piles of swede and carrots instead, which was no great hardship. And the real beauty was that I could eat as much meat as I liked – plenty of bacon, sausages, steak, chicken, fish – and I was actually losing weight!

The tough bit for me, though, was the lunches, because I'm a big sarnie fan. But bread was off the menu, so sandwiches were out of bounds. And the suggested alternative for a lunchtime snack always seemed to be salad, which as far as I'm concerned is a waste of space on the plate. Salad is just a few drops of water with the odd vitamin thrown in to make it seem more palatable.

FAST BOWLERS DO NOT EAT SALAD!

So the lunches were a bit of a struggle, but generally I had a pretty good time on the diet. I ate loads, but lost a few kilos and then picked up my training regime again for the start of the tour to Sri Lanka. Job's a good 'un.

I think that's probably all you need to know about me and my slightly unconventional eating habits. If you see a nutritionist any time soon, give him my regards. And maybe offer him a packet of crisps.

Writing this chapter has made my belly start to rumble. I'm off for something to eat. Jam and cornflake sarnie, anyone?

BIG CHEF HOGGY'S
à la Scorecard Menu

JAM AND CORNFLAKE SANDWICHES

You will need: 2 slices bread, jam, cornflakes
To make: (1) slap jam on bread (2) bung in cornflakes (3) scoff

MASH AND STASH

You will need: mashed spuds, raw onion, tuna, mayonnaise, sweetcorn
To make: (1) put mash in a bowl (2) chuck in other ingredients (3) scoff

SOUPED-UP VEG

You will need: leftover veg from Sunday roast – parsnips, carrots, whatever. Plus random sauces and spices that are lying around the kitchen
To make: (1) chuck all veg in a blender (2) see what's lying around the kitchen – I like cinnamon and brown sauce (3) throw those in and mix (4) scoff

SUPERSONIC NOODLES

You will need: Super Noodles, bacon, sausage, mushrooms, eggs
To make: (1) Pour boiling water on noodles (2) lob all the other stuff in a frying pan (3) mix everything together (4) scoff

KNACKERED NIGHT'S NOSH

You will need: phone, takeaway menu
To make: (1) ring number on menu (2) think of something nice to eat (3) answer door (4) scoff

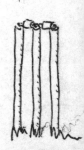

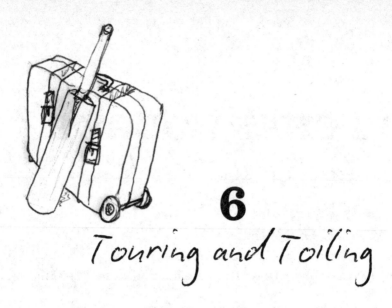

6
Touring and Toiling

It's a great job being an England cricketer, a fantastic way to earn your crust. We all have to work in life and if I was going to be able to do my work out on a cricket field, playing for my country, I was going to be a fairly happy bloke. The one big problem is that there is always the possibility that someone else will come along and nick your job; or that the boss will decide it's time to give someone else a go, so you might be given your cards and sent on your way. During the summer of 2002 I'd been an ever-present in the Test side and, in theory, being given a central contract should have given me an element of job security. But as I was well aware at the time, and as would be proven to me over the next couple of winters, there is no such thing as job security for an international cricketer.

That especially applies to England cricketers around the time of an Ashes series. Consistency of selection is all very well, but it can only go so far if you're being stuffed game after game. Something – anything – has to be done to try to improve fortunes, and careers can be put on the line as a result. Until the minor miracle of 2005, those stuffings happened on a regular basis and I got my first dose of them on the tour to Australia in the winter of 2002–03. For me as a bowler, and for the England team in general, this was the usual reality check about how far we still had to go. We were up against a very good Australian side, probably one of the best teams in history, and in 2002 they were not too far from their best.

It was the first time I had played against Australia and I had the misfortune to run into Matthew Hayden at the absolute peak of his game. Or maybe I should say that he ran into me, and then ran over me. In the first Test at Brisbane, he hit 197 in the first innings, 103 in the second and never looked back from there. I wasn't the only one to suffer, of course, nor was he the only one to dish out the punishment. We lost by 384 runs at Brisbane, then went on to Adelaide and lost by an innings there. Welcome to the Ashes.

When anybody asks me who was the best batsman I bowled at, I'll always say Hayden. In some ways, that may seem odd, because in the next couple of Ashes series I got him out plenty of times. But during that series in 2002–03, he was just horrible to bowl at. If I bowled it full, he would smash it straight back past me, or bludgeon it through the covers. If I tried to bowl it a little bit shorter, he'd just rock back and pull me for six. Hmmm, going to have to think of something else, Hoggy. What next? How about bowling it a bit wider, make him either leave it or go reaching for it? All the more room for him to swing his arms and hit it even harder through the off side. A touch straighter? Bosh, he's whipped me away through the leg side.

I DON'T KNOW WHERE THE F**K TO BOWL AT HIM!

Not a nice feeling, that, when whatever you tried just didn't seem to be good enough. It made me feel very small. And when you're running in to bowl at someone as big as Hayden, that's not a good way to feel.

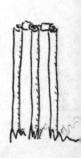

I didn't know it at the time, but my struggles in that series were really just a reflection of my inexperience and the lack of alternative tricks up my sleeve for when the ball wasn't swinging. In particular, I hadn't really learnt my angles, something that Duncan Fletcher was always very keen on. I hadn't figured out, for example, that if you're bowling right-arm over to a left-handed batsman and you bowl down the line of off stump, if the ball is not swinging it will be outside off by the time it reaches the batsman. So Hayden was able to keep cutting me from what I thought was a good line on off stump, when in fact he had more width than I realised. A couple of years later, when I had a few more miles in my legs and a few more cells in my brain, I'd learned from this experience and I was able to bowl much more effectively at Hayden, and left-handers in general, even if the ball wasn't swinging. I got him out three times in England in 2005 and twice more in Australia.

In that 2005 series we came up with an unusual fielding position for Hayden, putting a man on the straight drive, right next to the pitch on the off side, a couple of yards in front of the non-striker. He was very keen on hitting in that area, it was one of the ways he liked to assert himself, and we were really keen to cut off this scoring area. A while later, during the following Ashes series in Australia in 2006–07, Hayden told me that we had got to him by putting a man in that position in 2005. He said that he should have backed himself to hit the ball past or through that fielder, but it had got into his mind and created indecision. That was a great piece of strategic thinking from Michael Vaughan and Fletch. And I was surprised that Hayden was so honest about it, because we were still playing against him at the time.

For a long time, apart from not enjoying bowling at him, I really used to dislike Hayden as a bloke. I thought he was righteous and arrogant. But as we got to know each other better, and as the battle between us started to even up, we were able to have a few beers together after a game. During the last Ashes series down under, when he found out that I was planning on staying out in Australia for a holiday after the series, he even offered us the use of his beach house on an island just off the coast of Queensland. It sounded really nice – a lovely setting, with dolphins swimming up to the pier – but I would have felt a bit uncomfortable about accepting. Still, it was good of him to offer.

Anyway, back to my first encounters with that nice Mr Hayden when he wasn't quite so nice to me. After the mauling of the first couple of games, I lost my place for the third Test in Perth to Chris Silverwood, my mate from Yorkshire. I suppose if someone's going to nick your job, it may as well be one of your mates. But after he'd bowled four overs, he crocked his ankle. What a happy time we were having.

For obvious reasons, it wasn't a huge surprise to be dropped, because I was really struggling. Up to that point in my career, whenever I wasn't taking wickets I'd always been able to call on the lessons I'd learnt in Bloemfontein and find an awkward line and length that the batsman would struggle to score off. But Hayden and Co just hit through the line and knocked me off my length. I would need more than that if I was going to compete against the best.

And when I was struggling on that tour, I didn't feel as though there was much support coming from the management. It was a tough time. I'd failed to come up with the goods and I really felt as though I'd let people down. There are times playing under Fletch when you just don't know where you stand with him. If you're scoring runs or taking wickets, he'll talk to you as much as you like. But if you're not doing the business, or if you're injured, it just felt as though he didn't want to talk to you. As a young player making your way, that can feel like a pretty unpleasant way of treating people.

There was, mercifully, a small measure of consolation before the end of the series when I came back into the side for the fifth Test in Sydney. We'd lost the third and fourth Tests as well so they must have been looking for anybody that fancied a game by that stage. I took four wickets in the first innings, then Andy Caddick bowled brilliantly to take seven in the second and we managed to win by

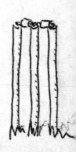

225 runs to avoid a whitewash. I suppose I really ought to mention the one wicket I took in the second innings: ML Hayden lbw Hoggard 2. That was the first time, but it wouldn't be the last!

Any victory over Australia is not to be sniffed at, and it gave us a huge lift at the end of the series to do the stuff in Sydney, but we knew that wins don't count for half as much once the series has gone.

There was one other problem I had to deal with during that series that I hadn't encountered before: How to keep a straight face when you're batting and Darren Lehmann is standing at short leg. You know how Aussies are supposed to be really nasty, sledging the life out of anyone who comes out to bat against them? Well, all that Boof did was try to make me laugh. And he succeeded.

There I was in Brisbane, playing in the most important game of my life, with Glenn McGrath and Jason Gillespie steaming in to bowl at me in front of a crowd of umpteen thousand at the Gabba, and I was just trying to stop myself from giggling at the crease. Every time I kept a ball out, he'd be crouching under the lid, three feet away from me, taking the piss. I'd better not tell you what he was saying, because it was rather rude, but it succeeded in cracking me up.

How am I supposed to concentrate when I've got his nonsense coming at me from short leg? Never mind the sledging. Put the funniest bloke in your side at short leg and see if the batsman can concentrate then.

I have been on some long tours over the course of my career, but that winter of 2002–03 really was something of a marathon. I was still involved with the one-day side in those days and we had started off in Sri Lanka in September with the Champions Trophy. No idea what the results were there, those tournaments are much of a muchness after a while, but I'm pretty sure we didn't win it. Then there was three months playing against Australia in the Ashes and a one-day series, all of which was followed directly by the World Cup in South Africa and Zimbabwe. In the six months between the middle of September and the middle of March, we were away from home for four and a half months. That is a long time away when you are losing a lot of cricket matches.

It is even longer when you're not playing in those matches, and I didn't play a single game in the World Cup, which took up the last month of that longest winter. You've got to try and keep yourself keyed up, try to ensure that you're ready to play in case those in front of you fall over at some stage. But inevitably it's harder to motivate yourself for carrying drinks and batting gloves than it is for playing cricket. There are only so many times you can tell yourself to be the best drinks carrier in the business.

Homesickness[†] goes with the territory. Some feel it more than others and I've been lucky that I've never been one of the worst sufferers. I've always been content to disappear to my room with a good book if I've been feeling a bit fed up, and that doesn't usually last for long. But if you've been working away for five or six months, however nice the place you're staying in, who wouldn't start to think about the green, green grass of home every now and then?

In the last few years, those days when you're feeling a long way from home have been made a lot easier with Skype and video calling. Now you can ring home every day, if you want, and check that your family still love you (if they ever did) and that the four walls at home are still standing. Back in 2003 that wasn't an option, so you could go an awful long time without seeing the faces of your nearest and dearest.

[†]**HOGFACT:** It has been claimed that the colour light green is helpful to those suffering from homesickness. Especially for people who are a long way from England and missing their mushy peas.

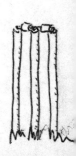

Having said that, we've been quite lucky in my time because our other halves have been allowed on tour a lot more than they used to be. Usually, they'll come out for a couple of weeks in the middle of the tour, whereas five years ago, when I started, it would have been just for a few days. Mind you, it's all very well saying that if you've actually got someone to come out and see you. If you're one of the single lads, or if your other half isn't coming out, it can be bloody hard work once everybody else is coupled up.

The atmosphere on tour changes completely when the girls come out. On the team bus, instead of a load of laddish larking about, all those silly boys suddenly start behaving very sensibly, as though they've had a personality transplant overnight. And so the single lads are left to sit together and you just know that they're secretly thinking: 'This is rubbish. Can't the women get another bus?' I can remember being hit by that feeling when Sarah didn't come out to the West Indies in 2004. Almost everybody else was married by that stage and, for the fortnight or so that their families were visiting, there was only me and Simon Jones left on our tods. No disrespect to Jonah, but that was a long couple of weeks.

It was in South Africa during the World Cup that I first developed a useful way of dealing with being away from home. For a couple of years I had been using visualisation as part of my preparation for a game, closing my eyes and training my brain in what to expect in a certain situation. More of which I'll tell you about a bit later on in the book. But one day in Durban, I was missing home and missing walking the dogs.[†] I suddenly thought to myself: 'Hey, why don't I go for an imaginary dog walk?' So I went out for a stroll on the beach and imagined I had the dogs running alongside me.

[†]**HOGFACT:** In Oklahoma you can be arrested for making ugly faces at dogs. Quite right too; they're very sensitive creatures. But how do really ugly people avoid doing this?

It worked. I felt a lot better afterwards, and I've repeated the trick plenty of times since, although not always on the beach. I'll lie back on the bed in my hotel room, close my eyes and set off from home. I'll go out of the gate and into the fields, remembering exactly where the trees are, where the stones are, picturing the places where I have to pick my feet up because it's muddy. I can recommend it. I've always enjoyed my splashes through the Yorkshire mud while I've been holed up in a hotel somewhere in the back of beyond. The really good news is that you don't have to dry the dogs' feet when you get back home. And there's no technology required to get this little slice of home, just a moderately well-functioning brain. It can't be that difficult if I can do it.

I was first introduced to visualisation by a sports psychologist who came in to talk to us at Yorkshire. He told us that our minds are powerful tools and that they can always influence the way our bodies work. He gave us an example. If you think about having sex with a beautiful woman, he said, there is a fair chance that you'll get an erection. 'Bloody hell, he's right,' I thought. 'This bloke must be onto something ...'

There are other, more practical uses. When I'm preparing to bowl, I can picture a ball pitching on off stump and swinging away, I know what that feels like and I can feel my body doing it. (No erection this time, though. Not even if it's a really good ball.) The repetitive nature of cricket means that much of our preparation is about muscle memory, trying to get your body to do the same things over and over again, and visualisation is a useful tool in that.

Sometimes on a practice day on tour, we'll go to the ground, run through some exercises and warm-ups and then there will be an optional net session. Those that fancy it can go for a bat and a bowl, those that don't can suit themselves. On those occasions I'll be inclined to say: 'Oh, I think I'll just have a mental net today, thanks.' So I'll lie down in the dressing-room, close my eyes and have a little snooze. Then someone will come back in and say, 'How's

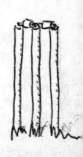

the mental net going, Hoggy?' So I try to sound as though I've been awake the whole time.

'Fantastic, thanks. I've taken eight wickets so far. Don't interrupt me again.'

The spirit in camp can fluctuate like mad in your time on tour, especially if you're away for as long as we were that winter of 2002–03. Clearly, whether you're winning or losing makes a big difference, but it's not always so straightforward. Sometimes, bizarrely, I've found that the greatest feeling of togetherness comes when you've just lost a game but still have the chance to play your way back into the series. I'm not saying that I recommend going 1–0 down in a three-match series (although I know it might often have looked as though that was our plan), but for some reason those situations seem to bring a touring squad together. You're in a hole, I suppose, and you're relying on your team-mates to help you dig your way out. Is that a siege mentality? A backs-to-the-wall situation? Whatever it is, it brings a certain mood of giddiness to the camp.

Other than that, spirits tend to be at their highest at the beginning and towards the end of the tour. Those are the times when the players either haven't had time yet to get on each other's nerves, or we know that there isn't long to go. If a series has just been won in the final game, and everyone is about to go home, then it really is party time. On our tour to Pakistan in 2000 I'd had a fairly dull few weeks, spending the entire trip as twelfth man and drinks waiter, but once we'd won the final Test in Karachi, when Graham Thorpe and Nasser Hussain saw us home in the dark to clinch the series, the atmosphere on our two little buses driving away from the ground was incredible. Everybody was dancing around and singing the theme tune from *The Great Escape* and those buses were rocking so much that it was amazing we didn't come off the road.

If you haven't got many victories to celebrate, the middle weeks on tour can be the hardest, apart from the time when you're joined by your missus. These are the weeks when you've stayed in so many hotels that you struggle to distinguish one from another. Living out of a suitcase is something that you quickly get used to as a professional cricketer, but you stay in so many hotels that some of them just pass you by. Even when you're in England during the summer, you get used to treating hotel after hotel as a temporary home. In my early days with Yorkshire, I used to hate staying in hotels night after night, I could never get to sleep. But fairly quickly I realised that when you get in bed and turn the light off it looks the same wherever you are.

You're all right then if you manage to sleep through until morning, but if you wake up during the night needing a wee there can be problems, especially on tour when you're staying in a different hotel every week. I've lost count of the number of times that I've climbed out of bed, then groggily tried to make my way towards the bathroom, only to walk straight into a wall.

After a few weeks away, it's not just the room layouts that all tend to blur into one. On a long tour, you can start to forget which room number you're staying in, or even which floor you're on. Quite often I'll come back to the hotel after a day's play or practice, get into the lift and someone will ask me: 'What floor?'

'Fourth. No, fifth. No, that was last week. What floor are you on?'

'Seventh.'

'No, it's not the seventh. Let's try the sixth.'

And then, when you eventually find your floor, there is the bigger problem of remembering where your room is. Hotel keycards don't usually have room numbers on them these days, so there can be a lot of guesswork involved. One hotel corridor is pretty much the

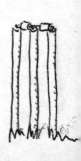

same as the next, so you walk out of the lift and wander off slowly in the direction you think you *ought* to be going. After a while, with a bit of luck, you might spot a landmark, such as a fire extinguisher, and think: 'I remember, I was third door on the left after the fire extinguisher.' You just hope then that you've got the right fire extinguisher. And that the room third on the left after the fire extinguisher wasn't your navigation plan from the previous week's hotel.

This business of forgetting my room number can be a complete pain in the arse. I'll go down to the restaurant sometimes and be asked on the way in which room I'm staying in. I won't have a clue, so I'll have to scoot off to reception to ask them my number before I can get any food. Or on a day off, I might get a phone call in my room from Jimmy Anderson, who will have rung through reception to ask if I fancy going out for lunch.

'I'll be round in ten minutes,' Jimmy will say. 'Which room are you in?'

'Erm, not sure, hang on a minute.' And I'll put the phone down, nip over to open my door and have a look on the other side – 'Oh, 412. I'd never have guessed that' – before returning to tell Jimmy where to come.

Thankfully, almost all the hotels we stay in these days are top notch. The only dodgy ones tend to be in places that are completely off the beaten track, such as Guwahati in India, where we went for a one-day match in 2006. And just as importantly, on an England tour these days everybody gets his own room. I usually do with Yorkshire as well now that I'm a senior player, but that wasn't the case when I was younger. You never knew who you were going to share a room with and you never knew what you were going to get from them. One of the worst people I ever shared with at Yorkshire was one of my oldest mates, James Middlebrook, formerly of Pudsey Congs and now with Essex, and I was lumbered with him a few times in our early days in the first team.

Not only did he snore like a pig, he also talked in his sleep. One night when he'd switched his light off and I was lying in bed, reading a book, he started chuntering away in a loud, angry voice.

'Hoggy, if you do that again, I'm going to hit you!'

'What am I doing, Midders?'

'You're pushing in.'

'Pushing in where?'

'Pushing into t'queue.'

'Which queue?'

'Queue for t'Big Dipper.'

Then he rolled over and shut up for the rest of the night, so I never found out if he got on the Big Dipper. But the next night he was at it again, this time mumbling away at David Byas (nickname 'Gadge'), our captain with Yorkshire at the time.

'No, Gadge, I'm not gonna do it. Why do I always have to do it? I'm not doing it.'

I looked up from my book. 'What you on about, Midders?'

'It's Gadge. He always makes me bowl into t'f***ing wind.'

Which was followed by a big sleepy sigh, a roll over in his bed, and then presumably Midders was off, stomping down to fine leg in his sleep. I was lying on my bed, chuckling away, ready with my tale to tell in the dressing-room the next morning. The lads were most amused.

I might have been missing out on entertainment of that sort by having my own room, but on balance I think it's a price worth paying. Having the chance to get away in your own space, however briefly, is something that's very important on a tour, especially on a winter like we had in 2002–03. Touring remains one of the best parts of being an international cricketer, and when it's good it's very, very good. You get to visit some fantastic places and have a lot of fun. Occasionally it can be hard work, but luckily I didn't have any other winters as long and drawn out as that one.

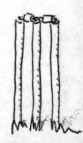

The following summer, in 2003, I only played in one Test match because I knackered the cartilage in my right knee, which kept me out for much of the season. A few days after I'd played in the first Test against Zimbabwe at Lord's, I turned out for Yorkshire in a C&G Trophy match against Worcestershire at New Road and with my first ball of the day I had Graeme Hick caught at third man, but hurt my knee as I bowled. I tried to stamp if off and then bowled two more balls which, with hindsight, may not have been the brightest thing to do. That was on 28 May, and the next time I bowled for Yorkshire's first team was on 24 August, having missed the whole of the Test series against South Africa in the meantime. Throughout my career, I've always been fairly laid-back about injuries. They're intensely annoying at the time, but as a fast bowler you know you're going to get 'em, so there's no point getting too down in the dumps when it happens.

Fortunately, I hit my straps pretty quickly after coming back from that knee injury in 2003 and in my first four-day match after injury I took seven for 49 against Somerset at Headingley, still the best first-class figures of my career. And that was quite timely, really, because I only had a few weeks to bowl myself into the England squad for the tours to Bangladesh and Sri Lanka before Christmas. I just about did enough.

The tour to Bangladesh was reasonably straightforward. We won both Tests, I picked up a few wickets – seven in the first game in Dhaka, two in the second at Chittagong – and I was named Man of the Series, although that was nothing to get excited about because the opposition weren't the strongest.

Then we moved straight on to Sri Lanka, where the heat and humidity can make life bloody hard for a fast bowler. After a few winters away on tour, you get used to bowling in hot weather, but the humidity in Sri Lanka adds another dimension. As luck would have it, though, we had a magic solution at hand this time, ingeniously provided by those wise folk at the ECB. To help us stay cool, we were going to wear ice vests. These were a special thin layer to wear under our shirts; they had gel in them and had been kept in a tub of ice. The theory was that the gel would remain cold and so help to keep our body temperatures down when we were sweating our nuts off out in the middle.

All good in theory. The problem was that these vests ended up dripping with water. And before we knew it, everything else that we were wearing was soaked: shirt, trousers, the lot. So we didn't wear them for long because the players got fed up with them. Another time, the medical staff recommended that we try wearing ice collars, which worked on a similar basis, but were just like a rolled-up hankie that you tied round your neck. And guess what? I put them on at first and thought: 'Oooh, yes, this is nice and cool.' Half an hour later in the field, though, I felt something trickling down my back. Oh yes, it's water from my ice collar. How annoying. So that would be ripped off and chucked away as well in the bin marked 'bad ideas'.

Sometimes I wonder whether people are coming up with these gimmicks for the sake of it. Presumably, somebody at the ECB must have seen a bit of scientific research or something from another sport and thought it would be worth a go in cricket. A few months later there was probably another bit of research that disproved the last lot.

I feel much the same way about ice baths, something we've been treated to in the last few years of my career. I wonder whether this is a medical fad that will have passed in a few years' time. This is the ritual we perform after coming off the field, which involves jumping into a wheelie bin full of ice. I realise what it is *supposed* to do. The idea is similar to the way you treat a bruise: by putting ice on it you keep the swelling to a minimum. An ice bath after a day's play is supposed to do the same for your muscles, but I wouldn't be surprised if, in a couple of years' time, some

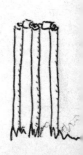

research will be produced that recommends hot baths only after exercise, opening up the blood vessels and giving everything a good chance to flow around the body.

If that were to happen, and ice baths became a thing of the past, you wouldn't find many cricketers shedding tears. Ice baths can be horrible, horrible, horrible. There will be just the odd time when you come off from playing somewhere really hot and think that a dip in the ice would be just the job to cool you down. But the rest of the time they are sheer hell.

In the England team, everybody was made to have an ice bath by Nigel Stockill, our physiologist. We were supposed to buddy up with one of our team-mates and do the baths in pairs, but occasionally I would try to hide to avoid going in. Nige always kept his beady eye on me, though.

'Hoggy, have you been in the ice bath yet?'

'Yes, Nige. It was horrible.'

'Who did you go in with?'

'Fred.'

'Fred hasn't been in yet.'

'Oh yes. I went in with Harmy.'

'Harmy hasn't been in yet either.'

'I remember now. I went in with Straussy. Sorry, Nige, my brain's frozen up after that ice bath.'

'No, you didn't go in with Straussy. He went in with Vaughany.'

'Bollocks. I suppose I'd better get in then ...'

The wheelie bins are about half full, so the ice goes up to your belly. If you want to try it at home, just run a cold bath, go in it up to your tummy and see how long you can stay in there. We were made to go for a minute in an ice bath, then a minute in a hot bath, then back to the ice bath, and so on, three or four times. It's never a pleasant thing to do. There's a song that nicely describes the experience, to the tune of 'The First Cut is the Deepest', by Cat Stevens:

♫ *The first bath is the coldest, baby I know*
The first bath is the coldest
When it gets to your toes, it hurts
When it gets to your balls, it's worse ... ♫ ♪

So roll on the new research proving that ice baths are a load of rubbish. I might even do it myself, once I've become a Professor of Fast Bowling Studies in my retirement. It would be one way to make myself very popular with a lot of sportsmen.

But back to our tour of Sri Lanka, where the ice vests weren't doing us much good at all. Well, they certainly didn't do me much good. We drew the first Test in Galle, finishing nine wickets down in our second innings. I helped Ashley Giles to bat out for a draw at the end, but otherwise I had a steady game, taking just the one wicket but not going for too many runs.

I didn't think I'd bowled that badly, but somebody did, because I then found myself dropped for the second Test in Kandy. The news came as a bit of a bombshell because I'd been chuffed with how I'd worked my way back into the side after my knee injury. The worst thing about it was that the selectors went for James Kirtley instead, like me a skiddy swing bowler. He was effectively a like-for-like replacement, so that was a pretty bitter pill to swallow.

This was my first winter playing under the captaincy of Michael Vaughan, as he had replaced Nasser Hussain the previous summer while I was out injured. It took me a while to adjust to playing under Vaughany because I'd played with him at Yorkshire since I started, but never as captain. So when I was dropped, and he was one of the selectors, I went to Nasser to talk about it. Nass was still around as a player then and, for all my England career up to this point, he'd been the man in charge. Very much in charge, given his style of captaincy. Understandably, Vaughany wasn't very happy about this and he called me into his office and said: 'Look, if you've got

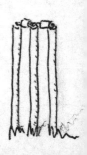

a problem, you need to speak to me about it. I'm the captain now, not Nass.'

Worse was to come in Colombo before the third Test. With the series poised at 0–0 with one to play, the selectors opted to leave out a batsman and go for an extra bowler. But rather than picking me, they went for Jimmy Anderson, another skiddy swing bowler, another like-for-like replacement. Now it seemed as though I was third-choice swing bowler, not to mention the other seamers who'd been picked ahead of me. I found that really tough to take at the time, because Jimmy hadn't even been bowling that well on tour, and I didn't think I'd been bowling that badly.

But what if my best just wasn't good enough any more? What if I was destined just to fall short of the class required for Test level, and even if I was bowling well it wouldn't be enough? I'd played twenty-two Tests by this stage, but this was the second time I'd been dropped in just over a year, and it was starting to look as though this awful possibility might prove to be true. I thought that my England career was over.

Sri Lanka won that last Test by 215 runs and then we went straight home for Christmas. No giddy end-of-tour parties for me this time. And I think it would be fair to say that it wasn't the happiest festive season ever held at the Hoggard household. Mention that Christmas to Sarah and she'll shudder. I was, apparently, an absolute nightmare to be around that Christmas. Scrooge would have been better company. I was the bear with the sore head, feeling desperately sorry for myself and mooching around the place, unable to stop thinking that everything I had worked for in my career was coming crashing down around me.

I just couldn't see a way back. Fletch didn't rate me, I didn't know whether Vaughany wanted me in the side, there were other bowlers around who were quicker than me. At this stage I was 26 going on 27, and I should have been coming to my peak. But that Christmas I was in the lowest trough of my career so far. I didn't think I stood a hope of being picked for the tour to the West Indies in the New Year and I was dreading seeing the list of players without my name on it. I wasn't even sure when the squad was going to be named. I didn't want to know when.

On 6 January, two weeks after I had got back from Sri Lanka (it felt like two months for those who had spent Christmas with me), we were sitting at home when Sarah got a text message from her mum that said: 'Congratulations.' She sent a reply saying: 'Congratulations for what?' Surviving the last couple of weeks with a grumpy sod without killing him, perhaps? Sarah's mum replied: 'After your horrible Christmas, it's all worked out okay and Matthew is going to Windies.' I didn't have a clue at this point, but Carole had seen the news on teletext. When I realised that she was right, I think I cried. It was a massive release of tension.

Strange to think that a player should have to find out something as important as that from his mother-in-law. Another fine example of ECB communications. But I didn't really care how I found out at that point. Thank you, thank you, thank you, wise men of the selection panel. Such a fine bunch of men, such good judges of a player. Happy bloody Christmas everyone! I was going to get another chance.

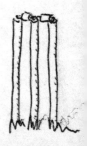

LEAGUE TABLE OF COUNTRIES TO VISIT ON TOUR

T here really aren't any bad places to go on a cricket tour. The weather's almost always nice and the people are almost always friendly. Except in Australia, where some of them yell abuse at you all day long, but that's only because they can't hold their booze.

1. SOUTH AFRICA

Great country, lovely scenery, and it was where I learned to drink. Any tourists who happen to wander anywhere near the Pirates clubhouse in Johannesburg should be advised that they are unlikely to come away sober.

2. WEST INDIES

Beaches, cricket, laid-back folk. And Barbados is a very nice place to take a hat-trick. In the times when Brian Lara was still playing, the traveller needed to immunise himself against flatwick-etitis in case of encountering the master batsman on a belting pitch in Antigua.

3. NEW ZEALAND

Beautiful place, some stunning countryside, and they love their rugby. There are some great outdoor pursuits too, but I don't recommend being dropped from the great height of the England cricket team while in New Zealand. From my experience, the landing can be quite painful.

4. AUSTRALIA

This would be higher up the list if we hadn't lost so many bloody games there. Visitors should beware of the wildlife that lurks in the stands at cricket matches. The native creatures found there can be highly uncivilised and should not be approached alone.

5. ZIMBABWE

Great shame what has happened in this lovely country, for cricket as much as everything else that is going on. My visit there in 2001 was almost cut short when Nasser Hussain, the captain, objected to me making chicken noises and threatened to send me home.

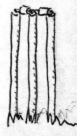

6. SRI LANKA

Watch out for cobras lurking beyond the boundary's edge. I picked one up and regretted it instantly. Tourists should also beware of the bumpy roads, especially if suffering from a bad back, as I was in 2007. I spent most of a 3½ hour journey from Kandy to Colombo lying on the floor of our coach. Not to be recommended.

7. INDIA

There are some amazing, never-to-be forgotten places, like Delhi and Calcutta, but on the one-day leg of our tour in 2007 we were sent to some places out in the sticks such as Guwahati and Jamshedpur where the hotels were yet to be finished. And there didn't appear to be any communications. I think we must have upset someone.

8. BANGLADESH

They might be second from bottom of my table, but there are still some amazing places to see there and some fantastically friendly people. We haven't had any memorable tours there yet, though. Any cricketers feeling a long way from home in Bangladesh at least have the consolation that victories tend to be fairly easily come by in this country.

9. PAKISTAN

There are some incredible parts to Pakistan, but in recent years we've had to spend too long in our hotels there due to the security situation, which was a great shame. But I don't think cricket teams will be going there for a while after the tragic events involving the Sri Lankan team in Lahore.

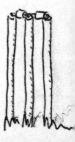

7
Physical Jerks

When you are on tour with England, you bump into all sorts of people: cricket fans, well-wishers, nutters, the lot.

Some just want to say 'hello', some will ask for an autograph, others you will end up chatting to you for quite a while. And if there was one good thing to come out of that tour to Sri Lanka in late 2003, it was a chance meeting I had in our hotel gym in Galle with a short, squat, extremely tough-looking ginger-haired cricket fan.

He was lifting some fairly monstrous weights in the gym and we got talking. I soon discovered that he was from Leeds, his name was Gary Simpson and he was on holiday watching the cricket. I told him that the gym was the last place you would find me on a holiday, but he said that he was a fitness trainer, so keeping fit sort of went with the job. Before I knew it, I'd signed him up as my personal trainer for three sessions a week, starting after Christmas. I'm not sure I knew what I was letting myself in for.

Whatever you do for a living, and however much you like your work, I think everyone has parts of the job that they don't enjoy. For me, and for many cricketers that I know, the one bit of the job that we really hate is the fitness training. It's a bloody ball-ache.

I suppose we're fortunate in that cricket is a sport that doesn't require you to be superfit, unlike rugby or football. But clearly you still need to be something more than a couch potato to play at the highest level. There are exceptions, but there aren't many fat boys around these days.

Everywhere in the world, international cricket teams are becoming fitter year by year, and nobody wants to be left behind, even if some coaches tend to overdo it. However fit you are, it's not much use being fit enough to run up Ben Nevis with a rucksack full of rocks on your back if your middle stump is getting knocked out first ball every time you go out to bat. But still, as much as we might hate it, the fitness training has to be done.

In terms of motivation, it's not so bad making yourself buckle down to the physical jerks during the season itself. As long as you're playing week in and week out, you basically concentrate on topping up your fitness levels as you go. And it doesn't take too much motivation to nip to the gym for half an hour during a match, while your team is batting, if there are another few lads around to do the same thing.

The time when motivation is really required is during the off-season, when there isn't that peer pressure to get you to the gym in the first place, or to help you make the most of it when you get there. If I was preparing to go on tour with England, for example, back in 2003 we were given guidelines as to the sort of fitness programme we should be following, but then we were pretty much left to our own devices to get on with it. Which requires plenty of motivation and self-discipline and general va-va-voom. Or you could hire a personal trainer to do all that for you, which is where Gary came in.

During my time as an England player, the attitudes towards fitness changed dramatically. When I started out, some players were happy just to ensure that they were fit enough to play cricket, that they didn't keel over after running a three and that they could conceal their beer guts by breathing in whenever the television

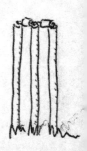

cameras were on them. But once central contracts had been introduced by the ECB in 2002, greater attention was paid to players' physical condition and higher levels of fitness were expected. This was made clear to us by Nasser Hussain and Duncan Fletcher. Although Nass hated going to the gym, he realised the importance of fitness and, as captain, he was determined to set an example.

The emphasis on fitness increased further when Michael Vaughan took over from Nasser as captain and then even more so when Peter Moores succeeded Fletch as coach. On the tour to New Zealand under Moores in 2008, we suddenly found ourselves being asked to do an extra fitness session at the end of a day's play in a warm-up match, even if we had just bowled fifteen overs. Everyone was a bit shocked by that.

Mooresy is something of an Iron Man himself, and fitness clearly meant a lot to him. Fitness levels, I suppose, are something that a new coach can always look to improve to stamp his mark on a squad, and I don't think we'll ever see a new bloke coming into the job and saying: 'Right, for starters, I think you lads are all a bit too fit. Nets are cancelled and we're all off down to the local greasy spoon for a decent fry-up.' Shame.

My own new and improved fitness regime started with Gary shortly after I found out from the mother-in-law that I had scraped into the squad for the West Indies tour, which was to start in late February. So I had a good few weeks to see how much I could benefit from working with a personal trainer, and I decided to throw myself into it.

In his infinite wisdom, Gary persuaded me that we ought to get our sessions out of the way first thing in the morning, so that I then had the rest of the day to do my own thing. Exercising at that time also has the advantage of raising your metabolism and, in theory, it wakes you up for the rest of the day. Or as I found out, it often makes you so tired that you often just want to go home and go back to sleep.

Three times a week, I would struggle to get myself out of bed at six in the morning, ready to make the twenty-minute drive to meet Gary at 7 a.m. in Headingley, where we'd do a session in the indoor cricket school or in a gym just down the road. That was an achievement in itself, because I'm not the greatest of morning people. I'm sure that plenty of other folk were starting New Year fitness regimes at the same time as me that year, getting out of bed to find it dark and cold and then deciding that life was much better back under the duvet. And I'd probably have been the same if I didn't have a scary personal trainer to crack the whip.

Without that to spur me into action, if I'd made it out of bed at all at 6 o'clock, I would probably have got down to the gym and thought: 'God, I'm tired. I'll do twenty minutes on a bike, twenty minutes on a treadmill, and then I'm off home.' But it's a bit different when you've got someone there to say: 'You're not doing twenty minutes, you're doing half an hour. And when you've finished that, you're going to do some weights. And then you're going to do some boxing on a punchbag.' In short, I had someone to kick my arse whenever I was in danger of slacking. I'm sure anybody would benefit from that.

Perhaps my instinctive aversion to these fitness sessions stemmed from my first experience of them, back in the days when I had just joined the academy at Yorkshire. I was still at school, in fact, when Yorkshire employed a new fitness trainer, a fearsome New Zealander called Dean Riddle, who rounded us up on a Wednesday evening to flog us half to death. In these sessions with Dean, we'd be made to sprint up the steep hills around Headingley, lamp-post by lamp-post, followed by endless step-ups on the kerbs when we were at the top, then down on our backs for sixty sit-ups, back up for another set of sprints, down again for a load of press-ups. And so on and so on, ad nauseam (literally, in some cases).

These were hard, hard sessions and I had never known anything like it. The day before a session, I used to dread them. Then, once

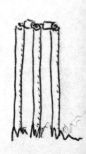

I'd got home afterwards and gone to bed I used to have nightmares about Dean barking orders at us.

One moment I'd be sleeping peacefully, the next I would suddenly find myself sitting bolt upright.

'What, Dean? Sixty sit-ups? Sixty press-ups? Sixty squat-thrusts?'

And then I'd stop, look around and think: 'Oh, thank God for that, I was only dreaming. I can go back to sleep.' A couple of hours later I'd wake up again.

'What, Dean? Which lamp-post? Where do we run to? How many times?'

And then I would come to my senses and realise that I didn't need to run to any lamp-posts or do any sodding sit-ups. Not until the following Wednesday, anyway.

The next day I would end up going to school completely knackered. Not necessarily due to the arduous fitness training I'd done, but because of all the times I'd woken up during the night.

So that was my chastening introduction to intensive exercise sessions, but it was never quite so traumatic with Gary. Perhaps that was because I didn't have to go to school the next day and try to keep my weary brain tuned into a chemistry lesson. But the great thing about the sessions Gary planned for me was that he varied them to keep them interesting. Or at least as interesting as fitness training gets.

He knew, for example, that I liked boxing on the pads and punch-bags, so one day he brought along a former professional boxer to join our session. This bloke was bald, much smaller than me and had his nose splattered all over his face. He must have been in his mid-40s, but I could see that he was still as fit as a fiddle. Once Gary had introduced us, the boxer put on his headguard and body

Short dungarees and long white socks: smart lad.

One man and his machine...

A rose between two thorns.

Karen   Me   Julie

Butter wouldn't melt...

No, honestly, we had a great time on hols.

Me and Bonnie, my Nan and Grandad's dog. Ecstatic.

Three Pirates: with Michael Lumb (left) and Grant Elliott.

Breakfast time in Pirates' clubhouse.

Car-sick? Beer-sick? Or both?

Simply gorgeous.

above Nicky and Barry Skjoldhammer, my second family in Jo'burg.

left Am I really this ugly? So it would seem. I look like Sloth out of *The Goonies*.

below Free and easy in Free State: me and Sarah with AD and Tina.

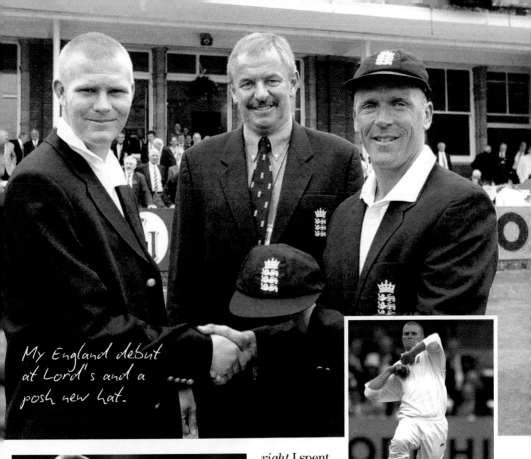

My England debut at Lord's and a posh new hat.

right I spent most of my debut suspended in mid-air.

above Nass telling me exactly what to bowl and how to bowl it. And if I didn't...

right Fletch pointing me in the right direction. Or maybe telling me where to go.

On my way to a seven-fer, Christchurch 2002.

above left Everyone needs a little love away on tour. Me and Nelly, Zimbabwe 2001.

above right They don't all swing out, Sachin! Tendulkar bowled at Lord's by one that nipped back down the slope, 2002.

left My first Test wicket, Younis Khan lbw at Old Trafford, 2001. It wasn't out, and he doesn't look impressed. I don't seem overly concerned.

That's right, Hoggy, eyes on the ball.

Ryan Hinds is caught at slip to complete my hat-trick in Barbados, 2004. Even Nasser (wearing helmet) looked happy with my bowling then…

The North of England male voice choir, celebrating victory in Barbados.

Despite his pathetic begging to be spared, Graeme Smith was lbw here, the first of my 12 wickets at Jo'burg in 2005.

armour, and said to me: 'OK, let's get started. You put your body armour on now. But don't worry, you won't need a headguard, because I'm not going to hit you on the head.'

'**PARDON??!!**' I said. 'What do you mean you're not going to hit me *on the head*? That sounds suspiciously like you're going to be hitting me somewhere else.'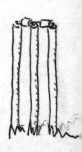

'Erm, yes, I think that's the general idea, isn't it, Gary?' he said. 'But only on the body.'

Gary nodded and smiled mischievously. 'Oh, marvellous,' I said. For the first three minutes, the boxer said, I was to try to hit him on the body, but he wouldn't be hitting me back. (Some consolation.) He would be keeping his hands by his sides, just trying to avoid my punches. So off we went, and for those three minutes he bobbed and weaved around, dodging right and left and stepping in close so I couldn't get any really decent shots in. Then he said: 'Right, we've had three minutes of you hitting me. I'll hit you now.'

'Do you have to?' I spluttered. He might have been smaller than me, but he looked an awful lot harder.

But Gary had obviously decided that I needed toughening up, so I went in the ring and took a few body blows, though the boxer was obviously being gentle with me. Good job, too, because I wasn't half as light on my feet as he was. We had a few rounds like that and then, for the last couple of rounds, I was allowed to aim for his head. I connected with one punch and bust his nose. Nothing new for him, clearly, but I certainly connected. And it turned out to be a foolish mistake because he then started punching me a little bit harder. Always on the body, but he certainly made sure that I didn't bust his nose again.

So that was an insight into how Gary was intending to keep things 'interesting' for me. A few weeks later, I turned up to meet him in the indoor cricket school at Headingley and he had chalked off a section of the floor in a square. 'I've got a surprise for you this week,' Gary said. 'I've got another mate of mine I'd like to introduce you to.'

Shortly afterwards, a Smart car drove into the car park. It only looked like a tiny little car, but it must have been a Tardis inside, because when the door opened, out stepped a six foot four, eighteen-stone monster. 'Matthew,' said Gary. 'Meet Andy, my mate.'

I felt like a 12-year-old being introduced to a proper grown-up. 'Erm, hello, Andy,' I said, in what felt like a very high-pitched voice. 'You're going to be boxing together today,' Gary said. I just gulped.

The area that Gary had chalked off in the cricket school, it turned out, was our boxing ring, and Andy was my 'surprise'. Lucky me. I could cope last time when the other bloke was smaller than me and twenty years older. This guy was bigger than me, a lot wider and probably a couple of years younger. It turned out that Andy was preparing for his first professional fight in a couple of weeks' time, so this wasn't a guy who was winding down at the end of his career.

The plan was that we would go in the ring for four three-minute rounds. He was going to keep me honest, he said, and I had the licence to batter him, if I could. He would try to avoid my punches, at the same time as keeping me honest, whatever that meant. And this time there was no body armour.

So I tried to hit him, as hard as I could, and he just brushed me off as though I was a particularly irritating fly. I was jabbing away, as hard and fast as I could, but I was barely troubling him.

And every so often he would suddenly unleash a big haymaker in my direction, which would miss my head by a few inches, but not by much. Each time one of those punches whistled past my head, it was close enough that I felt the rush of air past my head. So that's what he meant by keeping me honest. 'Christ,' I thought, 'if one of those punches connects with me, I won't be waking up until next week.'

All this time, whenever I wasn't trying to remember whether I'd made a will or not, I was continuing to throw my best shots at him. Occasionally, I'd connect with a glancing blow, but he never even flinched. Now I know that I'm no professional boxer, but I'm not the smallest of lads and a few of my punches, I thought, were fairly decent shots. But by the time those four rounds were finished, I felt fairly small and insignificant.

Thankfully, the airshots that he kept sending past my bonce were well directed and I survived. And, as intended by Gary, I was absolutely knackered. Mainly that was from physical exhaustion, but I think I'd also used up more than an ounce or two of nervous energy while those punches were flying round my head.

What Gary was trying to do in these sessions, apart from making me very scared, was coming up with exercises that kept my brain going as well as my body. Admittedly, sometimes I came close to having my brain knocked out of my skull, but he was certainly challenging me. Whereas some people thrive on the routine and discipline of doing the same exercise programme all the time, I was much more likely to push my body to the limit if there was plenty of variety in the activities. And even better if there was an element of rivalry to satisfy my competitive instincts.

Take long-distance running, for example, which I have never enjoyed. I'd go further than that, in fact, to say that **I ABSOLUTELY DETEST IT**. My boredom threshold is much too low. I know that you can run against the clock[†] and I could compete against myself that way, but that wouldn't motivate me anywhere near as much as competing against other people.

My dislike of running surprises some people, given the amount of time I spend walking the dogs. Why not just treat running like a glorified dog walk? Well, walking the dogs feels like an escape, a chance to breathe in fresh air and let your mind wander for a while. Running just feels like hard work and I get bored shitless.

[†]**HOGFACT:** One day in 1945, Big Ben was made five minutes slow when a flock of starlings perched on the minute hand of the famous CLOCK. Imagine if they did that just as the bongs were about to go on *News at Ten*. What would happen then?

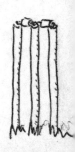

And yes, I have tried running with the dogs a few times. Molly, the Border Collie, just used to run in front of me all the time and try to trip me up. And Billy, the big daft Doberman, just thinks it's the greatest game ever and jumps up at me all the time, trying to bite me. Not ideal conditions, I'm sure you'll agree. Can you imagine Paula Radcliffe running a marathon with one dog getting under her feet and another leaping up in her face? I think not.

It has sometimes been suggested that stamina is one of my strong points as a fast bowler (a big arse and a wild haircut being the others), but that stamina certainly does not come from pounding up hill and down dale for hours on end. Don't get me wrong, I do go out running every now and then, when I feel I ought to, usually over the moors near home or round a golf course. On occasions I almost find it bearable. The problem is that we live in a very hilly area, so there aren't many flat stretches to intersperse with the ups and downs. I've scouted around to see if I can find an easier route to take, but it just can't be done. So whenever I go for a run from home, I know that I'm in for some bloody hard work.

I also feel that the relevance of long-distance running to cricketing fitness is fairly limited (well, he would say that, you might think, but bear with me). As a bowler, you will perform your role an over at a time, comprising six fairly explosive bursts of energy. Then you go down to fine leg to graze for five minutes. During your over off, you might have to chase a ball once or twice, but basically this is recovery time when you gear yourself up for another burst of action in your next over. And then, at the end of your spell, you get a much longer time to recover as the captain finds somewhere suitable in the field to hide a lumbering fast bowler.

One bright side to the niggling back injuries I've had over the last couple of years has been the instruction that I should be careful not to overdo the jogging, concentrating instead on sharp, short sprints. Picture my expression when I was told that. I could barely keep my face straight. And I am, as instructed, remaining on my very best behaviour and being very, very careful not to overdo the jogging.

The sprint work, by contrast, I have always been able to cope with. I've always preferred the anaerobic stuff – the intensive exercises that really get your heart going – to the aerobic, endurance-based activities. Much of the fitness work that I do on my own these days involves sprint repetitions up short, steep hills. This, I feel, mirrors much more closely the sort of exercise I have to do on a cricket field.

One hill near my house, up a steep path by the golf course, is an absolute killer, but it does the job and I find myself drawn back to it time after time. I think I've almost developed an affection for it. Maybe it has satisfied my need for competition and I look on the hill as a tough but respected opponent. I never want to let it beat me.

The hill is about 50 metres long and its gradient is about one in four. I start sprinting up it, my head down and my legs pounding away, and then I look up to see how far I've got and realise that I'm moving at the pace of an arthritic snail. Just when you think I'm almost at the top, this cunning, evil hill goes round a bend and suddenly gets even steeper. At that point, my thighs start burning and my lungs start heaving and I begin to think that the hill might beat me. Eventually I'll get there, bend over with my hands on my knees and try not to be sick. And then I'll stagger back down to the bottom and do the whole thing again. Six of those followed by a jog back home and I feel I've done a decent session. And if I'm ever struggling through a difficult spell on a flat wicket at the end of a long hot day in a Test match, I can always think to myself: 'At least I'm not running up that sodding hill.'

Another option for exercising when I'm at home is to go up to the local cricket and rugby grounds in Baildon. I'll jog up there from home, then work out a course for myself, either using the painted markings on the rugby pitch or by putting some chairs out on the cricket field, marking a rectangle of about 50 metres

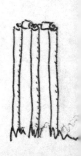

by 20 metres. Once my course is complete, I'll set off on a sprint
diagonally across the rectangle, turn right at a chair, then jog across
the straight edge of the rectangle before sprinting across another
diagonal, and so on, always turning right at the chairs, until I get
back to the start. In total, that will be four sprints and four walks.
I'll then have a short breather and do the same thing again, but
this time turning left at each chair. After six sets of these four
jogs, I'll set off for a dizzy-headed jog home, blowing hard and looking forward to collapsing in the bath. That's a regular exercise
session for me.

   The whole idea of all this donkey work during the off-season
is to get yourself into decent shape for the fitness tests at Loughborough University that come before every England tour. These
boot camps are held at the ECB Academy, where we gather as a
touring squad for a couple of days to be inspected thoroughly,
de-loused and generally checked over to make sure that we are
fit and proper persons to represent our country on a cricket tour.

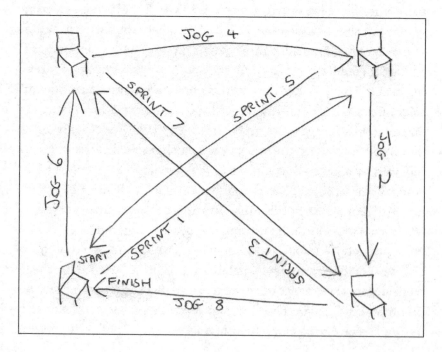

And as far as the fitness is concerned, they want to make sure that we haven't spent our few weeks away from the game staggering constantly between pub and curry house.

If anyone had been overdoing their rest and relaxation, they would soon be found out by the notorious fitness challenge. This funfair of a gym session took you through a series of stations: a 1,000-metre climb on the VersaClimber, 500 metres on the rowing machine, then press-ups, sit-ups, shoulder presses, bench presses, step-ups with weights and an inclined run up a steep gradient on the treadmill. Makes me feel knackered just thinking about it. The whole thing only lasts for twenty minutes or so, but it's intensive stuff designed to test out every bit of your body, and by the time you finished you were pretty much pooped.

At night, we would have a team meal together, then go to bed early ready to be up and in the swimming pool the next morning by 7 a.m.

Swimming, I am led to believe, can be a delightful activity first thing in the morning, a gentle exercise and a soothing way to get rid of the aches and strains of the previous day without placing too much stress on your body.

Not for me, it ain't. Far from it. If, like me, you're not too good at swimming, splashing up and down in a relay race against several much better swimmers can be a gruelling business.

Since I was young, I have never been much of a water-baby. I can swim competently enough and I think I got one of those certificates at school that says 'Matthew didn't drown today when we threw him in the pool.' Breast-stroke I can manage, but I never learned front-crawl as a kid because I had a problem with my ears. If they got too much water in, wax came pouring out of them, which wasn't at all pleasant. Poor me.

Those early-morning swims at Loughborough would be straight relay races, swimming front-crawl as fast as you can for one 50-metre length before handing on to the next man. And for those with a decent swimming technique, this was an absolute doddle.

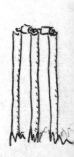

Kevin Pietersen, for example, is like a fish, as you'd expect from a boy who grew up near Durban. Jimmy Anderson is also pretty good in the pool, as is Steve Harmison. So while the superswimmers were all cruising away, I'd be thrashing around like a drowning cat, attempting my own version of the front-crawl but doing something that looked more like doggy-paddle. Some of them probably thought I should be wearing arm-bands. And I wasn't alone, thankfully, because Ashley Giles was similarly bad. At the end of the relay, the two of us would haul ourselves out of the pool, looking like we'd just swum the English channel, while KP and Harmy swanned off barely out of breath.

Where's the fairness in that, I ask you?

After breakfast, there would be further medical examinations before we were put through an all-round fitness assessment in the afternoon, which required us to lift a few weights, among other things. We were tested on how much we could bench-press, how much we could leg-press, how high we could jump[†] and how fast we could run between the wickets. We would be timed running a one, a two and a three, first with a bat in our right hands, then the same again with a bat in our left hands. Our results would then be measured against previous assessments to check that we were no more feeble now than we had been before previous tours.

The weight-lifting part of the assessments was never too popular, because not too many cricketers are obsessive about lifting big weights. For bowlers, especially, you have to be careful about the amount you lift because all those niggles in the shoulders and back can easily be aggravated if you don't get your lifting just right.

[†]**HOGFACT:** When flies take off, they JUMP backwards. That's one sport that hasn't been introduced at the Olympics yet, the Backwards Jump. If it was, presumably flies wouldn't be allowed to enter.

Among the England players, Ashley Giles and Marcus Trescothick were always among the biggest lifters. Alastair Cook is pretty strong, as is Matt Prior. And Freddie is very strong but, like me, he's not too bothered about lifting particularly big weights.

As far as I'm concerned, I'll pump enough iron to build and maintain my strength, but I've never been keen on doing weights for their own sake. I do have a weights bench at home and a few dumbbells scattered around, but they haven't seen a huge amount of use. The shape I am now is pretty much my natural shape, big and lumpy and reasonably strong.

I think I have a fairly high level of natural strength, something I've attempted to demonstrate on occasions by starting drunken arm-wrestling contests. If I needed anyone to vouch for my natural strength, I could probably call on most of the Sri Lankan cricket team of 2006 to testify on my behalf. More of which later.

As our final treat at Loughborough, before we were released back into the outside world, we had to undergo the dreaded bleep test. For those not familiar with this little bit of extra fun – and count yourself lucky if you're not – this is an exercise in which you have to run between two cones, 20 metres apart, for around a minute. You then move up a level and do the same thing again at a higher speed, all the time trying to complete each shuttle in time for the next bleep.

On the first level, the bleeps are widely spaced and allow you to start at a fast-paced walk for the first minute. You will then hear 'Start of Level Two', at which point the bleeps will be slightly closer together, requiring you to increase your speed to complete the shuttles in time. By the time you are on the eighth or ninth level, you will be sprinting the whole time. The highest level you manage before you fail to keep up with the bleeps is your score for the test.

This is never fun – let's face it, it's not supposed to be. But I always felt it was slightly tough on the bigger lads among us. If you're a little short-arsed batsman like Ian Bell, you're bound to be more nimble on the turn at the end of each shuttle than a big

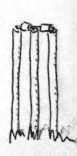

lump like me or Fred, who'd be like the QE2 in a cul-de-sac by comparison. And the time you take to turn effectively counts against you in a bleep test, not to mention the amount of energy used in turning.

So the sprinters among us would always do better in the bleep tests. Jimmy or Belly, for example, would run the 20 metres in, say, 2.8 seconds, whereas I would maybe take 2.9. And by the time you've reached levels seven and eight, you'll probably be running ten shuttles, so I would have that tenth of a second to make up on every shuttle.

The powers-that-be decided that the minimum score we should reach in the bleep test would be 12. I would usually tend to be mid-table in the squad, scoring somewhere between 12.5 and 13.5. Alastair Cook would usually be the best with about 14, and most of the others would be between 12 and 13.5, but just about everyone would reach 12. Marcus Trescothick was one of the worst at the bleep test, but then he was a big, heavy-footed lad who took a while to turn, so it wasn't really his sort of thing. He worked hard enough on his fitness, though, and nobody would ever have said, 'Sorry, Tres, you're not coming on tour, your bleep test wasn't good enough.'

In all my time of going to Loughborough for these sessions, there have been very few people who have turned up and fallen short of the required levels of fitness. Playing the game for a living tends to make sure that you stay in reasonable shape. Or at least it does for most people, because there has been the odd exception. I don't think it would surprise anyone to learn that, on the tour to India in 2000, Jimmy Ormond wasn't exactly a lean, mean bowling machine. And a few years later, when Ian Blackwell was chosen for our next tour to India, he didn't look as though he'd been competing in triathlons in his time off. Freddie has had his ups and downs over the years – not bad for a fat lad, he used to say – but most people in the core squad have generally been there or thereabouts.

In the last couple of years, the trend towards making cricketers stronger, faster, leaner and keener has continued. The ECB have been trying to make sure that county cricketers are in better shape by providing the funds for every county to have a full-time fitness coach. And under Peter Moores, with his fanatical dedication to fitness, the England team had probably never been fitter. They might have played some crap cricket at times, but hey, at least they were looking trim.

So fitness coaches are becoming a regular feature in and around a cricket team, but that doesn't mean that they're treated as just another one of the lads. Not by a long chalk. Those fitness coaches are, without question, the least popular members of any cricketing dressing-room. As a daily requirement of their job, they must attempt to motivate eleven cricketers, who have a natural tendency to laziness, to go to the gym rather than sit and read the paper or nip off for a coffee. And for their efforts, they get a fearful amount of abuse in return, some of it affectionate. They really are on a hiding to nothing. When I come to the end of my cricketing days and I'm considering future career options, I would not become a fitness coach in a team sport for all the tea in China.

It was different with a personal trainer such as Gary Simpson. I paid him to be nasty to me and, if I had any grumbles, the argument was one against one, rather than eleven against one. And of course, if I gave him any trouble, I was well aware that he had a few mates that he could call on to support him.

But once Yorkshire were able to employ a fitness coach to supervise my exercise routines and to kick my backside when necessary, there was no longer any need for me to employ Gary. He had, though, set me firmly on the right track.

From the time I started working with him in January 2004, I went on to play the next forty Test matches consecutively for England, which not many fast bowlers have done. Never mind the long-distance runs and the bleep tests. I think that is as good a measure of a cricketer's fitness as any.

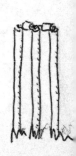

HOGGY'S HUTCH: MY BATTING BUNNIES

These are the batsmen that I'd like to thank for contributing most to my Test career by continually finding ways to get out to my bowling. As a token of my gratitude, I'd like to induct them into Hoggy's Hutch and award each of them a pair of ears appropriate for my batting bunnies.

MATTHEW HAYDEN (AUSTRALIA) – 6 TIMES

Pride of place goes to Mr Hayden. I attach these ears with particular pleasure after the bashings he gave me earlier in my career.

VIRENDER SEHWAG (INDIA) – 6 TIMES

If you don't get him early, he'll bat you all over. I managed to trick him out once or twice.

RAHUL DRAVID
(INDIA) – 5 TIMES

Even the most sensible of batsmen can't resist a drive at one of my dibbly-dobbly outswingers. I usually got him out snicking to the keeper or slips.

CHRIS GAYLE
(WEST INDIES) – 5 TIMES

It was either him or me. He once hit me for six fours in an over, so it was only fair that I got him out a few times as well.

WASIM JAFFER
(PAKISTAN) – 5 TIMES

With a name like that, you've got to expect a few balls with your name on them. I can only presume that I got him with five jaffas.

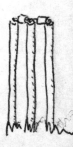

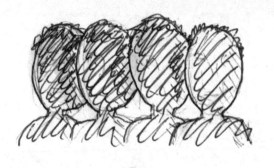

8

Getting Better All the Time

The names trip off the tongue, don't they? Everyone who followed cricket in 2004 and 2005 knows who they are. They all worked well together, they all offered something different, they were possibly one of England's finest fast-bowling quartets, key players in the famous Ashes win of 2005: Steve Harmison, Andrew Flintoff, Simon Jones and James Kirtley.

It could so easily have been that way, had the selectors plumped for James Kirtley rather than me for the squad to tour the West Indies in 2004. He had, after all, been chosen ahead of me for the last two Tests in Sri Lanka, and he had certainly not disgraced himself. I'm not entirely sure why the selectors had this apparent change of heart over Christmas, whether I had Michael Vaughan in my corner, or David Graveney, or Geoff Miller. I'd be surprised if it was Duncan Fletcher, because he was never my biggest fan, but you never really know with selection.

Although I was hugely relieved that my England career wasn't over, as it could have been, I felt really sorry for Kirts. When the squad was announced in January without his name in, he would have felt as low as I had been feeling a few weeks earlier when I was dropped in Sri Lanka. Kirts had been given a chance, taken the new ball for England in two Test matches and picked up six wickets in three innings, not a bad return. He must have thought that he had, at least, done enough to make the squad for the West Indies. But as it turned out, he was the one who would never play Test cricket again. It can be a cruel business sometimes.

And so it was that Hoggard, Harmison, Jones and Flintoff came together for the first time in Kingston, Jamaica, and remained as the four-man pace attack for the whole of the series. We didn't know at the time how long we would stay together as a fast-bowling pack, but it was soon apparent that our different bowling styles complemented each other well. And backed up by the shrewd spin of Ashley Giles, we seemed to have most bases covered.

Harmy got a ridonculous amount of pace just by turning over one of those very, very long arms of his. He got plenty of bounce and bowled a very different length from me with the new ball. Jonah was quick too, but from a much more skiddy trajectory, which could be especially useful with the old ball. Fred could bowl decidedly sharpish from the back of a length, hit the seam and, at the time of the West Indies tour, was just starting to use his wrist to get the ball to go away from the bat. Meanwhile I was the boring one, who swung the new ball for a few overs and then settled down to a good, solid shift of donkey work.

My role was summed up nicely by Michael Vaughan on that tour to the West Indies. It was my job to keep sweeping the shop floor, grafting away at the menial work while the other bowlers were grabbing the glory upstairs in the office. I wasn't to get ahead of myself and try to show the office workers how to do their job, he said. The captain and coach would be perfectly happy with me if I was just plugging away, keeping it tight and bowling my maidens, ensuring that the mess created by others was swept away. That analogy from Vaughany really helped, to have my role so clearly explained and to know exactly what was expected of me from the management. Having been dropped so recently in Sri Lanka, it was nice to know that I was fitting into their plans.

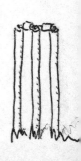

So all in all, with our four-pronged pace attack, we had different bowlers for different conditions and different stages of the innings. After a few Tests of bowling together, we started to get the feeling that if I didn't get someone then Freddie would, and if Freddie didn't, Harmy would, and if Harmy didn't, Jonah would. That's a nice feeling to have.

There was one other important reason why we made our mark as a foursome: we stayed fit. Take any four fast bowlers over any period of time and it won't be long before an injury crops up. When you start out your life as a professional fast bowler, you have to accept that there will be times spent sitting on the sidelines wrapped in cotton wool. But we stayed fit throughout that West Indies series. Jonah was in and out with injury in the summer of 2004, but we then played four out of five Tests as a unit in South Africa and then the first four matches of the Ashes series together. That timespan just happened to be England's most successful period for a long time. Coincidence or not? It's not really for us to say, but it's a great shame that we have never managed to get back together since the Trent Bridge Test against Australia in 2005.

An added bonus was that we all got on so well together. Me, Fred and Harmy had been good mates for a while – we're all from different parts of the North, but we all speak roughly the same language – and Jonah, being a Welshman, was an honorary northerner as far as I was concerned, so he fitted in nicely as well. All the southern batsmen had us northern riff-raff to do the hard work while they had tea and scones and scored a few runs from time to time.

Flintoff is possibly at his finest when he is taking the piss out of Harmison. The subject matter could be just about anything, but probably his best turn is when he does an impression of Harmy, back in his home town of Ashington, astonishing the locals with tales of his travels abroad. It was clearly Fred's opinion – and I couldn't possibly comment – that Ashington folk hadn't seen much of the world. You'll have to imagine the comical north-eastern accent:

'Gather roond, gather roond. I'll tell y'all a tale aboot when wuz went ter the West Indies, like. You wouldna believe it, but there woz these people there and thez faces were black. Not peented black or anything. Real proper black!'

'Haaa-wayyy, Steve! They nevvah did! Tell us another one!'

'Well, I went to this restaurant, like, and they had this stuff called sooshi. Honestly, you wouldna believe it, but it had raw fish in it. It wasn't even cooked, no batter on it or anything! And there woz people eatin' this stuff!'

'Haaa-wayyy, Steve! They nevvah! Tell us another one!'

I'm not sure how you prove it, and as far as I know there are no accurate scientific measures, but I've always felt that the quality of piss-taking in a cricket dressing-room is not a bad indication of how the team is performing. One of these days, maybe they'll bring someone into the dressing-room to monitor that sort of thing. We could even have a coach in charge of piss-taking. Why not? We seem to need a coach for everything else these days. When that day comes, I'll nominate Fred to take up the role.

Back in the West Indies, the tone for the series was set, in spectacular fashion, by Steve Harmison in Jamaica. In the first innings of that Test, when we bowled West Indies out for 311, Harmy had taken a couple of wickets. I got three, Simon Jones and Ashley Giles took two apiece, and it was a job well done. Our batsmen then sneaked us a lead of 20-odd before, unannounced, Hurricane Harmy blew into town in the second innings.

He bowled quickly, accurately and with some very steep bounce. Harmy can be horrible to bat against when he bowls like that, as the West Indian batsmen discovered that day. I was really

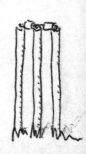

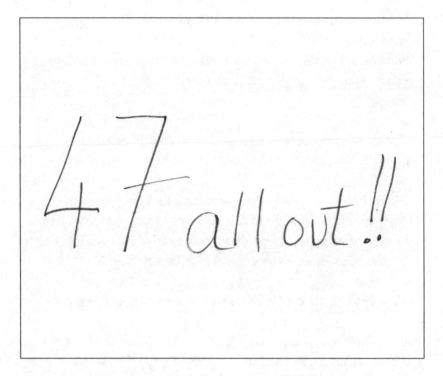

chuffed for him because he's the sort of bowler who gets some stick when he's not at his best, but he really came good in Kingston and had incredible figures of seven for 12. And we bowled them out for 47. That's **FOUR-SEVEN**. Forty-seven!!! I used to get more than that batting in a field against my dad with stumps six feet tall. Looking on as the bowler from the other end, I couldn't help but think: 'I'm not sure anybody else in the world could bowl as well as that.'

So that took us 1–0 up in the four-match series and we made it 2–0 in Trinidad with a seven-wicket win. Harmy was at it again in the first innings with six more wickets, then Jonah did the business in the second with five of his own. We were playing well, not stuffing the West Indies out of sight, by any means, with the exception of that 47 all out, but we were developing some momentum.

Then, in the third Test in Barbados, Fred decided it was his turn for a bit of glory, taking five wickets in the first innings as we bowled them out for 224. The new seam-bowling unit was firing on all cylinders. I'd been doing my bit, chipping in with eight[†] wickets in the first two Tests. But it's all very well knowing that the management are happy with me brushing up the shop floor; I wanted my team-mates to know that I was capable of pulling my weight as well.

We were just about level pegging after the first innings in Barbados and West Indies had reached 40 for two in their second innings. The game was in the balance and, if we had let them win this one, they would be back in the series at 2–1 with one to play. It was a pretty tense time and the atmosphere at the Kensington Oval was fantastic. The Barmy Army was out in force and England supporters outnumbered the locals by about three to one. And not many of them seemed to have come for a quiet day out at the cricket. They were a fairly rowdy bunch.

I was bowling my eighth over of the morning when I had Ramnaresh Sarwan caught in the gully with my fourth ball. We'd managed to tie him down for a while and, after three dot balls at the start of the over, he drove at an outswinger that wasn't quite there and edged straight into the safe hands of Ashley Giles.

The next man in was Shivnarine Chanderpaul, the crabby left-hander who can hang around all day if you give him the chance. In the first innings he'd stuck around for three hours while making 50. He can be a very frustrating man to bowl at, so it's best to get him early if you can. I ran in and bowled one that was full, swinging back into his pads he played all around it and was plumb lbw.

Then in came Ryan Hinds, another left-hander. As the ball was clearly swinging, I thought my best bet was probably to try the same thing again, and curve one back into his pads. But while I was running in to bowl, I suddenly thought, 'Nope, that's what he'll be

---

[†]**HOGFACT:** The dollar sign $ is a modification of the figure 8 that used to be stamped on the old Spanish coins called pieces of EIGHT.

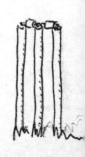

expecting,' and decided instead to push one across him. I don't think my brain made that decision, the body just seemed to take over. I pushed one across him, it nibbled a bit off the seam and he edged it to Freddie at second slip. I'm still not absolutely sure whether I did it intentionally or accidentally.

Whichever way, it did the job and the crowd went absolutely nuts. I didn't know quite what to do with myself. I sprinted over towards Fred but never quite got there because Nasser was running at me, Jonah was running at me and I got buried under a pile of players leaping on top of me. The noise around the ground was incredible and I couldn't hear myself think.

Not that I was in much of a mood for thinking anyway

Bizarre to think that I became only the tenth English bowler to take a hat-trick in a Test match. And that's in 120-odd years of Test matches!!! Ridonculous. After the game, I got a congratulatory text message from Darren Gough, who'd been the last man to do it in Sydney a few years earlier.

It's a strange thing, taking a hat-trick.

They happen so rarely that it's not something you ever really dream about doing. I suppose it's basically an individual achievement, and if I'm asked to choose the highlights of my career, the hat-trick wouldn't necessarily spring to mind. I'm more likely to think of the best victories we've had as a team. You come straight back down to earth after a hat-trick, but after a good Test match win, the feeling stays with you for quite a while afterwards.

The only time I'd taken a hat-trick before had been for Pudsey Congs third team in the Dales Council when I was 14. One of those was caught, one was bowled and the other was a stumping – not an ideal dismissal for an aspiring fast bowler. In Barbados, I'm glad to say, Chris Read, our wicketkeeper, was standing back to me and there was no chance of me getting a batsman stumped.

The best thing of all about my hat-trick was that we were now in a position to go on and win the match. West Indies were now 45 for five; we quickly bowled them out for 94, knocked off the runs and the series was won that night. Great place to do it, great way to do it. We were the first England team to win a series in the Caribbean for thirty-six years and you can imagine how good that felt.

There was still the small matter of the fourth and final Test to come, to be played on a pitch in Antigua that had runs written all over it. And for some reason I developed a nasty illness that meant I could only bowl 18 out of 202 overs while West Indies racked up 751 for five. I was puking up and generally feeling grim, but it could have been the instinctive reaction of a fast bowler who has seen a very good batting pitch and Brian Lara looking hungry for runs. *Flatwicketitis*, I think is the precise medical term. Funnily enough, Gilo had gone down with the same condition earlier, so Gareth Batty came in and made a bit of history with two for 185. Stop sniggering, Gilo.

Of course, that was the game when Lara made 400 not out. It was an incredible innings, but we had been absolutely convinced that he edged Harmy behind before he had even got off the mark. We all went up, we were all sure he'd edged it, but the hands of Darrell Hair, the umpire, remained clasped behind his back.

I brought the subject up with Lara a couple of years later when we were doing a testimonial event together. We were up on the stage and I said: 'Right, Brian, let's talk about your wonderfully magical innings of 400 in Antigua. What people don't realise is that you were out on none when you snicked Harmy behind, didn't you?' He just looked at me and smiled.

'Four hundred for one, more like,' I said. 'That's as many runs as I've managed in my entire Test career!'

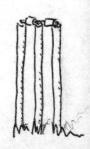

So we'd beaten West Indies 3–0, something that hadn't been done for a while, but one good series didn't make us a good team. The following summer, though, there were plenty more signs that we were, at the very least, on the way to becoming a decent side. Our two opponents, New Zealand and West Indies, were not among the world's strongest teams – those challenges would come later – but we beat New Zealand 3–0 in a three-Test series and West Indies 4–0 in a four-Test series, and you can't do much more than that. I don't think that winning all seven Tests in a summer had been done before and there's a fair chance that it won't be done again.

The great thing about the summer of 2004, looking back, was that it enabled us to become a settled side. Our confidence and belief were developing by the game and most of us managed to stay fit, so the team was pretty much picking itself. The game becomes so much easier when the team is doing well. I know that sounds obvious, but it's noticeable how much less anxiety there is around when you're winning. Even for those who have not performed well, there is less scrutiny of their performances, less chance that anybody will be dropped for the next game. If you're winning, poor individual performances tend to be hidden away.

The opposite applies when your team is losing. After a defeat, the players who have underperformed get all the unwanted attention, while even the best individual performances can be glossed over. That's just a part of our culture, really, when you're playing a team sport in the public eye.

It's also easier for a winning team to welcome the occasional new player into the dressing-room. I had always remembered how awkward it was to walk into an England dressing-room for the first time, and I was determined that, once I was a slightly more senior figure in the team, we wouldn't make it so daunting for the new lads. I really hope we managed to do that.

In 2004, whenever a new player came into the side, he seemed to do well. Andrew Strauss came in and scored runs straight away against New Zealand, Rob Key was recalled and hit a double-hundred against West Indies at Lord's, and Ian Bell made 70 when he made his debut in the final Test of the summer at the Oval.

That was also a credit to Michael Vaughan's captaincy, which was proving to be very different from the previous regime under Nasser Hussain. Every captain is different and their style of captaincy will always reflect their own personality. Whoever followed Nasser was always likely to be a bit more laid-back, but Vaughany was much, much more chilled out. And that is not to knock Nasser, who was a great captain in his own way. His style of leadership was exactly what England needed at the time.

I think I've mentioned how I got used to having Nasser fielding at mid-off while I was bowling and, whenever I bowled a bad ball, I'd begin the long, lonely walk back to my mark watching Nasser kicking the dirt or cursing under his breath. Vaughany fielded at mid-off too, but there the similarities ended. When I walked back past Vaughany after I'd been hit for a boundary, he'd just roll his eyes at me in mocking fashion and say something like: 'Hmmm, trying too hard to get up those office steps again, Hoggy. Back down to the shop floor, please, and bowl us some dot balls.'

Vaughany really stamped his mark on the captaincy in 2004. Like the team, his confidence in his own leadership grew with every win. He thinks about the game a lot, he'd move fielders into positions that might have seemed strange at first, but there would always be some sound reasoning behind the move. He was more one of the lads than Nasser, and their styles of motivation were very different, but in their own ways they were both highly capable of getting the best out of people.

As a group of bowlers, we were still ticking over quite nicely that summer. Simon Jones was in and out of the side because of injury, but Harmy was carrying on from where he'd left off in the West Indies, while Fred and I were chipping in here and there. It was probably no coincidence that lurking in the background at this time we had another key figure who was pretty good at getting the best out of people, and fast bowlers in particular.

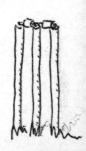

Troy Cooley had been the ECB's fast bowling coach for a year or so by that time, and most of us had been impressed by his work. In his time, he'd played a bit of first-class cricket as a fast bowler for Tasmania, but he had since become a much better coach than he ever was a bowler. After his playing days were over, he had spent a lot of time studying the biomechanics of fast bowling and he was clued up with the latest video and computer technology to analyse a bowler's action.

So Troy had plenty of technical know-how, but his real strength was that he had the man-management skills to back it up. When you're playing international sport, there shouldn't be an awful lot that a coach needs to change about your technique. You must have been doing something right to get there in the first place, so the amount of tweaking that a coach needs to do should be minimal. If the engine of a decent car has a problem, you don't strip the whole thing down and rebuild it, you just do a spot of fine-tuning. The trick for the coach is to be confident enough in his knowledge and secure enough in his job not to feel the need to justify his position by suggesting unnecessary changes.

From this point of view, Troy was outstanding. Every now and then he would make a suggestion – 'Hoggy, your front arm is dropping a bit,' something like that – but he knew when was a good time to offer his advice. And because he got to know our actions and our personalities so well, he knew how to make each of us feel good about our bowling. To get the best out of Jimmy Anderson or Simon Jones, for example, may need something completely different from getting the best out of me. Troy had the knack of knowing how to treat each of his bowlers. I think he was as good a man-manager as I've come across in the game. There aren't many people who have his level of technical knowledge and can combine that with an understanding of how to treat international cricketers.

We were all amazed when we found out that the ECB had allowed Troy to return home to work with Australia in 2006. He'd have been happy to stay in England if he'd been given a two-year deal, but he was only offered one year and got a better offer from the Aussies. Everyone in the England team – and not just the bowlers – was staggered that we hadn't hung onto him. That was a huge, huge mistake by the ECB. Troy has been badly missed since he went back to Australia.

So just how good a team had we become by the end of the summer of 2004? As a player, I don't think you ever really stop to consider anything like that at the time. It's for other people to judge, really, you're more concerned with what could happen in the next game, or the next series, and by this stage of my career I was all too aware that we could be bitten on the bum at any time.

We'd won the last Test against West Indies by ten wickets at the Oval, completing our 100 per cent record for the summer, but we had only really beaten two teams in New Zealand and West Indies that we would have expected to overcome. A better measure would come with the tour to South Africa that started a few months later. In terms of quality, South Africa were a further step up, especially in their own backyard, and if we were to build up any genuine confidence for the Ashes series the following summer we really had to perform against South Africa.

On a personal level, it was nice to be back in the country where I'd had such a great time in my younger, wilder days. I'd been back briefly as part of the squad for the World Cup in 2003, but I'd hardly played a game then. Now I was back as a grown-up – relatively speaking – and it was time to show how far I'd come in the last few years.

We started off in Port Elizabeth, a pleasant place by the sea that I will always associate with Darren Gough. It was there, on a pre-season tour for Yorkshire a few years earlier, that I'd managed to educate Goughie about the differences between playing at sea-level and playing at altitude. I had joined the tour after spending the previous few months playing for the Pirates in Johannesburg and Goughie was impressed by how fit I was when I turned up. I

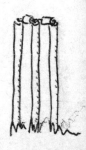

explained to him that Jo'burg is 1,500 metres above sea level, so I'd been playing and training at altitude, where the lack of oxygen makes your lungs work harder, so you tend to get fit pretty quickly.

We were having this conversation in the lift at our seafront hotel in Port Elizabeth. As we got to the bottom, I could see that Goughie was thinking hard about what I'd said. We walked out of the lift and into the hotel lobby, which had a glorious view out to sea straight through the front doors. Then Goughie piped up.

'If Johannesburg is 1,500 metres above sea level,' he said, 'what altitude do you think we're at in Port Elizabeth?'

I just pointed out of the front doors towards the sea. 'If you look over there, Darren, there's the beach. I would guess that we're approximately 12 metres above sea level at the moment.'

I am happy to report that we both managed to avoid altitude sickness on that visit and, back in Port Elizabeth in 2005, the series started in some style. I had Graeme Smith caught at slip by Andrew Strauss with the second ball of the series which, as it turned out, was quite a symbolic success. We went on to win that first Test by seven wickets and both Straussy and I would go on to have the most productive series of our careers up to that point.

Straussy had come into the England side the previous summer, making an instant impression with a century on his debut, and here in South Africa he had an incredible series, hitting three hundreds in the first four Tests. At Port Elizabeth he got a ton in the first innings, then saw us to victory with a cool, calm 94 not out. And that made it eight Test wins in a row.

Regardless of all the runs he scored, Straussy would make an immediate impression in any dressing-room he walked into because, apart from anything else, he has the most incredibly loud[†]

[†]**HOGFACT:** It is possible to bore holes in solid matter with a noise of 210 decibels. If Andrew Strauss shouted really loudly, I think he might manage this.

voice. It's not as though he shouts. He could just be having a normal chat across the other side of the room, but you would still hear this booming, posh voice drowning out everybody else's conversations. Even when we went to big functions on tour, such as a High Commissioner's drinks reception where there'd be hundreds of people, nobody ever needed to ask: 'Has anyone seen Straussy?' You only had to listen. Now that he's England captain, he shouldn't have any difficulty commanding attention when he makes his team talks.

When he first came into the side, he was christened Lord Brocket after the dodgy aristocrat who was on telly at the time. Dodgy? Maybe that doesn't apply to Straussy, but posh he most certainly is. As he's an Old Radleian and I'm a common-as-muck Pudsey Pumper, you could say that we're chalk and cheese. But for some reason we've always got on extremely well.

Moving on to the second Test in Durban, Straussy scored another century as we fought back from conceding a first-innings lead of 193 to push for victory on the final day. Marcus Trescoth-ick and Graham Thorpe also hit tons, enabling us to set South Africa a fourth-innings target of 378. I got Smith out early again and we soon had them 173 for six. It would have been an incredible win if we could have finished it off, but Shaun Pollock and A.B. DeVilliers put up some solid resistance.

Then we ran Pollock out and we were two wickets away from victory with Makhaya Ntini and Dale Steyn, a pair of rabbits, coming in as their last two men. But the light started to close in and the umpires, Darrell Hair and Simon Taufel, asked the batsmen if they wanted to go off. They didn't need to be asked twice.

It had been a long, hot Test match and we were gutted that all our hard work was going to be in vain. The batsmen, DeVilliers and Ntini, marched off, the umpires followed them and we ambled over towards the changing-rooms. But we ended up staying outside, just sitting on the edge of the outfield, tearing our hair out with frustration. I'm not sure if it ever became a fully fledged protest, but we were certainly pissed off that they were being let

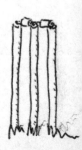

off the hook at a time when we felt we were about to take a firm grip on the series.

Whether the light was still okay or whether we allowed ourselves to be caught up in the heat of the moment, I'm not really sure. If you're the team bowling to get a victory in such a situation, you always tend to feel that the light is not too bad. And the opposite applies, I'm sure, if you're batting to save the match: you probably always think that the light is worse than it really is. In fading light, I don't think you'll ever get two teams to agree on the point at which the light becomes unacceptably gloomy.

Eventually, we were told to get our backsides into the dressing-room before we got into bother with the match referee. I can't remember if it was Fletch or Vaughany who brought the protest to a halt, but I'm sure it was the right decision. We had to stop being such naughty boys and go and deal with our frustration in the privacy of the pavilion, where we could slam our fists against walls and swear loudly without being heard by television microphones.

Sometimes cricket can be a bloody infuriating game

To make matters worse, we were stuffed in the next Test match in Cape Town by 196 runs. From being on the brink of taking a 2–0 lead in the series, we were suddenly 1–1 with two Tests to play. Ouch. That hurt a lot, and the resilience of a side that had become used to winning was being given a stern test.

Our pride wasn't the only thing to be dented in Cape Town, either. While we were warming up in the nets before play, I was walking away from the practice area when I was hit on the back of the left heel by a low, skimming drive from Andrew Flintoff. He was batting in the nets some 30 metres behind me, but when Freddie bashes the ball, it tends to stay bashed. I went down in a heap and I was in so much pain that I couldn't field later that day. Even to this day, if I knock my heel I can still feel the pain from that blow. That Flintoff bloke should come with a health warning. I'm quite surprised, thinking about it now, that I recovered in time to play in the next Test.

Given the time I had spent in the city a few years earlier, you might have thought that I'd be really looking forward to the next Test match in Johannesburg. And I was indeed relishing the chance to visit the place again. I went down to the Pirates club, caught up with a few old friends and reminisced about all those silly nights out. And best of all, I had a lovely meal with the Skjoldhammers, my 'second family' who had put me up (and put up with me) on my first stay in South Africa.

But as for playing at the Wanderers, I was not looking forward to it one little bit. While I was living in Jo'burg, because I was playing club cricket, I'd never played in the Bull Ring stadium that is used for Test matches. I played for the Pirates against the Wanderers club across the road, but I didn't play in the Bull Ring until I came over as a visiting player with Free State. And on both occasions that I had played there for Free State against Gauteng – one four-day match and another one-day game – I had bowled a pile of poo. In the four-day match, I bowled twelve overs for 82 and then dropped a catch at extra-cover off Nicky Boje, the captain, breaking my finger in the process.

There was no particular reason why I should have bowled badly there, no slope that disrupted my rhythm or fierce breeze to run into, it was just one of those grounds where it hadn't happened for me. In fact, the only decent game I'd had at the Wanderers was when I was working on the bar during the Test match against England nine years previously. I didn't do a lot wrong on that occasion.

True to my form in the Bull Ring, I did not bowl well at all in the first innings against South Africa. My 34 overs went for 144 runs, which my dad, who's a maths teacher, could tell you is more

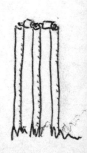

than four an over. Somehow I picked up five wickets along the way, I'm not quite sure how. I must have bowled some decent balls amongst the dross, but in general I wasn't feeling at all happy with my bowling.

Then, in the second innings, something clicked. As soon as I started bowling, I felt able to put the ball exactly where I wanted it, at a good pace and with a decent amount of swing. I can't explain how or why that happened, it was just one of those things. I'd been bowling well earlier in the series and suddenly it all came flooding back. When you're feeling out of sorts, you just have to battle away and try to limit the damage. And then, when another wave of form comes along, you just enjoy the ride.

It was the last day and we had set them 325 to win after Tres hit a magnificent 180. But we only had two sessions in which to bowl them out, so we needed to rip through their top order. In my third over I had DeVilliers lbw trapped on the crease. A couple of overs later I bowled Jacques Rudolph, a left-hander, with a ball that swung back through him and knocked out two stumps, middle and leg, which doesn't happen very often. Another sign that things were going my way.

Next ball came a dismissal that I will always be proud of. Jacques Kallis is a fine player and he'd been in fantastic form that series, but he got a ball with his name on it in Jo'burg and was caught by Tres at first slip. It was not far from being a perfect dismissal as far as I was concerned. No matter how good the batsman, they are always vulnerable first ball, and on this occasion I got Kallis's first ball in just the right place. He had to play, he came forward, covered the line and didn't push at it, the ball swung a touch and he snicked it to slip. He didn't do much wrong, but I'd got him out.

There was no hat-trick this time, but when I came back for my second spell I took a wicket in each of my next two overs and ended up taking the first six to fall. Freddie, who had been bowling really well at the other end, then chipped in with a couple. But Graeme Smith, who was injured, came in down the order and hung around for a while, and it began to look as though we might run out of time. But eventually, with only eight overs remaining, I picked up the last wicket, my seventh, having Dale Steyn caught behind by Geraint Jones, and we were 2–1 up in the series with one match to play. I think we all went a bit loopy.

Now that was a *really* satisfying performance. I was told later that my match figures of twelve for 205 were the best by an England bowler since Ian Botham twenty-five years earlier. **TWENTY-FIVE YEARS!** I was only three years old! In the next few hours I had a shedload of texts from my South African mates at the Pirates, pleasant messages such as 'Well done, Hoggy. You bastard!' But as with my hat-trick, the most pleasing aspect of the performance was that it put the team in such a good position in such an important series. We went on to draw the final Test at Centurion Park, and our most significant series win so far was in the bag.

While we were all celebrating like mad on the field after I had taken that final wicket at Johannesburg, somebody grabbed me a stump, I think it may have been Vaughany. I'm not exactly sure where that stump has ended up, probably tucked away in a box in our spare bedroom at home. I haven't had a rummage around in there for a while, but I think there are a few stumps down the bottom somewhere. I've never been much of a memorabilia man, but it might be nice in a few years' time, when Ernie is telling me what a useless old git I am, to show him that stump and say that once upon a time, when he had a bit of luck, Daddy wasn't such a useless cricket player.

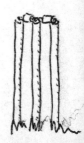

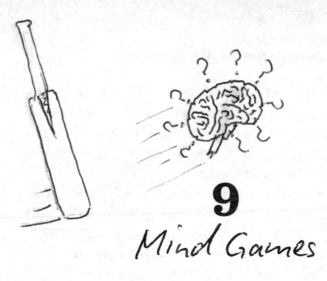

9

Mind Games

I know that there are some people who think that cricket matches go on too long. If you're one of those impatient people with a ridonculously short attention span, don't worry, this book will start getting interesting *really* soon. Having said that, I know what they mean at times. When I've been slapped around the field on the first day of a Test match and taken none for plenty, those next four days could stretch out in front of me like a 24-hour plane†flight to Australia, when I've been seated next to a fat, sweaty man. Who snores.

But the thing about the gentle pace of a cricket match is that it gives everyone plenty of time for thinking, whether you're a spectator or a player. Even when you're right in the thick of the action – a batsman taking strike, or a bowler in the middle of an over – you've still got the time in between balls when you become painfully aware of whatever is going on in your brain. I can't speak for

---

†**HOGFACT:** In Alaska it his considered an offence to push a moose out of a moving PLANE. So presumably it's okay if you stop the plane to do so.

anybody else, but I know that the garbage inside my head would not be a pretty sight at times.

Needs a bloody good clearout, a bit like our garage at home.

So if you see me on the telly, walking back to my mark between balls, what is likely to be going through my mind? Well, that really depends on what sort of ball I've just bowled. If I've sent down a crap ball and been hit for four, I'll probably be huffing and puffing, chuntering away and giving myself a severe bollocking:

'You stupid f***ing prat, why, why, why did you bowl a frigging half-volley on leg stump? You know he's strong through there, so why bowl there, pillock? Useless, sodding sod. Don't do it again. And stand up straight when you're bowling!'

All under my breath, of course, because there might be television cameras zooming up close as I walk back to my mark. And as cricket tends to be on telly before the nine o'clock watershed, such language certainly wouldn't be appropriate for a family audience. So I have to try to remain calm on the outside while giving myself a good kicking on the inside.

If, on the other hand, I've just bowled a decent ball, I'll be much less agitated, simply telling myself to run up for the next ball and do exactly the same thing again. And again, and again, and again. 'Don't waste those good balls now with a bad 'un. Keep it there or thereabouts. One bad ball and all your hard work will have been for nowt.'

But the best frame of mind to be in when you're bowling is when you're so happy with everything – happy with your run-up, happy with the way you're landing at the crease, happy with the way the ball's coming out – that you don't really think about bowling at all. On those rare occasions, when everything feels hunky-dory, I'll be wandering back to my mark, thinking, 'Ooh, I hope it's bangers and mash for tea tonight.' I might even be singing a song to myself

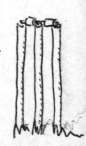

that I've had on in the car that morning, perhaps a bit of Dolly Parton.

🎵 *Islands in the stream, that is what we are*
No one in between, how can we be wrong?
Sail away with me to another world
And we rely on each other, ah-ha
From one lover to ... 🎵 🎵

Before I know it, I'll find myself halfway down the pitch, having bowled another ball. 'Hang on a minute! How on earth did I get down here?' It's like the times when your mind switches to automatic pilot in your car and you arrive at your destination before you've thought about how to get there. It doesn't happen very often, but it's marvellous when it does, and it usually means you're bowling well.

I've always thought that Dolly Parton is a vastly underrated bowling coach.

If your bowling machine is slipping into automatic mode like that, the chances are you'll be at ease with your game, at ease with yourself, and you're letting everything happen naturally. In sporting terms, I suppose it's generally known as being **IN THE ZONE**.

Sounds great, doesn't it? What a marvellous place to be, In The Zone. I think I'll go there for my holidays some time. I'll stand in the high street outside Headingley, flag a cab down and shout: 'Taxi to the zone, please.' In which case, I would probably find myself in a grubby nightclub somewhere on the outskirts of Leeds.

The problem is that, as any sportsman will tell you, the zone is desperately difficult to find. Nerves, dips in confidence and the small matter of eleven blokes on the other team all have a habit of obstructing the route to the zone. It's a place we'd all like to visit on a regular basis, but nobody has a reliable set of directions.

I heard a story about how Jack Russell, the former England wicketkeeper, protects his privacy by blindfolding anybody he takes to his house. Maybe he lives in The Zone. I think I might try sending a letter to him, with the envelope addressed: Jack Russell, The Zone, Gloucestershire. I wonder whether I'll get a reply.

SO HOW THE HELL *DO* YOU GET THERE?

Into the zone, I mean, not to Jack Russell's house. Well, as the saying goes, if I had the answer to that, I'd be a millionaire. Or at least I *would* become a millionaire once I'd retired from playing cricket. Until then, I'd keep the magic formula to myself, wait until I'd taken 1,000 Test wickets and scored a couple of hundreds, then hang up my boots and reveal my secret to the world.

But in actual fact I haven't got a chuffing clue. Being in the zone is a mindset that can click into place any old time. For a batsman, it can be one good shot that takes you there. For a bowler, you can start a new spell after a change of ends and suddenly feel like a completely different bloke. Most of the time, it seems to be completely random. But that doesn't stop any of us – captains, coaches, sports psychologists, players – from agonising over our mental preparation, wondering how we can recreate those special moments when everything slotted into place, working out how we might get ourselves back into that bloody zone.

For what it's worth, here's a rough idea of my preparation on the day of a Test match. Say we're playing at Lord's; the day before the game I'll have bowled a couple of practice spells out in the middle, one from the Pavilion End and one from the Nursery End, each time until I felt absolutely comfortable. I might bowl four overs, I might bowl five, it could be more or it could be less. Then on the morning of the match, once we've done our warm-ups as a team, I'll have another bowl on the edge of the square from both ends until I'm loose and the ball feels to be coming out all right.

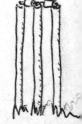

Once I'm feeling comfortable, I'll have a stroll over to the pitch we're going to be playing on and have a quiet sit-down. Firstly, I'll plonk myself down on the crease and visualise what it will feel like to bowl from there during the game. I'll do that from both ends, then I'll go to the end of my run-up and sit down there for a couple of minutes, look down the pitch and think myself through an over or two. How's the pitch going to play? How will I need to bowl? Who am I going to be bowling at? How will I need to adjust? I'll picture where I want my first ball to land. I'll visualise the ball coming out of my hand. And I'll try to anticipate the different situations that are likely to crop up during the game.

When all that's done and dusted, I'll take my kit back up to the changing-room, get myself a coffee and sit down and have a chat and stop thinking about bowling for a while.

Having got myself into this routine, I wouldn't want to go without my preparation processes on the morning of a game. Going through the same routines helps you to feel comfortable, helps your mind and body know what is coming up over the next few hours. And you need to be sure that you've done as much as you can to prepare yourself for the game.

But how much effect does all this have on my performance? Much of the time, probably none whatsoever. There have been times when I've bowled for twenty minutes before a game, struggled to find my rhythm and eventually thought to myself: 'Sod this, I could bowl all day here and it's never going to feel right.'

There was one time recently, playing for Yorkshire at Scarborough, when I bowled worse in the warm-up than I had ever done before a game. No matter how hard I tried, I just couldn't get the ball to go down the off side. I adjusted my action, adjusted my wrist, but the ball just kept squirting off down the leg side. It was really weird. I gave up in the end, and stomped off into the dressing-room in a really bad mood.

We lost the toss and took the field and, would you believe it, I proceeded to bowl a beautiful opening spell. I felt great, I was on the spot almost every ball, I could hardly have bowled better. So how did that happen? Perhaps I'd been so bad in the warm-up that I subconsciously relaxed and thought, 'Well, it can't get any worse.' Who knows? Sometimes it can happen the other way around: you'll feel like a million dollars in practice and bowl like a buffoon in the middle. Do we put that down to complacency? Answers on a post-card, please.

It stands to reason, you would think, that a player has a better chance of getting into the zone when he is feeling at his most confident. If you've had a decent run of performances behind you, you're much less prone to worry about the nuts and bolts of your game, much more likely to impose yourself on the opposition. But I'm not sure that is necessarily the case. Clearly, a good dollop of confidence doesn't do anyone any harm, but when I think of my best performances, they haven't usually come at the highest point of a smooth upward curve in my form.

When I took seven wickets in the second innings against South Africa at Johannesburg, for example, I was playing on a ground that I didn't like and I'd bowled poorly in the first innings (even though I picked up five wickets). I certainly wasn't brimful of confidence in the second innings, but within my first five overs I'd dismissed A.B. DeVilliers, Jacques Rudolph and Jacques Kallis and I was bowling like a dream.

The same would apply to my performance at Adelaide in the 2006–07 Ashes series. We'd just come away from a drubbing at Brisbane, where I hadn't been anywhere near my best with the ball. There were only a couple of days between the games, but I ended up taking seven wickets on a flat deck against the Aussies. In each case, I absolutely had no idea that a really good perform-ance was on its way.

You need luck as well, of course. There are plenty of times when I've bowled close to my best for little reward; and as many times, I'm sure, when I've bowled ordinarily and fluked a five-fer. It all

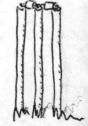

goes to show the seemingly random nature of those rare, wonderful days, when everything feels right and you finally find yourself In The Zone.

So what do you do the rest of the time, when the automatic pilot isn't switched on and you have to grind your way through the gears instead? Like any bowler who has ever played the game, I've had days when I've walked back to my mark, looked down at the batsman and thought to myself: 'I haven't got the foggiest idea where this ball is going to go.' These are the hardest times, when you have to try to prevent the self-doubt from affecting the way you bowl. You have to carry on regardless and, even though you're feeling like a bag of spanners, make him think that you're in the form of your life.

The danger is that you can start thinking about too many things as you're running in to bowl. Am I landing at the crease okay? Am I getting my wrist behind the ball? Am I following through as far as I should be? On days like this, I just try to remind myself that my job is not actually all that complicated. All I have to do is run in and land the ball on or around off stump, somewhere near a decent length.

The time for thinking in depth about your action is at practice. When you've only got a few cones to worry about, or you're bowling in the nets, you can have a good ponder about the various different parts of your action. By the time you go into a match, you need to have got all your fretting out of the way.

Unfortunately, it doesn't always work out like that. If that little lump of leather is being stubborn and refusing to go where you want it to go, it's only natural to think about what you're doing wrong and what emergency repairs can be carried out. So I have a short checklist of things to go through if I'm not bowling well.

1. Don't run in like a headless chicken. One of my strengths as a bowler is that I will always try hard. I'm always keyed up and engaged in the contest. But sometimes I'll try too hard and end up running in too quickly, which can upset my rhythm.

2. Stand tall when I'm bowling. As I go into my action, if I can get my front (left) elbow up high, then pull it through straight when I bowl, the rest of my action will probably fall into place. I'll be using my full height and my momentum will be going in a straight line. If I don't do this, my bowling arm won't be as high, I'll be delivering with a slingy action and that's when everything will start to go wrong.

3. Tickle armpit in follow-through. Once my right arm has let go of the ball, I want it to come all the way through to tickle my left armpit. This should ensure that there is enough energy in my action to give me a decent follow-through.

That may sound like a lot to think about, but it's all ingrained in my mind now, and all I really need to say to myself is: 'THINK TALL, TICKLE ARMPIT.' This mantra simplifies a lot of the technical guff that I could be getting bogged down with. So as much as I can, the only technical analysis I'll do while I'm actually bowling is to remind myself, while I'm walking back to my mark, to think tall and tickle my armpit. No matter how badly I'm bowling, I shouldn't be worrying about more than that during a game.

There will, of course, be days when everything you try is not good enough. If you're playing Test cricket and you happen to run into Brian Lara, Ricky Ponting or Sachin Tendulkar on a good day, there ain't a lot that little old me – or anybody else, for that matter – is going to be able to do to stop them. 'Hang on, Sachin, that was

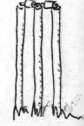

a good length ball outside off stump. You can't whip that through mid-on, that's not fair.'

He can. And he frequently does.

Now for this situation, as hopeless as it may seem, I do have a magic formula. It's a cunning ploy that I've managed to keep a secret for many years and I'm a little reluctant to divulge it now, just in case I ever need it again. But I suppose I've got to give you readers something for your money. So here goes.

When you're playing against a very good batsman, who's at the peak of his powers and treating everything he faces with disdain, the plan is this: hide from the captain.

For starters, try to stay out of his sight when you're fielding. Work out who the biggest bloke in your team is, say an Ashley Giles or an Andrew Flintoff, and try to position yourself behind them in the captain's eyeline (all the better if the bloke in between is a bowler).

Under no circumstances should you catch the captain's attention by doing anything fancy in the field, no spectacular dives or glamorous sliding stops (no danger there as far as I'm concerned). If the ball comes your way, a nice functional pick-up and throw should do the job perfectly well.

Also, don't shout too much encouragement. If you're going to do so, wait until somebody else has started shouting and make your noise at the same time. That way, you're still doing your bit for the team, but you're not drawing yourself to the captain's attention. If Michael Vaughan heard me shouting my mouth off down at fine leg when Lara had just reached 150, he might think: 'Oh, I forgot about Hoggy. He sounds in decent spirits, I might just give him a bowl. Let's see if he can stem the flow.' Bugger, my plan has been foiled. Any more bright ideas, Baldrick?

There is so much planning that goes into a Test match these days, you'd think that we ought to be able to spot the weaknesses of even the best of batsmen and plot how to get them out. Video analysis, Hawkeye, bowling coaches – we have plenty of resources at our disposal. But frustratingly, the other team's batsmen always seem to be in on the scam as well. So while we're watching videos of them batting, looking for technical flaws, they'll be watching videos of us bowling, looking for our weak spots. It probably all evens itself out in the end. Maybe we should just save everyone a lot of money and agree that we won't do any pre-match planning, we'll just turn up and see how it goes.

For every Test side we play against, we do put plans in place for the opposition batsmen, looking at where they score most of their runs and how they've been dismissed most frequently. It's well worth doing.

But in actual fact, how often does a plan really come off? How often is a batsman dismissed by an unplayable ball that pitches middle and hits off? Or one that draws him forward, makes him play, then moves away to get him caught at slip (that'll be my first ball to Jacques Kallis at Jo'burg)? I reckon that maybe only 10 per cent of dismissals come this way, when a batsman has been genuinely dismissed by the bowler's skill on that particular ball.

The rest will come about as a result of the pressure that has been created in the previous few overs. The batsman can't score a run, he becomes frustrated and he goes looking for runs when they're not there. Either that or he just plays a randomly crap shot. The trick is to make sure you're putting it in the right place when he does decide to press the self-destruct button.

If you're looking for a foolproof plan of how to bowl at any level of cricket, I can recommend an interview that I saw with Glenn McGrath and Jason Gillespie when they were at their peak. It went something like this:

'So Glenn, you're firmly established as the number one fast bowler in the world. What's your secret?'

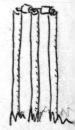

'Well, I run up, bowl and try to hit a length on or around off stump.'

'Yes, but what else do you do?'

'Well, I occasionally bowl a bouncer, but in the main I just run up, bowl and try to hit a length on or around off stump.'

'Come on, Glenn, you're the best in the world, there must be more to it than that.'

'No, I run up, bowl and try to hit a length on or around off stump. Oh, and one other thing. I generally assume the ball isn't going to swing. If it swings, I look on that as a bonus.'

'And you, Jason?'

'Er, pretty much the same, really.'

That's how simple cricket is. It might not have made for a particularly riveting television interview, but it was a strong message and it stayed with me. Yes, you can bowl wonderballs every now and then, and yes, sometimes the ball will swing round corners or seam about all over the place. But for the vast majority of the time you are just trying to find that old-fashioned line and length that batsmen find awkward.

In the England team, we used to joke when Duncan Fletcher was coach about his list of plans for opposing batsmen. Even before we went into the team meeting before a match, we'd have a fair idea that the letters T-O-O would be written against the names of most batsmen. This stood for the line and length we should bowl to the batsman, aiming to hit the Top of Off. So for South Africa, it might be Graeme Smith: Length: Top of Off. A.B. DeVilliers: Length: Top of Off. Jacques Kallis: Length: Top of Off.

There was some variation, of course. There would sometimes be a batsman who was uncomfortable playing the ball at hip height, so we'd bowl back-of-a-length to him. But for most of them it was good old T-O-O, the length that draws the batsman forward but doesn't allow him to drive.

There were more subtleties than this, and Fletch was a shrewd spotter of a batsman's weaknesses, but generally speaking the plans for any batsman will be a variation on this theme. If a batsman plays well down the line of off stump but opens the face of the bat just outside off, you'll try to bowl at an imaginary fourth stump, rather than the third. If a batsman's wagon wheel shows that he scores most heavily through the leg side, you might bowl a bit further out, at a fifth stump line outside off. A lot of Asian players will whip through leg from right outside off stump, so we might bowl a bit wider to them.

These were general plans, but it was left to each bowler to interpret them for himself. If we thought a batsman was vulnerable to a bouncer, Steve Harmison was much more likely to employ that particular plan than I was. And if Harmy and I were both going to try to get the ball around a batsman's hips, we'd have to pitch it in a slightly different place because our trajectories are not the same.

So while I would always bear in mind the plans for a batsman, the overriding aim would still be to follow that advice from McGrath and Gillespie and bowl my best ball six times out of six. My natural ball swings away from the right-hander, so if I can pitch it on or around off stump, on a good length, and move the ball away slightly, it's going to be quite difficult to play, or at least difficult to score from. Occasionally I'll try to bring a ball back in to get a batsman lbw, or tempt him with one that's wider, but most of the time I'm just trying to bowl my best ball, over and over again.

The skill, I suppose, comes in working out what your best ball is to each batsman on that particular wicket. If you are bowling to someone who stays back in his crease, for example, a good length to him could be a yard fuller than to a batsman who likes to get well forward. And pitches change from day to day, ground to ground and game to game, so you've always got to take that into account as well.

The area I try to land the ball in is about a foot square, the centre of which would be somewhere between 5½ and 6½ metres back from the crease, and around four inches outside off stump. When

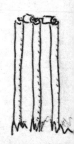

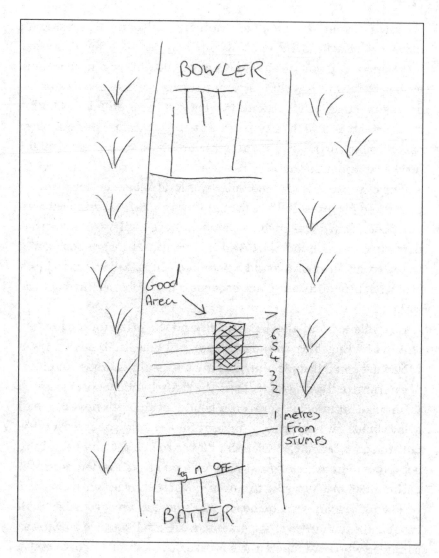

I'm practising on my own, I'll normally take five strides from the crease and put a cone down in front of me to aim at. I'll run in, bowl a few overs and try to hit that cone as many times as I can. Then I'll move it forward or back a bit and do the same thing again. Over the years, I've spent many an hour on my own with those cones, from the nets at Pudsey Congs, to the square at Heading-ley when there isn't a game on, and in nets at cricket grounds around the world. The cones don't offer much in the way of conversation, but they've been faithful assistants.

All those hours of practice have given me a fair idea of where my area is and how I need to shuffle it around for different batsmen. I was once bowling at Ricky Ponting and Fletch had told us not to bowl too straight or full at him early in his innings. Ponting liked to impose himself with a drive straight down the ground, so we were to bowl outside his off stump on a good length, which we'd worked out to be 6 metres from the stumps.

The first ball I bowled to him was driven straight back past me for four. What a prat I felt. That was exactly what we were trying to avoid. And sure enough, when we went off for lunch, Fletch called me into his office.

'Hoggy, I told you to bowl a good length to Ponting. So why did you go and bowl a half-volley straight away?'

'Can we just have a look on the pitch map, Fletch, and see where it pitched?'

We had a look on our computer, on which Hawkeye logs where every ball pitches. And on this occasion, that first ball to Ponting had landed *precisely* 6 metres from the stumps, a shade outside the off stump. It was exactly the ball I'd been told to bowl. 'Maybe that was just a good shot, Fletch,' I said.

I was let off the hook on that occasion, but there have been plenty of times when I've done something similar and been proved completely wrong. I might have been feeling a bit sorry for myself after an unrewarding day's graft out on the field, thinking I'd been a bit unlucky, and the computer would tell me that I had actually bowled like a fool. It certainly keeps you honest, this game.

It may not sound appealing to those who don't like cricket, and certainly not to those who think that the game goes on far too long,

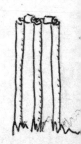

but much of the time as a bowler you are attempting to bore the batsman to death. Dot ball after dot ball, join those dots up into maidens, give him the rope to hang himself.

People who are bored do silly things in search of amusement, often getting themselves into trouble in the process. And when batsmen get bored, they play daft shots, desperate to hit a boundary to relieve the tedium, thinking they've seen a half-volley when in fact it's just another length ball. Even Geoff Boycott would have got bored eventually if you bowled enough good balls at him.

Boycs actually gave me some pretty good advice along these lines. He invited me to his house and sat me down in his living room – nice place, lots of Feng Shui – and he told me that, as a bowler, I should never forget that I'm in control of the contest with the batsman, because I start with the ball in my hand. Every ball, he said, I could make the batsman answer six questions.

Should he go forward? Or back?

Should he play it? Or leave it?

Should he play defensively? Or aggressively?

So in the space of an over, lasting about three minutes, you can pose him as many as thirty-six questions, which is more than Anne Robinson ever manages. And if you keep on asking those questions, sooner or later he is going to get one of them wrong, and that will be all it takes. 'You are the weakest link. Goodbye!'

And there's another factor, much underestimated, that can work in your favour if you're able to keep getting the ball in the same place time after time: the joy of natural variation. I don't know if you have ever noticed, but a cricket ball isn't completely round. It's got this nice big rope running around it, more commonly known as a seam. And the bigger it is the better, from my point of view. There's always a reasonable chance that the ball will land on this piece of rope, and who knows what it's going to do from there? And let's face it, if you don't know what you're doing with the ball, what chance has the poor old batsman got?

At Nagpur in 2006, Virender Sehwag shouldered arms to me in the second innings and was bowled off stump when the ball nipped back off the seam. He looked at me in surprise on his way off. In return, I attempted to give him a knowing look, as if to say, 'Didn't you spot the off-cutter then, Virender?' even though it was a complete fluke that it had jagged back at him. I also kept quiet in the post-match team meeting when we recorded Sehwag's dismissal as 'off-cutter, bowled off stump'.

So the seam will provide you with one type of natural variation, but there's also the guarantee that you won't get your action right every ball. Often, that can work against you, but sometimes it will work in your favour.

I remember the last time we toured Pakistan in late 2005, in the first Test at Multan I had Inzamam-ul-Haq lbw when he was expecting an outswinger, played no shot and the ball thudded into his front pad. The next day, Bob Woolmer, who was Pakistan's coach at the time, described it as the ball of the match, saying that I'd held the ball as though for an outswinger, changed the direction with my clever wrist action and completely bamboozled old Inzy.

My version of events was slightly different: I'd tried to bowl an outswinger, fallen away slightly in my delivery stride and the ball went straight on as a result.

But Bob was a clever bloke, far cleverer than me. Maybe he knew more than I did myself. Perhaps I conjured this bit of magic without even realising it myself. Who was I to argue with Bob Woolmer?

Maybe I am a genius after all.

This is one of the beauties of being a swing bowler. I wonder whether we have more natural variations than any other type of bowler. For all the scientific research and coaching mumbo-jumbo about how a cricket ball behaves in its journey through the air, one thing remains certain: sometimes a cricket ball swings; sometimes, for whatever reason, it just doesn't. Shortly after our Ashes victory in

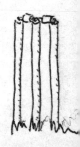

2005, a few of our players like Freddie, Harmy and KP travelled to Australia for those stuff-and-nonsense games between the Aussies and an ICC World XI. At the time, Tim Boon was our technical analyst and he went on to fulfil the same job for the ICC team.

When he came back, Tim told me that he'd been chatting to Graeme Smith, who was skippering the World XI in the 'Test' match. Apparently, Smith had been saying how much trouble, as a left-hander, he had found facing me during our series in South Africa the previous winter. 'The thing I'm never sure about facing Hoggy,' said Smith, 'is that I never know when he's going to make it swing and when he's going to make it go straight on.'

Well, Smithy, I've got news for you pal. Neither do I! Sometimes there may be an element of skill involved, but half the time it's just good old-fashioned luck. We all need a bit from time to time.

So much of a bowler's game is about putting doubts into the batsman's mind and then preying on them ruthlessly. When you've backed them into a corner, you don't ever want to let them out with a loose ball that could put you back to square one.

A lot of bowlers try to put doubts in a batsman's mind by sledging them, but that's something I've never gone in for. I might be a highly competitive person, but I've never been hugely confrontational. It's just not in my nature to sledge. I've always felt that, if you manage to beat a batsman, a bit of eye contact and a wry smile will reinforce the message just as well as a mouthful of abuse. The batsman's got a pretty good idea already that he looks a plonker because there are plenty of other people on the field watching everything he does, not to mention the thousands in the crowd and the millions on telly, if you happen to be playing Test cricket.

That's not to say that I disapprove of other bowlers sledging. It's a question of knowing how you perform best as an individual.

Andre Nel, for example, certainly seems to bowl better when he gets worked up and starts giving batsmen the verbals. He looks a goon while he's doing it, but I think he's well aware of that.

If I get angry with anyone while I'm bowling, it's more likely to be myself. So those times when I'm walking back to my mark, cursing myself after bowling a bad ball, I suppose I am, in effect, sledging myself. I don't think the match referee is going to come down on me too hard for that. The only time that I might have a go at the batsman is if he's nicked me behind and not walked, in which case I may venture the opinion that he's a cheating little so-and-so. Or words to that effect.

There might have been times, when I was younger and dafter, that I tried to prove my manhood by aiming a few choice swear words in the batsman's direction. One such time was in a four-day match for Free State against Eastern Province on another flat track at Bloemfontein. I was bowling well, I'd taken one for about 15 runs from as many overs, but I was getting frustrated because one guy, Louis Koen, had hung around for ages. He was edging it here, nudging it there, and we just couldn't get him out. Louis was a big lad, a huge dark-haired farmer, and eventually, when he inside-edged me for four, I just snapped:

'YOU SPAWNY F***ING C**T!'

He gave me a look, wandered slowly down the wicket, squared up to me and said, calmly: 'If you ever, ever call me that again, you little shit, I promise I will wrap this bat around your head.'

I wasn't quite sure what to say to that. I stomped off back to get my hat from the umpire and went down to third man, muttering away to myself. Then, in my next over, Louis did the same thing again, inside-edging me for four, just as he had done the previous over. This was more than I could bear.

'AAAARRGGHH!' I yelled.
'YOU SPAWNY F***ING ... DOOS!'

Which, for those of you not familiar with Afrikaner terms of abuse, is the local translation of the aforementioned c-word. On this occasion, Louis just laughed. And I think I started laughing back, perhaps in relief that he wasn't going to wrap his bat round my head. I reckon I learned an important lesson from that little exchange: don't swear at batsmen who are much bigger and harder than you.

There are times when it is part of a team's plans to give a batsman the verbals, maybe if he's the sort of player who can be goaded into playing a rash shot. Andrew Symonds was one player we fancied we could wind up when he came into the Australia side during the Ashes series in 2006–07. You don't just make a comment and expect the batsman to have a big whoosh from the next ball, not at Test level anyway. The only time I've seen that happen was the famous incident with Tino Best, the West Indies fast bowler, at Lord's in 2004. Freddie was fielding at first slip and could see Tino straining at the leash to have a swipe at Asley Giles. 'Mind the windows, Tino,' Fred said. Next ball, Tino strode down the wicket, tried to hit the ball over the Media Centre (thus avoiding the windows), missed by a yard and was stumped by a mile. Fred could barely contain himself.

That was the exception, though, and more often it's a case of having a gentle dig every now and then to try to get the batsman's adrenaline pumping to affect his decision-making. With Symonds, we'd try to get him to play more shots than he perhaps really wanted to, or at least felt he ought to. You try to get under his skin and hope that eventually he snaps. With Tino, that took one ball. For Symonds, and just about everyone else, it tends to take a bit longer to annoy them.

Not that those tactics can have worked particularly well with Symonds, as he averaged something like 60 in the three games he played. But the intention was there.

In those cases, I won't push myself into sledging, and I have never had a captain or coach who insisted that I should have a few words. It would sound forced and I would just end up looking and sounding like an idiot. I might make my stares a bit more pointed, a bit more prolonged, but there are always slips and the wicketkeeper who can make the clever comments, if that is what's required. Besides, I think a good stare can convey aggression just as effectively.

I remember when I was batting on my Test debut against West Indies at Lord's. Curtly Ambrose bowled one on the back of a length and I had a wild slog, which flew over mid-on for four. Curtly watched the ball's path with disdain and just stayed there, halfway down the wicket, eyeballing me with those great big eyes.

I'm not quite sure what I was doing – the adrenalin must have been pumping pretty powerfully at that stage – but I strode a couple of steps[†] towards him, patting the pitch and giving him a stare of my own. My best 'I may be No. 11, but I'm not scared of you' stare. And I was amazed when, in his team-talk before we went out to bowl at them in the second innings, Alec Stewart, the captain, said: 'Come on, lads, we've got to get out there and fight. Let's get in their faces. Look at Hoggy, staring down Ambrose in his first Test match. I want everyone to show that sort of courage.' Then we went and bowled them out for 54. I didn't actually get on to bowl, but it's quite clear that I deserved most of the credit for that victory.

So a well-timed stare can be a perfectly good way of getting your point across. As can a nicely observed period of silence. Just as some batsmen can, in theory, be unsettled by a few comments about their technique or their attitude, there are others who feel

---

[†]**HOGFACT:** The average person takes between 8,000 and 10,000 steps per day. No wonder we need a bit of a lie down every night, is it?

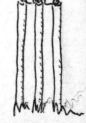

a little uneasy when all around them goes quiet. Or at least there are those, like Steve Waugh, who thrive on sledging, so you starve them of that motivational fodder. When a bouncer from Steve Harmison hit Ricky Ponting on the cheek on the first morning of the 2005 Ashes series, we all just kept quiet. No whooping, no back-slapping for Harmy, but no sympathy either. At the other end, Justin Langer said: 'Shit, boys, are we in a war here?' And I suppose that was the message we were trying to convey. We went on to get stuffed in that game, of course, but I think we'd still made a point about the aggressive intent we were determined to show.

I suppose it's up to the individual bowler to decide whether he feels that sledging a batsman will help his cause. And there is no doubt that some bowlers use it extremely effectively. At the highest level, the majority of batsmen have learned to turn a deaf ear to most of the stuff that is spouted in their direction, but the hardest bowler to ignore was Shane Warne. He just never stopped. He was engaged in a constant mission to make the batsman believe that he deserved a wicket every ball. And the umpire as well. Either that or he was just trying to annoy the hell out of them both.

Even if he bowled you a full toss that you smacked to the boundary, he'd still be shrieking: 'Awww, f**k!' as though you'd just survived one of the best balls in history.

The first time I faced him, I wondered whether something was wrong with him. Each ball was followed by this theatrical outburst, no matter what the result. Length ball, forward defensive, no run, 'Awww, f**k, jeez.' Widish ball, outside off stump, left well alone, no run, 'Awww, f**k, jeez.' Fuller delivery, turned into the leg side for single. 'Awww, f**k, jeez!' I thought he might have some sort of cricketing Tourette's.

But Warnie knew what he was doing, creating an atmosphere around the batsman and attempting to chip away at his self-belief. However hard the batsman tried to shut him out, Warnie just kept on going. And he did have one other small factor in his favour, of course: he was actually quite a useful leg-spin bowler.

While I was right at the other end of the scale from Warnie in terms of sledging output at Test level, I'm more likely to dole out a bit of abuse in county cricket. When I say abuse, it's more likely to be piss-taking than anything aggressive. And I'm much more likely to have a go at someone who I know will give me a bit back.

At the end of the 2008 season, I was playing against Sussex at Hove in Chris Adams's last game before his retirement. It was a great occasion for him. He'd captained Sussex for yonks, led them to three county championships, and this was his swansong on his home ground. When he came in to bat we did the decent thing and gave him a guard of honour and a round of applause on his way out to the crease.

Once he'd walked past us all, I caught up with him and put my arm around his shoulders. 'Grizz,' I said. 'Now that you're retiring, I've got a question for you. Does it work best when we chirp at you and try to wind you up at the crease? Or is it when we say nothing and leave you alone? When are you at your best?'

'When am I at my best?' he asked. 'That would have been about five years ago.'

Now that's the sort of answer you want to come up with if someone's giving you abuse. And incidentally, he was out for a duck shortly afterwards, so maybe my dastardly tactics actually worked.

Maybe it's not too late to become a sledger after all ...

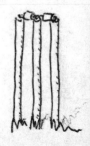

THE SCRUFF LIST

This is a quick guide to who have been the scruffiest and tidiest people in the England dressing-room in my experience. Some people are very organised, with all their kit neatly tucked away. Others have their gear spilling out all over the place as though a volcano has erupted in their kitbag.

Looking through the names below, there seems to be a batsman–bowler thing going on here. Maybe cricketing psychologists could look into the reasons for this ...

SCRUFFIEST PLAYERS

1. STEVE HARMISON

He's a very scruffy man. His stuff will be all over the shop and I've lost count of the number of times I've got home, dug the dirty kit out of my bag and found at least one of Harmy's shirts in there. So I'll send him a text to tell him, and he'll reply saying that he's got mine, too.

2. ANDREW FLINTOFF

His kit might start the day in his bag, but at some point it decides to get out and go for a wander round the dressing-room. Also no stranger to the accidental shirt-swapping antics. The problem is that the bowlers have often tended to sit next to each other in one corner, so these things are going to happen. At least we're all a similar size.

3. MATTHEW HOGGARD

Very glad I don't have to change next to myself. In reality, I should probably be right at the top of this list. But I don't need an independent adjudicator and it's my book, so I'm sticking myself at No 3.

TIDIEST PLAYERS

1. ANDREW STRAUSS

Everything is carefully arranged, nothing is spilling out, his kitbag is a model of organisation. I don't know how well all his different pairs of gloves and pads are arranged, but I imagine there'll be some meticulous system. I bet he's never got home and found someone else's shirt in his bag.

2. IAN BELL

It wouldn't be wise for me to change next to someone this tidy. He'd be constantly kicking my stray stuff back towards my bag and complaining about me flinging my boots off in his direction after I've just bowled 30 overs. Best we stay in our own corners, Belly.

3. ALASTAIR COOK

I'm guessing he had a very tidy bedroom when he was a little lad. He rarely has a hair out of place and there's never any mess around his stuff. Come to think of it, I wonder whether his mum packs his bag for him?

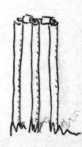

10
Time to Produce

O ne way or another, the summer of 2005 was going to be a pretty important time in my life. For the year or so leading up to that series, ever since we started winning Test matches consistently, everyone had been talking about the Ashes. In the England team, we tried to avoid it. *Shut up about the Ashes, we've got a few other games to win first!* But once we'd won that important series in South Africa and beaten Bangladesh at the start of the English season, it was finally time to start concentrating on playing the Aussies and trying to win the Ashes back for the first time in donkey's years. For any England cricketer, if you come to the end of your career and haven't played in an Ashes-winning side, it is something you would look back on with regret.

The other major goal I was hoping to achieve in those next few months was to become a dad. Sarah and I had tied the knot the previous October, on a fantastic day starting at St Margaret's church in Horsforth and going on to Rudding Park, near Harrogate. Like many a groom, I had been under strict instructions from my beautiful bride that day not to get too drunk. 'If you think you're just standing at the bar getting pissed with your mates all night,' she said, 'you can think again.' But it was only halfway through the night when I spotted my wife, holding half a Guinness in one hand, a big cigar in the other and pointing at me with her elbow as she was forbidden to point with her finger by some drinking game she'd become involved in. This was clearly a marriage made in heaven. It was a great day, the start of our family life together, and we were keen to add a little Hoggy (or Hoggette) to the gang as soon as possible.

So these really were exciting days, a time to start growing up off the field and to show how much me and the England team had matured as cricketers. As much as we wanted to play down the significance of the Ashes in the ridonculously overhyped build-up, we knew full well that England teams are judged on how they perform against the Aussies. And for a very long time – it had been eighteen years since we'd had the Ashes – England hadn't performed well.

We were desperate to change that pattern, and that meant making sure we didn't allow Australia to bully us. To do that, it was essential that we played aggressive cricket from the start to make them realise this wasn't the same old England. Don't get me wrong, we'd been playing plenty of aggressive cricket before – it hadn't been a friendly in the park in that Test series against South Africa. But against Australia we wanted to make sure that we began strongly and stayed tough throughout the series. This meant not saying hello and being nicey-nicey to them off the field, not being frightened to throw the ball towards them if they were in the way to make them move. They'd been doing that sort of thing to us for years. It was time for us to start doing it back.

After all the build-up of the previous weeks, there was an incredible atmosphere at Lord's on that first morning of the first Test on 21 July. Even when we walked out through the Long Room, where the members are normally very restrained, there was clapping, cheering and back-slapping as we went out to bowl first. There was a bit of adrenalin pumping that day, as you could tell from my reaction when I took the first wicket, bowling Matthew

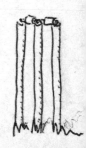

Hayden through the gate and yelling my head off in celebration. There was a massive release of tension in that moment. Besides, I had a bit of previous from the last Ashes series to sort out with Hayden. I owed him one or two.

Things really did go well at first. From Harmy's fast and nasty first spell to the aggressive intent we showed in the field, everything seemed to be going to plan as we bowled them out for 190. But then Glenn McGrath reminded us what a class act he is and bowled us out for 155. Things grew worse in their second innings when we dropped a bucketload of catches as they made 384. And by the time we had batted again, folding to Warne and McGrath for 180, there was only Kevin Pietersen left in any credit, having made two excellent fifties on his debut. The rest of us were looking worryingly like the same old England. Some tough guys we were proving to be.

But there was a real difference this time, and it came from the five series we had won on the trot over the previous couple of years. This time we could put the defeat at Lord's down to one bad day at the office **AND GENUINELY BELIEVE IT**. That sort of thing had been said hundreds of times before against the Aussies, more in hope than expectation, but we really thought we were capable of bouncing straight back in the second Test at Edgbaston the following week.

In the meantime, I had other things to worry about, because our efforts to create Hoggy Junior had been going about as well as that performance at Lord's. We'd been trying for several months by now, without any hint of success, and we were starting to feel the frustration, as Sarah will tell you ...

SARAH: *In hindsight, it probably wasn't the best of ideas for us to be trying for kids around the time of the Ashes. But we'd started trying pretty much straight away after we got married and, until you actually start, you don't ever think you're going to have a problem. Before you start, you seem to spend all your time trying not to get pregnant, so it's* *easy to think that when you decide you're ready, the babies will come along on demand.*

That certainly seemed to be the case in the England team at the time. In those couple of years leading up to the Ashes, there had been babies popping out everywhere. They weren't just prolific at winning cricket matches, those lads. There were little Flintoffs, Vaughans, Gileses, Trescothicks, Harmisons, Strausses appearing. Everybody seemed to be producing. We were probably the last ones of that group to get married and nobody else seemed to have had major problems conceiving, so why should we?

By the time of the Ashes in 2005, we had only been trying to conceive for around eight or nine months, which I know is not a long time by some people's standards. There are friends of ours who had been trying for ten years before they succeeded. And for other people, it never happens at all. But when you've been getting your hopes up month after month, the anxiety soon starts to build. Each month I would take a pregnancy test and each month we would be disappointed.

Quite often that summer, I wouldn't tell Matthew that I'd taken a test because I didn't want to burden him with extra worries. There was so much hype surrounding his cricket at the time that I thought he had enough on his plate. And as the summer wore on, the cricket was becoming more and more stressful by the game, for players and spectators alike ...

The last day of that second Test at Edgbaston was just ridonculous. There was no way it should have become such a nerve-jangler. Going into that last morning, we were home and almost dry. Chasing 282, they needed 107 to win with only two wickets remaining. Shane Warne and Brett Lee were both decent batsmen, but it should have been a doddle, shouldn't it? Yes, it should have been. But, as we were gradually finding out, nothing that summer was going to come easily.

In the crowd at Edgbaston that Sunday morning, there was a big group of Aussies who kept chanting out the state of the game.

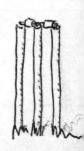

'Eighty-six runs to go, eighty-six runs to go ...' It became a bit of a soundtrack to the game. A couple of minutes later it would be: 'Sixty-five runs to go, sixty-five runs to go ...' After a while, Fred made Warnie stand on his stumps, but Brett and Michael Kasprowicz, the last pair, carried on as though batting was the easiest thing in the world.

'Forty-six runs to go, forty-six runs to go ...' Come on, lads, this can't go on for ever, can it? 'Twenty-two runs to go, twenty-two runs to go ...' What? Twenty-two? How did that happen? The target just kept going down, and those Aussies kept singing. This was getting scary, very scary. We weren't going to throw it all away, were we?

Before the game at Edgbaston, we had reminded ourselves how we'd come back from dismal defeats to produce good performances in the next game. A few months earlier in South Africa, we'd been stuffed at Cape Town but then fought back to win a crucial Test in Johannesburg. Those sort of experiences are worth a lot to a team in situations like this.

On the first day, we had come to Edgbaston and our batsmen had done exactly what was needed. Straussy and Tres put on 112 in twenty-five overs for the first wicket and we managed to score 407 in less than eighty overs, which was the best way of proving that a crap performance at Lord's didn't make us a bad side all of a sudden.

I then dismissed Matthew Hayden again, this time with my first ball, when he slapped straight to Straussy at short extra cover. That was most obliging of him because Straussy had been put there for precisely that reason.

We got a first-innings lead of 99, but then folded ourselves to 182 all out as Warnie got to work. Fred was the only one to do his stuff, hitting some big sixes in a knock of 73. So it was 282 to win for Australia, which would have pretty much clinched the series for them. They were probably just about favourites at this stage, but not by close of play on the third day. All the bowlers were contributing, and Fred bowled that brilliant over in which Langer played on and he had Ponting caught behind. Once Harmy had bowled Michael Clarke with a slower ball, it looked as though we would be able to come back on the Sunday morning, wrap up the last couple of wickets and tootle off home.

Back to those chanting Aussies. Over the course of the game, they'd been given more than a run for their money by the home supporters. The Edgbaston crowd is probably the loudest in the country and they had been giving us great support, as ever. But as the runs ticked down and the tension grew on that Sunday morning, they became strangely quiet. All we could hear was 'Fifteen runs to go, fifteen runs to go ...'

I was a bit of a spectator myself that morning as Michael Vaughan opted to rotate Harmy, Gilo and Fred. But we were getting desperate and, when about ten runs were needed, Vaughany asked me to warm up. I must have had half an eye[†] on him, hoping that he wouldn't be calling on me at this late stage, and I thought I'd seen him looking towards me a couple of balls earlier. Not now, Vaughany, not now. Give Harmy another one! But sure enough, he started swinging his arms to indicate that I should get myself loose and ready to bowl.

I think I pretended that I didn't see him at first. But then he did it again and he was definitely gesturing in my direction. I looked behind me in the hope that Simon Jones, or any of the other bowlers, might be standing behind me. But then I realised I was on the fine-leg boundary, so if he was asking anybody else to warm up it would have been some bloke in the crowd. At that stage, I think I'd have been happier for the bloke in the crowd to have a go. I was shitting myself.

[†] **HOGFACT:** The average duration of a single blink of the human EYE is 0.3 seconds. A little tip here: don't blink when Brett Lee is just about to bowl at you. That would be more than half your reaction time gone.

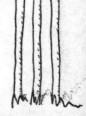

I wouldn't have minded so much if there had still been thirty or so required. You're allowed to bowl a bad ball then. But imagine coming on after just standing in the field all morning and they only need ten to win. Perhaps Vaughany was taking the piss. He must have been crapping himself as well by that time. I'm normally one to put my hand up in any situation, but this time I think I was only human in secretly thinking: 'Go on, Vaughany. Give Harmy one more over.'

Which would, of course, have been the right decision (you see, I had the best interests of the team at heart). Just in the nick of time, just as the Aussies were chanting 'Three runs to go, three runs to go ...', Harmy had Kasprowicz caught behind by Geraint Jones and we had got away from a very sticky situation. And I had got away without bowling. The sheer sense of relief that we all felt then was incredible.

Back in the dressing-room, we were all just looking at each other and smiling in disbelief for a while, but it wasn't long before we were having a couple of beers and a good old sing-song. And to their credit, the Aussies came to join us for a drink and a chat, which was big of them after such an agonising defeat. I think we all realised we'd been involved in something special.

It had been an astonishing Test match and I thought to myself as I drove away from the ground that it had been a privilege to play a part. Normally if I've been involved in a game with a close finish, when I speak to friends and family afterwards they always seem to have suffered from nerves far more than me, but I'm not sure that was the case at Edgbaston. At the time, we thought that finishes like that only came along once a blue moon. Little did we know there were a few more to come that summer. Maybe it was a good job that Sarah wasn't pregnant, because with all that tension, there'd have been a danger she'd have gone into labour in the stands ...

SARAH: *As it happens, there were actually a couple of the girls sitting with me who were expecting babies around that time. Nichola Vaughan, my best mate, was pregnant with her second child, which was a shame because it meant we couldn't get sloshed together when the cricket was getting stressful. But I did feel for her towards the end of some of those tight games because you're supposed to avoid stressful situations when you're pregnant. There were times when I was seriously concerned that I would have to play the role of emergency midwife.*

As well as the babies appearing all around us, there was another thing I noticed that summer that newly married couples have to contend with. I'd never really thought about it before, but it seems that as soon as you've got yourselves hitched, other people suddenly become incredibly interested in when you are going to have children. Nice that they show an interest, I suppose, but if you're having problems along those lines it can become a tad irritating. I'm sure anyone who has struggled to conceive will have experienced this, but there can be a lack of tact shown in these situations. 'Are we going to be hearing the patter of tiny feet soon? When's it going to be then?' Erm, well, I wish I could tell you, but ...

The baby digs were starting to grate and Matthew was getting the same thing. I didn't want to mention to the cricket girls that we were trying, because they'd only have been asking even more. During lunchtime at one Test match, I was sitting giving Rachael Flintoff's son, Corey, his bottle and one of the players' wives came up and said to me: 'For God's sake, Sarah, when are you going to stop taking everybody else's and get on with having one of your own?' See what I mean about a lack of tact?

Everyone was at it with the baby digs. I couldn't believe it. Even Camilla Parker-Bloody-Bowles got in on the act. We were still struggling to conceive a few months later when we went on tour to India, and Camilla was with Prince Charles at a reception we were attending at the British High Commission. She came up to

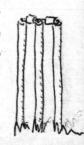

me while I was holding little Sam Strauss, who had a lot of blond hair and could have passed for mine. 'Now here's a lovely little boy. How old is he?'

Oh God, not you as well, I thought. But I said: 'I'm not quite sure. You'd better ask his dad. He's over there.'

'I am sorry, I thought he was yours,' she said. Was there no escape from those baby digs?

SARAH: *We forgave Camilla quite quickly, though, because she came back to us a short while later and said: 'I'm terribly sorry, but we're going to have to leave shortly.' Matthew was fairly fed up of the reception by this time, so he said: 'If you're going, can we come too? I'm really bored.' She smiled. I think she was quite amused. She was probably bored herself.*

So all these baby digs weren't helping the cause. And the longer the wait went on, the more I was thinking there could be something biologically wrong with one of us. Or at the very least, we should be getting ourselves checked out. But it just wasn't the right time to be doing these things. Not until the Ashes was over.

If any of us in the England team had been in the dark about how this Ashes series was catching on with the general public, it became perfectly clear on the team bus on the final day of the third Test at Old Trafford. That morning, we crawled through the streets of Manchester in our cars on our way to the ground. From our hotel at the Lowry it was normally a fifteen-minute drive to Old Trafford, but that morning it must have taken us at least an hour. A few of the players tried to drive down the wrong side of the road to get past the blockages, but the traffic police stopped us. So we told them why we were in such a hurry and they let us carry on. There were people everywhere, and we were told later more than

20,000 of them had been locked out of the ground. **TWENTY THOUSAND!?!** That has never happened before in my lifetime, and I don't know if it will happen again.

We were starting that last day with a simple equation of needing to take ten wickets. The night before, we'd declared our second innings and set them 423 to win. But more realistically, they had to bat out the last day. Wickets kept falling at regular intervals, but then they would put a partnership together and it would look as though we were going to run out of time. And throughout the day, Ricky Ponting would not be budged. He played magnificently for his 156 and, although he was caught behind down the leg side off Harmy shortly before the end, leaving Brett Lee and Glenn McGrath to negotiate the last four overs, it was Ponting who had saved his side.

We were, of course, really fed up that we hadn't finished them off and taken a 2–1 lead in the series. Would we get such a good opportunity again? But as we were walking off the field, we looked up to the pavilion balcony and saw the Aussies celebrating wildly. The sight of them larking about like that would normally be a cause for an Englishman to avert his gaze, but this time it was different.

It was amazing to see how ecstatically they were celebrating a draw. Yes, it had been another tense finish and they'd done well on that last day, but they were high-fiving, giving each other big hugs and generally looking as though they'd just thrashed us out of sight, rather than avoided defeat by the skin of their teeth.

That was the moment when I knew the tables had turned.

Those celebrations were the sort of thing that England teams used to do when they had drawn with Australia. I realised then that we had definitely got to them, that they genuinely feared us and that we had every chance of outplaying them again in the last couple of Tests. The momentum, I felt, had definitely shifted in our favour.

We now had the opportunity for a bit of a breather before the fourth Test at Trent Bridge in ten days' time. The second and third

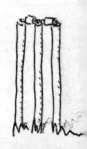

games had been back-to-back, which is always hard work, and we'd probably used up more than a little nervous energy over those past two weeks as well. So it was time for a short drive back across the Pennines for me and the chance for a few days at home with my lovely wife.

Over the last couple of weeks, the cricket had inevitably taken my mind off my attempts to become a dad, but in between games thoughts inevitably drifted that way again. But I was determined to remain upbeat about it. Sarah had a feeling that something wasn't quite right, but as far as we knew we could just have been waiting for the right day to hit the jackpot. And hey, look on the bright side, it's not the worst thing in the world to have to keep trying at. If nothing else, it's still a damn good excuse to get your leg over.

SARAH: *It would have been more convenient if my body clock had sorted its timings out to fit in with the Ashes series and the appearances of His Nibs in between matches. You have to get your timings right on these things, but that never seemed to be the case for us. And it wasn't as though we could ask them to postpone an Ashes Test match for a couple of days so we could have another go at getting pregnant. Don't think that would quite have worked somehow ...*

In these circumstances, you can't help but wonder why things aren't working. As a bloke, the last thing you want to hear is that you're firing blanks. A few months later, I did eventually take the plunge and go to the local clinic for a sperm count. It was just after we had come back from that tour to India in the New Year. We were having a load of work done on our house at the time, so we were living with Carole and Colin, Sarah's folks, for a couple of months. It was very kind of them to put us up, but it probably wasn't the best of times for me to be going for a sperm count.

Once I'd been up to the clinic, I came back down to Carole and Colin's house and wandered in through the front door with a plastic cup in my hand. Feeling more than a little embarrassed, with everybody looking at my plastic cup, I had to say: 'Erm, excuse me, I'm just going upstairs for a while.'

Off I went to do my business, then I came back downstairs and popped my head round the door: 'Just off back to the clinic. Cheerio.' However much you love your in-laws, that's not really the sort of thing you want to be doing at their house. Anyway, just for the record, the test results revealed that I was firing on all cylinders, so to speak.

SARAH: *Poor Mum and Dad. I don't think they knew where to put themselves then. Nor did I, for that matter. But I think the whole thing became easier for me once I'd told a couple of those closest to me about our situation, people like my mum and Nichola Vaughan. I hadn't wanted to tell any of the cricket girls initially, but Nichola was someone I knew I could trust. And as ever with something like that, you start to feel better about a problem once you've shared it with someone else.*

During the Ashes, I hadn't even been talking about it much with Matthew. I didn't want him to be coming home from one of those intense Test matches and plunging straight into a big discussion at home about what was going on, or what wasn't going on. None of the lads had ever been under as much scrutiny before as they were that summer, and they were bound to start feeling it. The boy Hoggard was expected to do well at Trent Bridge as well, which only added to the pressure on his shoulders ...

The really difficult thing was that it was becoming increasingly hard to switch off from the cricket between games. This was something I'd never really had a problem with before. Once I was away from the ground, I could go out with the dogs and completely forget about any worries I might have had with my job. Walking the dogs was still a release during the Ashes, but when I came home there would be something about it on the telly, even if we weren't watching sport. If I picked up a newspaper, I couldn't simply avoid the

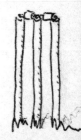

cricket by staying away from the back pages – it was on the front pages by this time as well.

So with the pressure steadily building, I was extremely grateful to Simon Jones when he told the press in the lead-up to the fourth Test that it would be Hoggy's turn to do the business in this game. He didn't mean to heap the expectation all on me, of course, he was just saying that the ball usually swung at Trent Bridge and so conditions should favour my type of bowling. But the way it was reported, it was a case of 'Hoggard must do the business here, or else ...' Thanks for that one, Jonah.

I hadn't taken a hatful of wickets in the series so far, but I'd been chipping in along the way. I hadn't bowled a huge number of overs because conditions had generally suited the other bowlers, but I'd picked up seven wickets in 56 overs, not a bad strike-rate, and six of them had been top-order batsmen. The important thing was that I felt I was bowling well and was confident that my day would come as long as I kept doing my stuff.

At tea on the second day, Australia finally bowled us out for 477. Mercifully, I had been batting at the end of our innings, which meant that I didn't have to sit around and think about my bowling for too long. The waiting is always the worst bit in these situations.

When we went out to bowl, there was a bit of cloud cover, which often helps a bowler like me. And yes, the ball was swinging. It took us a few overs to build up some pressure on the batsmen, and I came agonisingly close to getting Matthew Hayden lbw a couple of times, as he jammed his bat down to get an inside edge before the ball slapped him on the pad. But with the third ball of my fifth over there was no inside edge and he was bang in front, so he was on his way. That run-up from the garden was paying dividends against the left-handers again.

With the first ball of my next over I nipped one back into the right-handed Damien Martyn and we had another big lbw shout. The television replays showed afterwards that he'd got a massive inside edge, but thankfully Aleem Dar didn't spot it. Hey ho, you win some and you lose some. It was beginning to look as though it was my day.

Jonah had done his bit by getting Ponting lbw and both of us were bowling really well now. With conditions in my favour, Vaughany kept me going, and just as I was getting towards the end of my spell, with the third ball of my tenth over, Justin Langer insideedged onto his pad, the ball looped up and Ian Bell dived forward from short leg to take the catch. By the time I came off I had taken three for 28 from eleven overs and Australia were 62 for four. The feeling that I'd had at Old Trafford had been right. We were on top again and the momentum was definitely with us.

In the end, we bowled them out for 218 the next morning. On the way off the field we got in a huddle and decided that we would make Australia follow on. Then we started bowling in their second innings and Jonah broke down with an ankle injury. Bollocks. It was going to be a much harder job with only four bowlers.

And it did prove to be a long, hard slog in the second innings, more about boring them out. Our efforts were helped considerably, though by the intervention of Gary Pratt, our substitute fielder, who ran out Ricky Ponting with a brilliant direct hit from cover. Ponting then completely lost his rag. I could see that he was fuming as he left the field because he was giving me and Gilo a right old glare as he stormed past us. 'What are you looking at?' I said. It turned out that he was having a rant about our use of substitute fielders and on his way off, he spouted a load of abuse at Fletch, who was sitting on our dressing-room balcony. Most amusing. Apparently, Ponting thought that our bowlers were going off the field for a rub-down every time we finished a spell, but we were only ever going off for a pee. We take on board a load of fluid while we're bowling to keep our hydration levels up and occasionally we have to let nature take its course. So Ponting was wrong as well as run out.

It eventually took us 124 overs to dismiss the Aussies for 387, so we were left needing only 129 to win, with four sessions to do it in. Surely this would be straightforward. Surely we wouldn't have

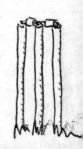

yet another nail-biter on our hands. Once Tres and Straussy had put on 32 in the first five overs, it looked as though it was to be a stroll this time.

Oh no it wasn't. Remember, nothing was going to come easily this summer, not as long as Shane Warne and Brett Lee had something to do with it.

Once the wickets started tumbling, they didn't stop. I'm not a brilliant watcher at these times and I retreated to the physio's room and asked him to massage muscles[†] and joints that really didn't need rubbing. Anything to avoid watching. And in the background, there would be the sound of another batsman coming back in, cursing and throwing his bat down into his kitbag. Soon enough, when the fifth wicket fell and we were 103 for five, I had to leave the physio's room to get my pads on. And three overs after that, Geraint Jones skied Warnie to long off and I was in. Seven wickets down, 13 still needed. Shit, shit, shit.

It's amazing what happens once you stop being a spectator and start to become involved. As soon as I got through the pavilion gate at Trent Bridge and began my walk towards the middle, the nerves just disappeared. How does that happen? For some reason, I suddenly started feeling weirdly confident. It was surreal. When I got to the middle, Ashley Giles did his best to dent that confidence. 'Warnie's turning it a long way, and Brett Lee is bowling 90 mph in-duckers,' he said. 'Good luck.' Cheers, Gilo.

But the next few overs turned out to be incredibly enjoyable. Gilo is always a good bloke to bat with, and every run we knocked off felt good. And somehow, from somewhere, with eight to win I pulled the shot of my life out of the locker to drive Brett Lee through extra cover for four. It was a widish full toss, I put a bit

---

[†]**HOGFACT:** A caterpillar has more than 2,000 MUSCLES, compared with a human being's 700. You should see the caterpillars down at my local gym. Put the rest of us to shame.

of bottom hand into it and, when the ball trickled over the rope, there was an enormous roar from the crowd. I think that was the point when everyone realised that we were going to win after all. I never had any doubts, of course.

Straussy told me afterwards that he had been sitting next to Fred and told him that he fancied me to nail one through the covers.

Freddie said: 'Piss off. When has Hoggy ever done that?'

Only on special occasions, Fred. If we'd needed a few more, it wouldn't have been a problem.

Then Gilo clipped Warnie through midwicket for two and we were home. We had a big, messy hug out in the middle – these things are never easy with bats in hand and helmets on – we shook hands with the Aussies, then I looked up to where the wives were sitting in the Radcliffe Road stand and gave Sarah a wave.

There had been a lot hanging on this game for me and, in the end, everything had come good. In those times you're always grateful for the support of those around you, and Sarah had been a big help to me.

SARAH: *I have never, ever been so nervous watching cricket as the closing stages of that game at Trent Bridge. It was bad enough that we were losing so many wickets, but when Matthew had to come out to bat, I was just shaking. Ruth Strauss was sitting next to me, trying to keep me calm, and when he played that shot off Brett Lee, I yelled, 'He's hit a four. I can't believe it. He's hit a four!' And when Gilo hit the winning runs, I just burst into tears with sheer relief. Most embarrassing. But it was all over, thank God. For another week or so, at least.*

You bump into all sorts of people at a Test match and that day we had found ourselves sitting just behind Piers Morgan during Australia's second innings. There were times on that day when it looked as though Australia would get enough runs to set us a big target in the last innings. Matthew didn't pick up any wickets for a while and Mr Morgan wasn't impressed. When Matthew was brought back on for another spell,

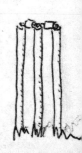

Morgan said: 'Oh God, we've got no chance with Hoggard on. He's a waste of time.'

At this point, Rachael Flintoff decided we'd heard enough. 'Excuse me,' she said, 'I think you should be careful what you say because Matthew Hoggard's wife is sitting right behind you.'

'Oh yes, very amusing,' he said. Then Rachael gestured towards me and he turned to look.

'Oh, Mrs Hoggard.'

'Don't you Mrs Hoggard me,' I said.

For the next few minutes, I was praying: 'Come on, Matthew, don't let me down, get us a wicket.' And a couple of overs later the boy came good. He got Michael Clarke caught behind and then had Gilchrist lbw a couple of overs later, which swung the game back in our favour. The former newspaper editor sitting in front of me turned round sheepishly and said: 'I think I owe you an apology, Mrs Hoggard. Your husband has just made me look a complete arse.'

'No,' I said. 'You managed that all on your own.'

So we were 2–1 up with one to play. And I wasn't quite prepared for how that victory at Trent Bridge would change the way I felt going into the last game at the Oval. Up to that point there had been a lot of pressure, but we had probably exceeded most people's expectations just by competing so well against such a powerful team. Now, after Trent Bridge, the fact that we were leading the series made the situation even more daunting. All of a sudden, the Ashes were ours to lose. If we were beaten in that last game, we would have thrown away the chance of a lifetime.

On the first morning of that Test match, I was ridonculously nervous. You tell everybody that you're not feeling the tension, but inside you're squirming. The worst time of any game is the thirty minutes before the toss, when you don't know whether you're going to be batting or bowling, and the half-hour before the toss that day was a horrible experience.

All the bowlers get giddy when we win the toss and bat, or grumpy if we lose the toss and have to bowl. It's the difference between sitting in the dressing-room for the day, putting your feet up and having a cuppa, or going out for one of the most important days' work of your life. I think the bowlers were seriously giddy when Michael Vaughan won the toss that morning and chose to bat first. We would have kept it quiet, though, out of respect for the opening batsmen.

As it turned out, we batted for a day and a half in making 373, with Straussy making a hundred, a top effort under pressure. The Aussies then batted for the next couple of days, which were interrupted at times by the great English weather. I've never heard of so many people in our country praying for rain. For a while, it looked as though Australia were going to get a massive score after Hayden and Langer put on 185 for the first wicket. But then they lost their last seven wickets for 44 and we sneaked a six-run lead. Freddie bowled a magic spell to take five-fer and I chipped in with four.

By the end of that fourth day we'd reached 34 for one, the draw looked a near-certainty, and now the Ashes really were ours to lose. That awful feeling I'd had before the Test match came back with a vengeance and, on that night before the final day, the stress of the situation really got to me. We had arranged to go out for a nice relaxing meal with Carole and Colin, but the evening didn't quite go to plan ...

SARAH: *When Matthew came in at the end of that fourth day, he was absolutely knackered and I suggested that we cancel the restaurant booking. My mum and dad wouldn't have minded; they would have understood if Matthew preferred not to go out. 'You've got a massive day tomorrow. Why don't we just stay in and order some room service?' I said. 'It's entirely up to you.'*

But he was adamant that he wanted to go out. 'I don't want to just sit in the room. I need to get out,' he said. Fair enough, it had to be his call that night.

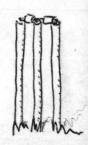

Unfortunately, my lovely husband then put the rest of us through a very uncomfortable couple of hours at the restaurant. He was grumpy, he was snappy, nothing was right. The tension had got to him all right, which was hardly surprising at this point. I tried to be tolerant, but at the end of the meal I made some sort of comment implying that we would have been better staying in.

And that was it. He got up and stomped out of the restaurant in a massive sulk. He must have waited for the rest of us outside because we caught him up, but he was still in a huff when we got out there, and he stormed off ahead on his own. The restaurant was on the south side of Tower Bridge and the hotel was just to the north side, so we only had to get across the bridge and we would be back. My mum said to me: 'Catch him up quick and make friends, Sarah. You can't leave it like this tonight.'

Wise woman, my mum. I ran and caught up with him on the middle of Tower Bridge, and we had a little chat. He apologised to me for being such an idiot. I told him that it was absolutely forgivable under the circumstances. We walked back to the hotel hand in hand, and by the time he left for the ground in the morning we were the best of friends again ...

What we really needed on that last morning at the Oval was someone who could bat all day. You know, somebody sensible, a batsman solid in defence and restrained in their strokeplay. What we got was Kevin Pietersen.

I started trying to watch, but after a while it just got ridonculous. The bloke was playing shots left, right and centre and I couldn't handle watching it any more. Hooks just over the head of fine leg, huge cover drives. Kev doesn't do things the way others do them and this wasn't most people's idea of batting all day.

'Gilo,' I said. 'Get the cards out.'

With Gilo as my fellow sufferer, I retreated to the coach's office out at the back of the dressing-room and we sat down and played cards for an hour. Rather that than watch what was going on out in the middle. Every so often there would be a roar, so one of us would poke our head round the door and ask what had happened. 'Kev's hit another six,' was usually the reply.

But wickets were falling as well, and before long Gilo had to get his pads on. When Geraint Jones was out and we were 199 for seven, the game was still in the balance. So out went Gilo to get a closer look at what exactly Kev was trying to do. The answer was to make us safe as quickly as possible. The faster he scored the runs, the more the Aussies would have to chase, and once Gilo had hung around with him for a while, the draw was as good as secured.

There was still time for me to go out to have a quick bat and, far from having given up the ghost, Brett Lee bowled me probably the fastest spell I've ever faced. He looked really angry too. I asked him if I'd done something to upset him. 'Nah,' he said. 'I'm just pissed off.'

You could hardly blame him. I'd have been pissed off if I'd just lost the Ashes for the first time in eighteen years. Thankfully, on this occasion, I was on the other side. We'd done it.

WE'D WON THE BLOODY ASHES

All the preparation, the practice, the fretting, the tension, the arguments with the wife, they were all worth it. One of those life-long ambitions I had wanted to achieve this summer had been fulfilled.

As soon as I could, I tried to make my way up to the box where Sarah was sitting, but the whole of the Oval was in chaos. It took me about fifteen minutes to work my way through a maze of corridors. One door was locked, I couldn't get through another door, some corridors were blocked off. And then, when I finally got there, I discovered that she had left two minutes earlier. Bugger.

Never mind, I needed to get back downstairs sharpish anyway. There was a little urn to gaze at, for starters, and there was some serious drinking to be done ...

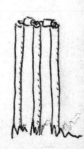

SARAH: *Before I left the hotel on that last morning at the Oval, after Matthew had gone, I counted up in my diary and it had been exactly nine weeks since my last period. After our long wait, I was finally convinced that I was pregnant. How amazing would it be, I thought, if the lads win the Ashes today, then Matthew comes off the field and I can tell him I'm pregnant. It seemed too good to be true, but I really felt that both things we'd been longing for could have happened on that same day.*

In the end, I put my sensible head on and decided to wait one more day before I took the pregnancy test. Another day wouldn't make any difference either way, and there was enough to worry about that day with the cricket.

Once the game was over, the girls knew that the lads' celebrations that night would be a boys-only affair, but there was reason enough for the girls to go to town as well. It was a great night, but I was convinced enough about my pregnancy to be really conservative with my drinking. And there was champagne everywhere that night. I've never seen so much bubbly. I had a couple of small glasses, but from then on it was a case of sipping soft drinks. I told Nichola what I was up to, but kept a glass of champagne handy in case anyone else spotted what I was doing. After a while, though, I think most people were so pissed that they wouldn't have noticed anyway ...

As you would probably guess, I was not quite so conservative with my drinking that evening. We started in the dressing-rooms – we had to rub the Aussies' noses in it – and then went on from there, from bar to bar, long into the night. I've no idea of the names of the places we went to, but they all seemed to be full of very friendly people and I don't think we had to pay for very many drinks that night.

I staggered back into our hotel room at some ungodly hour and I presumed Sarah must have been pissed herself before she went to sleep. Neither of us are quite sure what time I got in, but at some point she noticed me sleeping on the floor, stark bollock naked, and was good enough to cover me up with a dressing-gown from the back of the door.

But there wasn't much time for sleeping. We'd won the bloody Ashes and there was a champagne breakfast waiting for us downstairs. I made it down there in decent time and saw Freddie still sitting up in the bar. He hadn't been to bed at all. Gary Pratt, our supersub fielder from the Trent Bridge Test, was with him.

From the luxury food and drink that was on offer, I skipped the breakfast bit and concentrated instead on the champagne. We then had to get suited and booted because there was an open-top bus waiting to take us on a parade around London ...

SARAH: *It was madness in and around the hotel that next morning. There were people everywhere, cameras flashing and media waiting in a scrum that looked to be forty deep. The safest place to be was back in your room, so when Matthew went off to do some press stuff I decided that the time had come to take my pregnancy test.*

This was just before we were due to get on the bus to parade around London. It felt like the perfect time to be doing it and I was more convinced than ever that this time the result would be positive. So I did the test. And I waited three or four minutes, as usual. And as usual, it turned out to be negative. Nine bloody weeks I'd been waiting. Where was all this going to end?

Anyway, there was nothing else for it. Now that I knew I wasn't pregnant, I was going to go and get properly pissed on that bus ride. I'd got some catching up to do after turning down all that booze the night before. I was gutted, of course I was, but there are worse ways to deal with disappointment than drinking free champagne on an open-top bus ride around London.

I was worried that there wouldn't be anybody out to see us on that parade. I thought it might be a bit embarrassing. How many cricket fans would be able to take the day off work at such short notice? More to the point, how many people would really be inter-

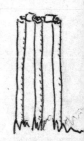

197

ested in watching a group of hungover idiots riding round town in a bus?

Well, the answer became clear as soon as we turned the first corner after leaving our hotel. We could see for half a mile and the pavement was lined with people the whole way. There were people sitting on roofs, folk hanging out of windows, this was going to be fun. 'Get back to work!' we kept shouting from the bus.

The first place we called in at was Mansion House, official residence of the Lord Mayor of London. We topped up there with a couple more drinks and were introduced to the Lord Mayor himself. He was there in all his finery: robes, chains, fancy hat, the works. This outfit clearly impressed Fred. As he was staggering past, Fred stopped and gave the Mayor's costume an admiring once-over. 'What have you come as?' he asked.

I needn't have worried about nobody turning out to see us that day. Trafalgar Square was crammed full, which was an extraordinary sight. Then we moved on to No. 10 Downing Street, where there were more people of great importance who apparently wanted to meet us. Mr and Mrs Blair hadn't been properly briefed, though, because when we arrived the only drinks on offer were pineapple juice and water. Perhaps things were a bit tight at the time, but we managed to persuade them to produce something stronger after a while. Eventually, a few glasses of red and white wine appeared. The white was slightly warm, but it was certainly better than the pineapple juice.

As we were leaving the Prime Minister's gaff, Mr Blair himself was seeing us on our way. He was shaking everybody's hand as we walked past and, as I stopped to thank him for the pineapple juice, he spotted all the photographers who had gathered outside.

'Oh God, what do they want?' he said.

'A photo, you knob,' I replied.

Well, ask a silly question and you get a silly answer. What else would a load of photographers have been there for? And to think he was the Prime Minister. Still, probably not the way you're supposed to address such an important person. I might have jeopardised my chances of a knighthood there. But he's not in charge any more, so maybe there's still hope.

So back to those two goals I'd been hoping to achieve in that summer of 2005. The Ashes win made it one down and one to go. Sarah didn't tell me until a couple of days afterwards about that test she had taken before the bus ride. And not long afterwards she was diagnosed with polycystic ovary syndrome, a problem that one in twenty women suffer from and which affects a woman's fertility.

For a while, she took some fertility drugs that had been prescribed by a consultant, but they didn't agree with her. The next summer, on the day that we'd been invited to go into the Royal Box at Wimbledon, she collapsed with some dreadful stomach pains. Sarah was devastated, because she'd wanted to go to Wimbledon for ages and had got all frocked up for the occasion. We made it into the grounds, but instead of dazzling the Royal Box with her posh new dress, Sarah was pushed out of Wimbledon in a St John's Ambulance wheelchair – wearing a pink silk dress and a pair of silver high heels. I was running alongside, hanging on to her silver clutch bag. What a sight we must have made.

Anyway, after that disaster, we switched consultants and Sarah was prescribed a series of injections. This was not long before we were due to go out to Australia for the next Ashes series, so she was hoping for something she could administer herself and these injections seemed to fit the bill.

But before she could start the new treatment, the consultant rang her up and told her that she wouldn't be able to start the course of injections. Her face just dropped and she wondered what was wrong this time.

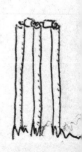

'Why not? What is it?' she said.

'It's because you're pregnant,' the consultant said.

She put the phone down and started crying, and this time it was my turn to ask: 'What's wrong now?'

'Nothing's wrong,' she sobbed. 'I'm pregnant.' And then I started crying.

This came completely out of the blue for us, because Sarah was between treatments and we thought we would have to wait for the injections to work their magic before we could hope for any progress. It was early stages – she was only two or three weeks pregnant – so we couldn't get too carried away, but after almost two years of trying since we got married in October 2004, this was unbelievable news.

If all went well, I was going to become a dad; the second of those two goals was finally going to be fulfilled. As with the Ashes, there had been a load of emotional ups and downs to get through before reaching this point, but once we got there I felt like one lucky, lucky lad.

'Daddy, Daddy, please can I do some words for your book?'

'Not now, Ernie. The nice people want to read all about how much Daddy likes his drinkypoos.'

'But even Mummy has done some words Daddy.'

'Maybe later, Ernie, if you're a good boy …'

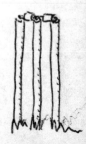

TOP ACTIVITIES ON AN ENGLAND TOUR

There are some tours when you're able to get out and about and occupying yourselves is never a problem. But there are others when you spend long hours cooped up in the team hotel, so entertainment has to be found. These are the ways that we've tended to amuse ourselves on tour ...

1. DARTS

Steve Harmison is the king of the oche. Takes his own darts board on tour, his own stand, his own darts, with his own bag to keep them all in. You should see the faces of the airport staff when he goes to check that in. It weighs a ton.

2. POOL AND SNOOKER

Jimmy Anderson is snooker champ. When I say he's the best, a break of 20 is probably as much as anybody manages on tour. And that's when all the balls have been over the pockets and just need nudging in.

3. TABLE TENNIS

Andrew Flintoff is very good at pinging and ponging, Paul Collingwood is pretty good, I'm not too bad. I've been known to have the odd game of drunken table-tennis in my garage on a makeshift table late at night. Makes for very good practice.

4. PLAYSTATIONS

When we were stuck in our hotels for a long time in Pakistan or India, the likes of Vaughan, Collingwood and Giles would often set up football leagues and play a game every night. You wouldn't believe how seriously they took it.

5. M*ST*RB*TION

Sorry about this one, you'd probably rather not have known. But this wouldn't be an honest list without it. The situation would be very different, though, if we ever toured Indonesia.[†]

6. READING BOOKS

Not many are bookworms, but I like a good read, as does Andrew Strauss. I used to swap books a lot with Phil Neale, the manager, sometimes with Duncan Fletcher and occasionally Nige Stockill, the physiologist. Straussy's stuff was usually far too intellectual for my liking.

[†]**HOGFACT:** M*st*rb*tion is illegal in Indonesia and the punishment is decapitation. Ouch.

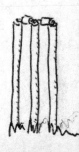

11
Drinking for England

Now I don't want all that stuff about post-Ashes piss-ups to make you think that the England team were a bunch of immature boozers, hell-bent on getting sloshed whenever the opportunity presented itself. Immature? Well, maybe, from time to time, but what else do you expect from a group of grown men who play with bats and balls for a living? But boozers? Only when the time was right. And the time was certainly right when we won back the Ashes in 2005.

Apart from anything else, the boozing that night (and the following morning, and then in the afternoon) did provide a pretty stern test of everyone's drinking capacity. We were given, for example, utterly undeniable proof that Andrew Flintoff belonged at the very top of the drinkers' league table. Not that there was ever any doubt about that.

As for me, I'd probably have placed myself somewhere around mid-table in the England teams I played in. I've got reasonable stamina, although I often get a bit sidetracked because when I've had a few I can become an argumentative sod. In the nicest possible way, of course. Then, when some of the others start to get a little silly, I'll probably tend to slope off to bed when no one else is looking.

From the lads I've played with, Ryan Sidebottom would prob-ably be somewhere down the bottom of the league table, living in constant fear of relegation to the Half-a-Lager League. Unfortu-nately for Sid, he has developed a bit of a reputation as something of a plant feeder. If you're on a night out or at a party with him, he can often be found loitering away from the main crowd, quietly looking for a plant that he thinks would benefit from the alcohol more than him. Many's the time I've been drinking with Sid and looked behind him to see a yukka plant swaying unsteadily in the background.

But as I've said, these booze-ups would only happen when the time and place were right, and that was usually in celebration of a job well done. It was a firmly established part of the team culture under Michael Vaughan and Duncan Fletcher that we should cele-brate our victories in suitably fine style. That didn't mean lording it around town and ordering eleven bucketfuls of champagne in every bar we went in. (Imagine the burping.) It simply meant enjoying each other's company the night after we had achieved something special together. Sometimes that involved considerable quantities of alcohol. Sometimes it might just have been a convivial meal out with a few glasses of wine.

Most of us had grown up with the custom that, at the end of a game of cricket, you have a few drinks with your team-mates and possibly a couple with the opposition as well. Whatever level of the game they're playing, most cricketers would agree that the social side of the game is one of the best things about it. Why should that be any different at international level?

Whenever we won a Test match, the ECB would always fork out to give us a decent kitty for the evening's entertainment. And the first round of drinks was normally on Duncan Fletcher, who'd set himself up at the bar and get the celebrations underway.

I know that the image most people have of Fletch is hardly that of a party animal, but he could be fantastic company on a night like that, when he allowed himself to relax and let himself go,

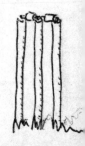

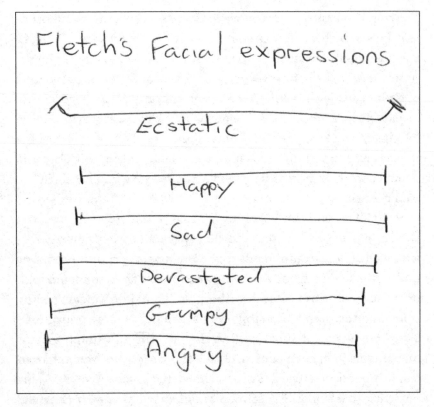

Fletch's Facial expressions

Ecstatic

Happy

Sad

Devastated

Grumpy

Angry

providing he was out of the way of the press. He had a fantastically dry sense of humour and, when he wasn't being a grumpy bastard, I could have sat and listened to him for hours. At a team meal, he would sit with a glass of wine, chewing the cud with Matthew Maynard and Dean Conway, his mates from his Glamorgan days. And that was a brave thing to do in itself because **BLOODY HELL THE WELSH CAN DRINK!**[†]

Fletch was always very keen that we should make these celebrations special occasions. Unless you've had an absolute stinker

---

[†]**HOGFACT:** In WALES, there are more sheep than people: about five million sheep to three million people. No further comment from me is required on this one.

personally, you're likely to be in a very good mood, everyone's feeling the warm afterglow of victory and the world generally seems a pretty marvellous place.

It is also on occasions like this that the bonds of friendship within a team can be cemented. These are the guys who, when it comes to the crunch in a Test match in front of 50,000 people, you're going to have to rely on. And if you think your team-mates are decent, trustworthy blokes, you're going to feel an awful lot better about going out to battle with them at your side.

As far as alcohol was concerned, we were certainly always trusted by the England management. There were, of course, the warnings from physiologists and nutritionists about how much your body can be affected by too much booze, but if you chose to have a glass of wine with your evening meal during a Test match, nobody would have complained. Having said that, I can hardly remember anyone in the England team drinking during a Test. Generally speaking, everyone was extremely professional and didn't abuse the trust shown in them. So there was never any need for an alcohol ban.

In fact, the one attempt at an alcohol ban I can remember was actually self-imposed. It came on the tour to the West Indies in early 2004, when Harmy and Fred decided that they weren't going to drink at all until the end of the trip, and I decided to join them. We were all working particularly hard on our fitness at the time and we knew it would be hot in the West Indies, so it seemed like a good idea to give our bodies every chance of performing at their peak.

I didn't think it was going to be a problem. Sure, there are plenty of temptations in the West Indies, nice warm evenings and all those beach bars enticing you in for a cheeky rum punch. But when you've been flogging yourself out in the heat all day, you tend to be fairly knackered and ready for a good night's kip. No booze? No problem.

Well, so much for good intentions. Shall I tell you how long our good behaviour lasted? Until the end of the first Test. And the

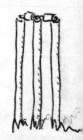

blame for our lapse lies squarely with that big gangly git from Durham. Going into that first Test in Jamaica, everything had been going to plan, a couple of soft drinks at the hotel bar and then off to bed with a good book for an early night. Then Harmison goes and takes seven for 12 in the second innings, West Indies are bowled out for 47, their lowest ever total, and we stormed to an incredible victory by ten wickets. What are we supposed to do then?

ERM, ELEVEN GLASSES OF LEMONADE, PLEASE, BARMAN. AND NOT TOO FIZZY, EITHER. OUR CHAPS ARE TAKING IT EASY.

No, I think not. The alcohol ban was suddenly forgotten and, as far as I can remember, I'm not sure that it was ever really reinstated. As ever, we were good boys between Tests and during the matches themselves, but we had another couple of victories to celebrate in Trinidad and Barbados over the next couple of weeks. And let's just say we were on a bit of a roll by then.

But again, this was an example of letting our hair down at the right time and in the right place. We were developing a habit of winning Test matches and we were also learning to celebrate our victories in the grand manner.

There was, however, one example during my England career of how I let myself and my team-mates down by going overboard on the booze in the *wrong* place and very much at the *wrong* time. This was by far the worst thing I ever did on England duty and I'm not at all proud of it, but sometimes these things happen.

It came just a few months before that trip to the West Indies, which was the tour when I really nailed down my place in the England side and the fast-bowling quartet of Harmison, Flintoff, Jones and Muggins here firmly established ourselves. But that had certainly not been the case during our trip to Bangladesh and Sri Lanka in late 2003, when I was still very much playing for my place.

During the 2003 season at home, I had only played one game for England before I knackered my knee and missed much of the rest of the summer. Thankfully, I won my place back for the tour to Bangladesh, played in both Tests there and took a few wickets as we won the series 2–0. We then went on to Sri Lanka, where I played in the drawn first Test in Galle and didn't really cover myself in glory – I only took one wicket – but didn't bowl appallingly badly.

Then, for the second Test in Kandy I was dropped, just as I thought I was becoming a regular in the side. The selectors opted to play an extra batsman and James Kirtley was picked ahead of me as the swing bowler.

Worse still came in Colombo before the third Test. Rather than playing the extra batsman, an extra seam bowler was added to the side, but instead of bringing me back they went for James Anderson instead. So that was Kirtley and Anderson who had been picked ahead of me, and the worst thing was that I didn't think I'd been bowling that badly, while Jimmy had clearly been bowling like a drain all tour.

I couldn't understand the selectors' thinking and I feared that they had come to the conclusion that I simply wasn't good enough. I thought that the writing was on the wall and that my time as an international cricketer was probably up.

On the evening before the match, there was a quiz at the Crick-eters' Inn in Colombo. There were quite a few of the guys work-ing for Sky, maybe two or three other players and all the Barmy Army there. Needless to say, when the Barmies are around, the evening wasn't going to be a quiet, sober affair.

As I'd just been told that I wasn't playing, I went along to try to cheer myself up. I allowed myself a couple of drinks, then that led to a couple more, which in turn put me on the slippery slope that makes you think: 'Oh, what the hell!' You'll have to forgive me if the memory's a little hazy, but I can remember drinking as though

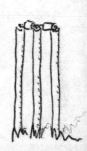

I was on a stag do. Pretty soon I was past caring about whether it was really sensible to have one more drink or not, and I kept going with the Barmy Army through the night. I was, I'm sorry to say, **COMPLETELY AND UTTERLY WANKERED**.

Whether I was playing or not, that was certainly not the right time or place to be supping myself senseless. It wasn't a good move. The problem was that, if any of our seamers had gone down injured the next day, I would probably have been called on to play. And the state I was in the morning after, I would have been in no fit state to play for a Barmy Army XI, never mind England.

Take the fielding warm-ups, for example. Mike 'Winker' Watkinson was our assistant coach on that tour and he was running the fielding drills before the game. Every single ball that he hit for me to catch, I dropped. The low, hard ones would thud into me before I knew they'd arrived. For the high, steepling ones, I'd hold my hands out in the general direction of the ball, but it was pot luck whether the ball hit them or not. In the end, Winker stood about 12 yards away from me and, with a weary grin on his face, he lobbed one to me underarm and said: 'Here you go, Hoggy. See if you can catch that one.' I only went and dropped that one as well. I just wanted to curl up and die.

At that stage, I think a couple of the lads suspected that I'd been out drinking. For a start, I must have stunk of booze. Luckily, none of the bowlers broke down and my duties were restricted to carry-ing out drinks with Rikki Clarke. But even that was a struggle and, after a while, Rikki said to me: 'I think you need to go and have a lie down.'

Out of the back of the pavilion, there was a roof terrace that was hidden from view of the general public and out of sight of those in the changing-rooms and pavilion, unless they chose to go out there. So I sneaked out onto the roof terrace, lay down and went to sleep instantly. I was in such a bad way that I slept for a session and a half. As far as I know, nobody saw me and I certainly never got the bollocking that I really deserved. But I felt like a complete pillock and, unsurprisingly, I've tended to steer well clear of the Barmy Army on the night before a Test match ever since.

Looking back, I can't believe I reacted like that to being dropped. The professional response, of course, would be to say to myself: 'OK, you're obviously not doing something right. Let's have a think about how you are going to win your place back.' But it's easy to say that now. At the time I'd only played a handful of Test matches, didn't really know whether I'd play any more and, I suppose, was pretty scared about what the future held. None of which excuses drunken stupidity, but I'm sure we all have our stupid moments that we live[†] to regret in the future.

So it's probably fair to say that the right time and place for a beer is probably not the night before a Test match, whether you're in the team or not. And the right people to choose as company are probably not the Barmy Army. They're unlikely to be taking it easy the night before a Test. They're merely limbering up for another five days of dutiful boozing and singing.

No, the time a beer tastes best is in the immediate aftermath of a Test match victory, sitting in your dressing-room, the main business taken care of. Boots off, sweaty feet up, kit strewn everywhere, lots of piss-taking to be done, beer in hand. Can't beat it. Sometimes it's nice to be joined by the opposition as well, depending on who you're playing and how the match has gone. This is not something that happens too often after a Test match these days, possibly at the end of a series. We've done that in New Zealand a couple of times, stayed in the dressing-rooms at the end of a series and taken the piss out of each other until fairly late into the evening.

The real exception over the last few years, when it became the norm to have a drink with the opposition after each Test, was in the last two series against Australia. In the 2005 Ashes series we

---

[†]**HOGFACT:** Only one person in two billion will LIVE to be 116 or older. I'm going to be one of them. I wonder who the other will be?

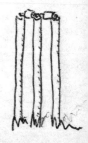

did it after almost every match, which is really unusual. I think that players on both sides got the feeling that we were part of something special and it was good to share that feeling with the opposition.

In fairness to the Aussies, they started the trend after we had beaten them at Edgbaston by coming into our dressing-room for a beer. We hadn't gone into theirs after they stuffed us at Lord's in the first Test, but at Edgbaston it was different. It had been an epic game, with an incredibly close finish, and both sides just thought: 'Wow!'

In these situations, the onus usually falls on the losing team to decide whether they want to join the other lot for a drink. That way, if some members of the losing side would rather jump in their cars and scarper, they can do so. Also, if it was left to the winners to take the lead, there would be a risk of seeming to gloat. If one side has been stuffed out of sight, the atmosphere would probably be a bit uncomfortable so, as at Edgbaston, teams are much more likely to get together after a close game. And just about every game was close in the 2005 Ashes, so it always seemed appropriate to go and clink a few bottles with the enemy.

More often than not, you'll find the bowlers from one side going to sit with the bowlers on the other side. The same applies to the batsmen. I sat and chatted with Brett Lee quite a lot in 2005 and, towards the end of the series, Shaun Tait came into their side and he seemed like a really good bloke. I suppose as bowlers we've got more in common with each other. But there's also the fact that you're not talking to your real opponents, the batsmen. It's not as easy to get close to them.

Having said that, during the next Ashes series in Australia I found myself chatting with Matthew Hayden quite a few times. We've played against one another a lot and know each other's games inside out.

In terms of fraternising with the opposition, that next Ashes series was much more difficult, as we were sliding to a 5–0 defeat.

There wasn't often the feeling that we'd been involved in a particularly great Test.

After the first Test at Brisbane, even though we'd been stuffed by 277 runs, it was decided that we should go into their dressing-room, despite the potential embarrassment factor. Part of that was because they had set the ball rolling at Edgbaston after a defeat in the previous series. But I think that a bigger reason was to say: 'Yes, you've beaten us, but we're not scared.' Hmmm, fat lot of good that did us for the rest of the series.

At the end of the next Test at Adelaide, after that horrendous last day when our batsmen threw away a perfectly good position and we ended up losing, some of our players went into the Aussies' changing-room, but I couldn't cope with that. I was too pissed off at how we'd let slip an opportunity to get back into the series and I just wanted to get away from the ground as quickly as I could. I've never been so thoroughly cheesed off in my whole career and, on that occasion, I wouldn't have been able to forget it all in such a short space of time, wander across the corridor and start trying to be cheerful. I just couldn't have done it.

By the time they had beaten us again in Perth in the third Test, it was game over as far as the series was concerned. That time, a feeling of grim resignation had set in and I think we all probably needed a drink to numb the pain. So we stayed in their dressing-room for ages and drank the night away.

The one time when cricketers are really let off the leash is at the end of a tour. Wherever we are in the world, we'll usually have a good old knees-up at the end of the tour before we go back home and enter the real world again. As a result, there have been some pretty messy end-of-tour piss-ups, and one particular example came on the last night of our tour to Pakistan back in 2005.

Now, as you probably know, Pakistan is a (mostly) dry country so it had been a pretty abstemious tour. But after the last Test in Lahore, we managed to set up our own little pub in our hotel, which

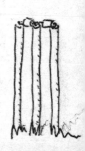

we called the Nag's Head. Unfortunately, we'd been trounced by an innings in that third Test and Pakistan had won the series 2–0, so there wasn't a great deal to celebrate. Well, the fact that we'd managed to find somewhere to drink might have been cause enough for celebration, but our performances on the field certainly hadn't put everyone in party mood. We also had to fly home the next day, so I didn't really feel like going overboard. I just had a few drinks and then left the Nag's Head to go to bed. But not everybody felt the same as me.

Late at night, at some silly time or other, there was a knock at my door. It was Warren Hegg, the chunky little Lancashire wicketkeeper, who was in Lahore for some reason that escapes me. 'I need your help, Hoggy,' he said. 'We need to get Fred to bed.'

'And why are you asking me?'

'Erm, cos I'm not big enough.'

'Can't you find anybody else?'

'Please, Hoggy, it won't take long.'

So I went back downstairs to the Nag's Head and we bumped into Fred in the corridor. He gave me a grin, then punched me on the shoulder, which was nice. 'Hello, Andrew,' I said. *Boom.* Another punch on the shoulder. 'Now come on, Andrew,' I said. 'We can either do this the easy way or the hard way. I don't really want to wrestle with you tonight, but it's time to go to bed.'

At that point, I looked around to check where Warren was, and he was nowhere to be seen. The cheeky little sod had pissed off back to his room. He'd obviously been in a few situations like this before with that nice Mr Flintoff.

'I need to peeeaaay my ruuurrrm bill,' said Fred.

'Okeydoke, let's go and get it paid. I'll do it for you,' I said.

He lurched over to the counter at reception and mumbled: 'Ceeeannn I peeeeeaaaaay my ruuuurrrrmmm bill plurrrse.'

I had to translate: 'Can we pay the room bill for room 107 please?'

At which point we noticed that there were half a dozen or so of the press there, so Freddie went and had a quick word with them.

Anyway, we got the bill paid and I took him back up to his room. He collapsed on his bed immediately and started snoring like a pig. I left the room, but took his key because I knew I'd have to wake him up.

So I had a few hours' kip back in my room, got up and went to wake up Fred. 'Freddie, Freddie, wake up, we're leaving.' He got up, I got him into the bathroom and went back to my room to get dressed.

When I returned to his room ten minutes later, he'd gone back to bed. I had to shake him awake this time.

'GET UP AND GET YOUR F***ING KIT ON, YOU GREAT OAF!'

Somehow I got him onto the coach to take us to the airport. He sat at the back, just behind Nasser Hussain, and I think that Fred must still have been drunk, because he was in a very irritating mood. He started giving Nass a load of grief, banging on the back of his chair. Nass humoured him for a while, then stood up and had a right old go at him.

Fred shut up until we got to the airport. I managed to avoid him for a while, but when we boarded the plane, sod's law, guess who was sitting right behind me. '*Boom!*' on the back of my seat. '*Boom!*' on the back of my seat again. '*Boom!*' on the back of my seat a third time. I knelt up on my seat and said: 'Fred, I looked after you last night, I put you to bed, I woke you up this morning ... twice ... I got you dressed and I got you on the coach. Now will you please, please, please, leaving me a-f***ing-lone.'

There was a pause while he thought about what I'd said. It took a while for the cogs to turn. And then, just when it was beginning to look as though he was going to be a pain in the arse all the way back from Lahore to London, a light bulb suddenly flashed above his head, he flashed me a big grin and said: 'You're right, Hoggy. You've been really nice to me. Thanks very much.' And with that,

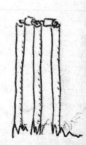

he put his head to one side, went to sleep and not a peep was heard out of him until we landed back in London.

I can't ever remember feeling more relieved in my whole life. (Apart from one time at a motorway service station when I was about 6 and we were stuck in traffic and I'd been trying not to wet my pants for about three hours. But that's another story.) I love Fred to bits and he's usually a perfectly pleasant person when he's drunk, but I'll never forget having to be his nursemaid in Lahore that time. If anyone ever knocks on my door again and utters the words, 'We need to get Fred to bed ...', I'm slamming it firmly shut.

Whenever I got Matthew Hayden out, I always felt desperately sorry for him. Just asking after his wife and kids as he wanders off to the pavilion.

Never in doubt: scampering the winning runs after Ashley Giles had clipped Shane Warne through midwicket at Trent Bridge, 2005.

A quiet moment's reflection on our Ashes victory in Trafalgar Square, with Kevin Pietersen, Andrew Strauss, Marcus Trescothick and Simon Jones. Look carefully and you can see Fletch smiling in the background. Or has this picture been doctored?

above left Best bib and tucker to pick up my MBE at Buckingham Palace.

above right Advising Tony on foreign policy over warm white wine at Downing Street. I have yet to abuse him at this stage of our visit.

right Very hot, very sweaty, very happy: celebrating with Fred after our victory in Jo'burg.

One beer down, umpteen more to follow. In the dressing-room at the Oval with Straussy and Super Gary Pratt after we'd clinched the Ashes.

Head: Full of useless information.

Face: Smiling as usual, must be early in the morning.

Don't forget to let go!

Left elbow: Should be higher, probably got hit for four this ball.

Does my bum look big in this? Yes, it always does.

Lack of grass stains on knees: been taking it easy in the field.

What's that? Blue clothes? Oh yes, one-day cricket. Dhoni bashed it hard that day in Jamshedpur. I never played again.

Must have been a good 'un to get through me: Glenn McGrath spoils my perfect nightwatchman's record at the eleventh attempt in Perth, December 2006.

Me and Ashley Giles visiting victims of the earthquake in Islamabad, Pakistan, October 2005. That was a heartbreaking experience.

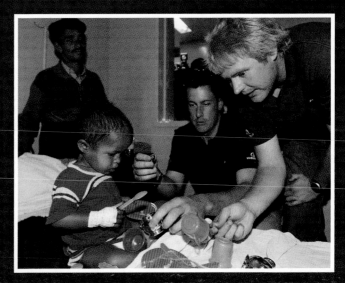

Can I drive all the way home on this thing? My best Steve McQueen impression with the Man of the Match prize in Nagpur, March 2006. Unfortunately, I had to leave it behind.

'Oh, God, he's sliced it again. Why do I always get stuck with this useless idiot?' Jimmy Anderson despairs of his golfing partner.

Trying to look immaculate after flight to OZ, November 2006. And fooling no-one.

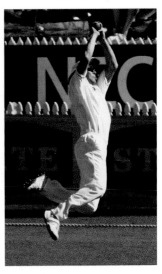

Stuart Clark becomes my seventh of seven at Adelaide, 2006. Looks like he was ready for a bowl.

Snake charming: I'd just foolishly picked up a six-foot cobra in Colombo, 2007. It escaped through a pipe and I'm watching it slither away

Taking a catch in my last game for England against New Zealand in Hamilton, March 2008. But I'll be back…

Pint of Hoggy's Nightwatchman, anyone?

That's me standing up with Dickie Bird, handing out Yorkshire puddings to Craig White, Michael Vaughan, Darren Gough and Ryan Sidebottom at Lord's. They look a bit soggy. Clearly made by a southerner. I'm giving Goughie a pair of Andy Caddick ears.

We don't scrub up badly with a bit of spit and polish. Our wedding day, 2 October 2004.

Me and Sarah on holiday in Queensland, pictured here at the Steve Irwin zoo. Ernie is cunningly hiding in this photo, in Sarah's tummy.

The wee man: Ernie on the beach at Scarborough, September 2008.

12
Swinging the Balance

That Ashes series in 2005 did some funny things to the world. Quite apart from people going loopy in London and skiving off work just to watch a few folk riding around town in an open-top bus, everybody in the country seemed to be a cricket fan for a few weeks.

For all that we play one of the major sports in this country, we don't tend to get recognised very much by the general population, at least not to the same level as footballers. I suppose it's a bit different for the likes of Freddie and KP, but for a backroom boy like me, I can go to the supermarket and nobody would know whether I was a butcher, a baker or a candlestick maker. And that suits me just nicely.

But the Ashes had caught on with a much larger audience, and for a few weeks I experienced the bizarre feeling of being recognised by complete strangers. I think my hairstyle probably had something to do with it. It had got longer and blonder as the Ashes series went on and I never quite got round to having it cut, except for the odd do-it-yourself trim of the fringe when it was getting in my eyes.

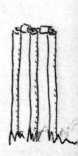

The attention was not unpleasant, by any means; there was nothing that made me go out wearing a big hat and false beard.[†] It was just unusual. Most of the people who approached me would say really nice things. A typical example was a bloke who came up while I was walking through Leeds train station. He just bustled up to me, shook me by the hand, and said: 'Thanks for everything this summer. You made me really happy.' And then he bustled off again. I presumed he was talking about the cricket. I wasn't aware of anything else I might have done for him.

A slightly more bizarre incident was when another bloke was walking along my carriage on the train. As he was about to pass me, he stopped in his tracks and stared for a few seconds, then broke into the broadest, silliest grin I've ever seen, and said: 'It's you, innit?' I wasn't quite sure what to say in return. 'Erm, yes, it's me.' The bloke just kept grinning at me, then all of a sudden he gave me a big thumbs-up sign with both hands, and promptly walked off. I was just left there feeling like a bit of an idiot.

One of the first times I'd realised how the series was catching on came a few days before the final Test, when I had been for a drive-through Burger King. As I got my wallet out and tried to pay, the lad behind the till wouldn't let me. 'Don't worry, it's free,' he said. 'But make sure you win the Ashes next week.'

Free Burger King, eh?
I must have really made it in life now.

The generosity continued in the weeks after we fulfilled the wishes of that lad behind the counter at the drive-through. Sarah and I had gone out for a meal once and a bottle of champagne suddenly

---

[†]**HOGFACT:** If the average man never shaved, his beard would grow to a length of $27\frac{1}{2}$ feet. And would presumably get very dirty and cumbersome around his feet.

appeared on our table. I tried to tell the waiter that we hadn't asked for any champagne, but he told me it had been ordered for us by the gentleman at the table in the corner. And it would, of course, have been rude to refuse such a generous gesture.

It wasn't just out and about in public that we were suddenly in demand; all sorts of strange invitations started coming our way. God knows why, but I was even invited to appear on the pilot of Graham Norton's new show. My brief was to be a 'celebrity' guest in a game that involved ripping up telephone directories. The first directory that they gave me to tear up was for the Barnet area. It was supposed to be a joke about my hair – you know, Barnet Fair and all that. The problem was that I had had all my hair cut off a couple of weeks earlier, so the joke fell spectacularly flat.

Now that I was firmly established as a star of stage and screen, I was one of a number of the Ashes squad invited onto a special cricketing edition of the BBC's *The Weakest Link* with Anne Robinson. I was standing next to Ashley Giles and we decided to team up, clubbing together to vote other people off and never voting for each other. After every round we'd whisper to each other to sort out our strategy. 'Gilo, who we gonna vote for this time?' 'Colly, we'll vote for Colly,' he'd whisper back.

And they say that cheats never prosper, but Gilo and I were the last two men left standing. The last round was a best-of-five questions and Gilo pipped me to the post, the bastard. I was gutted, but it was all good fun.

After all that showbiz malarkey, we were brought back to reality with a big bump on our tour to Pakistan before Christmas in 2005. From Anne Robinson to Shoaib Akhtar in a matter of weeks. I told you the world had become a strange place. It was time to get back to the day job and prove that we could still play cricket as well as

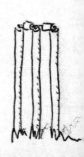

drink and rip up telephone directories. We competed well in patches against Pakistan, but that wasn't enough and we lost the Test series 2–0. Bitten on the bum once again.

For some reason, this was a tour on which I kept getting into trouble. The first time was in a team meeting early in the trip, when we were discussing our aims for the tour as a whole. The squad included most of the Ashes winners, with the exception of Simon Jones, who was unfortunately still injured. We also had some new young blood, with the likes of Liam Plunkett and Alex Loudon, and some new older blood in the form of Shaun Udal.

As usual, we had all met up before the tour at Loughborough to make sure that nobody had been overdoing it on the free champagne (or the Burger Kings) and to get together as a squad before our departure. I didn't know much about Alex Loudon at the time, except that he went to school at Eton and apparently his dad owns half of Kent.

I introduced myself to him, we had a chat and he seemed like a very nice lad. I gave him the nickname of Posh Twat, which was an affectionate way of welcoming him into the squad. Not very witty, I know, but I'm a fast bowler and I leave the wit to other people. I abbreviated the nickname to PT as a further sign of my affection.

Anyway, at that meeting once we had arrived in Pakistan, Duncan Fletcher was talking us through the potential difficulties of touring Pakistan. The security situation has obviously not been great there in the last few years so we would probably be spending a lot of time in our hotel, but we should try to keep a positive mindset at all times.

I'd better confess at this point that I'm not always the best at concentrating in these meetings. Fletch spoke well and always had intelligent points to make, but I'm afraid I found myself drifting off and daydreaming. I was probably only half-listening when he said something like: 'What we need as a squad on this tour is lots of P and T. Do we know what that stands for? Hoggy, any ideas?'

I was daydreaming, probably thinking about free Burger Kings, so I was a bit startled when I heard my name and I had to ask Fletch to repeat the question.

'PT, Hoggy,' he said. 'What does PT stand for?'

'Erm, Posh Twat, Fletch.'

'Interesting answer,' he said. 'I was thinking more of Patience and Tolerance. We need lots of patience and tolerance on this tour.'

Fletch clearly knew exactly what he was doing then. He'd heard about the nickname and he guessed what I'd say if he asked me about P and T. The wise old bird, he knew me too well.

I wasn't really in bother with Fletch then, but once the Test series started, I had an incident where I was made to feel like a naughty schoolboy.

The first Test was played in Multan and we got off to a very reasonable start, bowling Pakistan out for 274 and then scoring 418 ourselves, mainly thanks to a fantastic 193 from Marcus Trescothick. They then played themselves back into the game with 341, of which Salman Butt, the left-handed opener, made 122 before I had him caught behind. He pushed at it, got a huge nick and Geraint Jones took the catch. It had been such a big nick that I didn't bother to look behind me for the decision by Simon Taufel. There was no doubt in anyone's mind, I just jogged on down to thank Geraint.

For my troubles, I was reported to the match referee for celebrating the dismissal prematurely. And to make matters worse, this came under the category of excessive appealing. So I was done for excessive appealing, for not having actually appealed. Do you follow? It certainly baffled me.

I thought that I was treated pretty harshly. I'd never been warned before, it was my first misdemeanour in forty-five Tests and I'm not the sort of bowler who gives the umpire any gyp. But they nabbed 20 per cent of my match fee for that. So I made sure I appealed and appealed again for everything else that series,

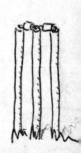

whether it was a catch to the keeper or I'd knocked the batsman's middle stump out of the ground. What had I ever done to deserve my harsh treatment? Maybe it was the time the previous winter in South Africa when I went to introduce Sarah to an umpire I knew and liked.

'Sarah, this is Russell Tiffin,' I said.

'Pleased to meet you, Sarah,' said the umpire. 'I'm Simon Taufel.'

The only other time I had come close to getting into trouble in a Test match was on my first tour to Sri Lanka in 2001, when I spent the whole Test series doing twelfth man duties. In the second Test at Kandy, we were trying to waste time towards the end of a day's play, and I was sent to take towels, fresh gloves and drinks out to the batsmen, as often as the umpires would allow. On my way back from the middle, I would carefully place a towel on the edge of my shoulder, so that when I started running off the field, the towel would disappear five yards behind me and I'd have to trudge back and pick it up. Then I'd drop a batting glove and have to wander back to pick that up. Whoops, clumsy Hoggy! Butterfingers! After a couple of these pantomime attempts at time-wasting, one of the umpires, Rudi Koertzen, came up to me and said: 'Hoggy, if you drop anything else on your way back to the pavilion, you're in bother.' So I didn't.

I usually get on well with umpires, Rudi is one of the best and Simon Taufel is all right when he's not reporting me for excessive non-appealing. One umpire I used to get frustrated with was Steve Bucknor with his 'slow death' decisions. For those who haven't seen him, he takes forever to make up his mind then lifts his arm ridonculously slowly. If you're a bowler waiting for a decision, it can feel like a lifetime.

'For God's sake, Steve, is he out or not? Just tell me!'

Except you wouldn't shout that, or you might get into trouble with the match referee. And we wouldn't want that, would we?

Back in Multan, we were left chasing 198 to win the first match in a three-Test series, which should have been a doddle, and it would have put us in a powerful position to win the series. We reached 67 for two and looked to be cruising but then, somehow, we disintegrated to 175 all out against Danish Kaneria and Shoaib Akhtar. It was quite some achievement to lose a game from that position. We basically had one bad session – one awful session – from which we never recovered in the series. We drew in Faisalabad and were then stuffed by an innings in Lahore. In a three-match series, it's tough when you go one match down, especially on the subcontinent, and Pakistan made us pay for that one session when we took our eye off the ball.

Maybe it was inevitable that we were going to struggle in the next series after the Ashes. It was, inevitably, a much less highly charged atmosphere in Pakistan than we had encountered against Australia a few months before. But that's no excuse. A Test match is a Test match, we didn't produce the goods and we suffered because of it.

It wasn't looking good for our next tour, either. After Christmas we had another three-match tour to the subcontinent, this time against India, and we were going with a severely weakened squad. By the start of the Test series, there was no Vaughan, Trescothick, Giles or Simon Jones. India are a difficult team to beat on their own turf at the best of times, but with almost half a side missing we suddenly found ourselves as serious underdogs, just a few months after we'd beaten Australia.

One of the lads who stepped into the team for the first Test in Nagpur was Alastair Cook, who had only just arrived on a flight from the England A tour to the West Indies. I'd barely seen Cooky bat before, having played against him only once in a county match at Chelmsford when he didn't score many runs. So it was an eye-opener for me and several others to see this whippersnapper hop

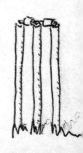

off the plane, stroll to the crease and score 60 in the first innings and a ton in the second, helping us to a very creditable draw. And the lad was only 21. He'd still have been wearing short trousers when I made my Test debut. He didn't even look 21 either; I thought he was about 12.

Paul Collingwood also got a maiden Test hundred in the first innings, helping us to 393, and then I had a very enjoyable time when India batted. It was a flat wicket, but the ball swung, conventionally with the new ball and reversing with the old. I took six for 57, which was probably up there with the best performances of my career. The state of the ball certainly helped, but I felt really good that day. The ball landed where I wanted it to land and things generally went my way.

By this stage of my career, I had quite a few more tricks up my sleeve than I had when I was younger. I'd always been able to bowl reverse-swing, but you need to build your experience of how to bowl when the ball is reversing. And for England, there had usually been other slightly quicker bowlers, such as Jonah and Fred, who had been used more than me when we got the ball in a condition to reverse, rough on one side and smooth on the other.

I think it's a popular misconception that reverse-swing is created by the bowler, when it is actually all about the condition of the ball. It's not something that a bowler needs to learn; providing he can bowl relatively quickly, reverse-swing will happen automatically once the ball is in a suitable state. If I bowl with my normal outswinger's action and the ball swings in, I know the ball is reversing. I don't have to do anything different. I can then bowl again with exactly the same action and the ball turned the other way around and it will become a normal outswinger.

So once the ball starts reverse-swinging as it was in Nagpur, depending on which way round I held the ball, I could bowl an outswinger with my outswinger's action (conventional) and an inswinger with my outswinger's action (reverse), plus an inswinger with my inswinger's action (conventional) and an outswinger with an inswinger's action (reverse).

Confused? Well, it can certainly be confusing for a batsman, and that's the general idea. Reverse-swing is harder for a batsman to face because the bowler can change the direction of swing without changing his action. To change the direction of swing normally, a bowler will need to modify his wrist position and possibly his whole action, which the sharp-eyed batsman could pick up on. But the only available clue to a batsman when the ball is old is which way round the bowler is holding the ball, and that is usually very difficult to spot.

I remember bowling at Nasser Hussain in the nets on tour to Sri Lanka in 2003. We had been working on bowling reverse-swing with Troy Cooley, the bowling coach, and the batsmen were practising facing it. We had prepared a few new balls to reverse by scuffing one side against concrete and leaving the other side shiny, and they were zooming round corners. I was bowling huge in-duckers at Nasser in the nets and, after a while, I thought I'd test him out, so I turned the ball around and made my next one swing away.

It beat him all ends up and he wasn't happy. He picked the ball up and belted it back over my head, miles out of the nets. 'If you're going to bowl with that f***ing ball,' he shouted, 'you only make it go one f***ing way.' I was under the impression that the batsmen were supposed to be practising against that sort of thing. But Nass obviously had a different take on the situation. Not for the first time in our careers.

Everyone knows much more about reverse-swing these days since Wasim Akram and Waqar Younis made it popular in the 1990s. Their secrets eventually filtered through to the rest of the game, partly from the time they spent playing county cricket, but also just from playing against them at Test level and watching what they did. And the key is to get one side dry and rough, and the other side as smooth as possible. It doesn't necessarily have to be shiny,

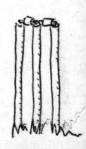

but it does have to be smooth. Dull smooth can be as effective as shiny smooth, as long as there is that contrast between the two sides.

As bowlers, we would have literature fed back to us from scientists who had been commissioned by the ECB to look into these things. They would put the ball on an axis in a wind tunnel and see how it reacted when a load of air was thrown at it, just like the aerodynamics of a car are tested by forcing a lot of air past it. I think NASA were involved at times (that's the American space agency, not the angry former England captain), but I'm not sure that much of practical use ever came from their experiments. For a start, the ball in the wind tunnel was stationary, quite different from a ball propelled by a bowler, which will have a number of revolutions on it, depending on how big a flick the bowler has given it with his wrist. I think they're over-rated, those NASA blokes. I mean, what they do is hardly rocket science, is it?

But that's enough science for now. Most teams will put one person in charge of looking after the ball, so they know which side is to be smooth and which one rough. And if you're trying to get reverse-swing, the fewer people that handle the ball, the better. Unless you're playing in England in April, fielders are likely to have sweaty palms, and if you're trying to keep one side of the ball dry, it needs to go through the minimum pairs of hands.

Tres was usually our ball monitor and he would be standing at slip, the man with the mints. He would give the ball a good shine or polish then throw it straight back to mid-off, who would have a towel to dry his hands before he caught the ball. And mid-off would then pass it back to the bowler, who would probably be sweating like a pig, but would try not to undo the careful work of his team-mates.

At the start of a tour or series, we would experiment with a batch of balls in the nets to see what worked best on them, because balls vary from country to country and from batch to batch. There are some theories that you can get a ball to reverse-swing by making one side really wet with spit, so to test that we would dunk one side of a ball in water, bowl with it in the nets and see what it did. We'd scratch one side of another ball to bits to see how it would perform after it had been bashed against hard ground and boundary boards for thirty or forty overs.

We'd do the same with the saliva from mints, to see how well that particular set of balls polished up. The sugary coating from the mints helps to shine one side of the ball and make it smooth. If I'm sucking a mint, I'll sometimes rub my finger straight onto the mint rather than just getting saliva, because that will get you more sugar on your finger than just from the saliva.

Is that cheating? Well, you're allowed to use bodily fluids, but it's quite a grey area in general. When a bowler rubs sweat from his forehead on the ball, is it cheating if he's got suncream on his forehead? I think every international team knows exactly which types of suncream help to add shine to the ball and which ones don't. Some bowlers use massaging wax, which feels a bit like Vaseline, but smells a lot nicer. They'll put a bit on their forearms or the back of their hand and allow it to mix in with their sweat. It might be a touch on the naughty side, but everybody has had their own ways of trying to put a bit of extra shine on the ball since W.G. Grace was a lad.

I've mentioned before about how, when I was a teenager, I'd put shoe polish on my ball and take it up to the nets at Pudsey Congs and impress everyone with my swing bowling. Another thing I tried was hair lacquer, which was also pretty good. I'd take an old ball, spray it with hair lacquer and leave it overnight. It used to swing all over the shop when I took it to nets the next evening.

I can't remember whether I bowled at V.V.S. Laxman with that ball in the nets at Congs, but I certainly undid him with some reverse-swing in that Test match in Nagpur. The ball was about fifty overs old and reversing nicely, and I'd just got Wasim Jaffer caught at slip with a ball that swung away. For my first ball to Laxman, I turned the ball the other way around and reversed one

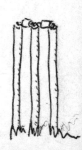

into his pads and he was plumb lbw. And that turned out be the only ball I bowled to him that series, because he didn't play in the next two Tests.

The second Test was at Mohali and we started to live up to our underdog billing there and were well beaten by nine wickets. Anil Kumble, that wily old customer, took four wickets in our second innings as we were bowled out for 181, then their batsmen knocked off 140-odd with ease. So once again we were one game down in a three-match series on the subcontinent, this time with only one to play. Against India's powerful batting line-up, with our badly weakened side, there was surely no way we could get back into the series, could we?

We managed to get a first-innings lead of 121 in the third Test at Mumbai, but it looked as though we would run out of time to force the victory that we needed to square the series. Come lunch on the last day, India had reached 75 for three, chasing 313 to win. It didn't look as though we were going to lose, but nor did it look like we'd have the time to bowl them out, especially as they had Dravid and Tendulkar at the crease, with plenty of batting to come and a 1–0 lead in the series to protect.

It had been an intensive three-match series and we were all pretty knackered by that stage. Towards the end of the lunch interval, Fred asked me to put some music from my iPod on in the dressing-room. He suggested 'Ring of Fire', by Johnny Cash. I'm quite a fan of country music – perhaps as a result of all those barn dances I went to while camping with my parents as a lad – and on that tour to India we had been playing a lot of my stuff on the team bus and in the changing-room; Kenny Rogers, Dolly Parton and especially Johnny Cash. There had been a few airings for 'A Boy Named Sue' and 'Ring of Fire' had also gone down well.

I don't think Fred had particularly planned it as a team sing-song, just a bit of music to get the blood pumping through tired limbs again. But it just happened that everybody was in the changing-room when the music came on. Nobody was in the loo, nobody was outside having a stretch, we were all in there together. And within the first few lines of the song, everybody was singing and clapping in time to the music.

> *♫ I fell into a burning ring of fire*
> *I went down, down, down, and*
> *   the flames went higher*
> *And it burns, burns, burns, the ring of fire*
> *The ring of fire. ♫ ♪*

I've been part of a few dressing-room sing-songs in my time, but I've never known anything quite like that. The singing was probably horrendous, but it didn't matter. As we went through the verses, there were some people dancing on chairs, others playing invisible trombones. What the Indian team in the next room must have thought, I have no idea, but it must have made a hell of a noise. It was one of those special moments that couldn't be planned, where you bond with everybody else in the room, and we went out after lunch feeling ten feet tall.

Maybe their heads were still spinning from that ear-bashing in the dressing-room, but within 15.2 overs of the afternoon session, India had contrived to lose their last seven wickets. I took the last catch, a steepling skyer to dismiss Munaf Patel off Shaggy Udal, who had a great day, taking four for 14. It was a surreal session of play. India just self-destructed and we could hardly believe that we had scraped a 1–1 draw in the series.

For the Man of the Match award, it was a close-run thing between Andrew Flintoff and Johnny Cash, but they gave it to Fred, who'd had a brilliant game as captain, as well as scoring runs and taking wickets. Maybe the backs-to-the-wall scenario suited his

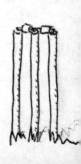

style of captaincy. He didn't take things too seriously, he was the same old Fred. And it was nice, for once, to have a bowler in charge, who understood what you were going through when you were blowing out of your arse after eight overs, and didn't say: 'Just a couple more, please, Hog.'

We tried to recapture the 'Ring of Fire' moment on a couple of other occasions, but it never had the same effect. Such spontaneous moments can't be recreated. They just have to happen.

One spin-off from my own success in that Test series was that I was added to the squad for the one-day series that followed. That was a compliment, I suppose, a recognition of how well I'd bowled in the preceding few weeks. Even though I hadn't been a regular in the one-day side for some time, the powers-that-be thought that I might still be able to do a good job against India's powerful batsmen.

But with very good reason, my lovely wife didn't quite see it that way. This was the third time in my career that Sarah and I had planned a holiday together, only to be forced to cancel it when I was unexpectedly called back into England's one-day side. The first holiday to go by the wayside was a planned trip to Mauritius in 2000, when I was selected for the Champions Trophy in Kenya and never played a game. In South Africa in 2005 I was whistled up for the one-day matches after I'd had a decent Test series, which meant we couldn't travel to Rome† to watch a Six Nations rugby match. Finally, in India, our scheduled holiday in Goa went down

---

†**HOGFACT:** Did you know that there is a place called Rome on every continent? Well, you do now.

the pan as I was sent travelling to various outposts around the country for the seven-match one-day series.

I was less inclined to see my call-up as a compliment when I didn't play at all in the first three matches of the series. By the time they picked me for the fourth game in Cochin, and then for the sixth game in Jamshedpur, I'd spent two weeks travelling all over India, not playing any cricket, and my rhythm had gone. I went for five or six an over in both games and was left wishing I'd spent the time lying on a beach in Goa instead. With the benefit of hindsight, the selectors probably thought the same thing.

And that turned out to be the last time I played one-day cricket for England. After I first started playing international cricket, I was highly thought of for a while as an opening bowler with the white ball, which always used to swing when it was new. From the time of my debut in Zimbabwe in October 2001 to the Champions Trophy in Sri Lanka in September 2002, I played eighteen one-day matches for England. But I don't think that Fletch ever really rated me as a one-day bowler; he thought I was too predictable, and at that stage of my career he was probably right.

The problem was that, once England had told me that I would only be playing Test matches, I didn't play many one-day games for Yorkshire either. Once I was on a central contract, which placed a greater emphasis on rest for fast bowlers between Test matches, the one-day matches for Yorkshire were a good opportunity to give my body a break. This meant that I never really built up my experience in one-day cricket. As Fletch himself used to say, you need to play about forty one-day international matches before you really get used to the game, and I never reached that level. The game moves on, I probably didn't adapt quickly enough, and then I didn't play enough one-day county cricket to stay in touch.

Perhaps I could have helped myself by playing more one-dayers for Yorkshire, but English seasons are so overcrowded that the decisions I took were right at the time. If I had played more one-day cricket, I probably wouldn't have stayed fit to be selected for

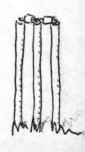

forty consecutive Test matches. So it's not something that I lose a great deal of sleep about.

We lost that one-day series in India 5–1, but while most of the team were struggling, Kevin Pietersen kept on scoring runs. That winter had been the first time I'd been away with KP for a prolonged period of time and it soon became clear that here was a bloke who had something different about him. And it wasn't just the accent or the haircuts.

There was one incident during that one-day series in India that struck me as fairly typical of why he has become such a brilliant player. It was during the first match in Delhi, where we were chasing 203 to win and were going nicely, needing around four an over. Kev had made 40-odd when, despite the fact that we didn't need to accelerate, he tried to hit Yuvraj Singh out of the ground and was caught on the midwicket boundary. From that point our innings unravelled and we lost by 39 runs.

After the game, in the dressing-room, everybody was mightily pissed off and most people were disappointed with the shot that KP had played, Fletch included. He was so annoyed that he thought it better not to say anything, and he left it to Matthew Maynard, our batting coach.

'So come on, KP, what were you thinking with that shot?' Matt said.

'Yeah, sorry, I mishit it,' Kev replied.

'What do you mean?'

'Well, if I'd have hit it well, it would have gone for six.'

'Yes, but it wasn't the best choice of shot when we only needed four an over.'

'Yeah, but if I'd hit it better, it'd have gone for six.'

'So you're saying it was the right shot, you just didn't hit it right.'

'Yeah, I should have hit it for six. Sorry about that.'

Kev was adamant that there was nothing wrong with the shot, there was never a trace of doubt in his mind that he should have done something else. He was immensely confident in his own ability, very much his own person, and that single-mindedness has helped him to become the player he is today.

Remember what I said about having Andrew Flintoff as captain, how it was great to have a fellow bowler in charge, someone who had a good idea when you were starting to suffer for your art? Well, I was sorely tempted to revise that opinion after the first Test of the following summer, against Sri Lanka at Lord's. And 'sorely' is the right word. This was the game in which we declared on 551 for six, then bowled Sri Lanka out for 192 in 55 overs in their first innings. I took four for 27, which included my 200th Test wicket, Farveez Maharoof caught and bowled. Nice landmark, but it was no more exciting really than my 199th or my 201st.

It was also around this time that I was told by someone in the England dressing-room that I was ranked as the fourth-best bowler in the world in Test cricket. 'How do you know that?' I said. 'Have you watched everybody bowling at once?' Maybe everyone else was injured at the time, or there wasn't much cricket on. That sort of thing is fairly meaningless in my eyes, just a load of numbers thrown into a computer and a few names spurted out the other side. Maybe they accidentally did it in alphabetical order that month and I was fourth on the list.

Anyway, we were well on top against Sri Lanka at Lord's, and midway through the third day we made them follow on, hoping for an early finish. The small matter of 199 overs later we were still hoping. At the end of the fifth day they were 537 for nine and we were bloody knackered. Having been in the field for two consecutive innings, we'd bowled 250-odd overs on the trot. That's nearly three full days' worth. And of the 199 overs in the second innings, I bowled 46 and Fred, who must have been feeling guilty for making

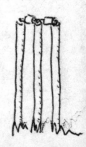

them follow on, bowled 51. That's a whole lot of overs for no reward at the end.

The thing that really sticks in my mind, though, is not so much those frustrating last couple of days at Lord's, but the day after the match ended. In their infinite wisdom, while we were down in London the ECB had arranged for us to go and shoot the photos for some billboard advertising for Sky Sports. And guess what, that meant bowling some more.

I was very, very sore that next morning. I struggled to find a part of my anatomy that wasn't aching. It hurt just to stand up straight. But in a makeshift studio somewhere in London, I had to run up and bowl, and that was something I really didn't want to do. I couldn't really just amble in off a couple of paces and turn my arm over, either; that wouldn't have looked too good on the billboards. They wanted some shots of me in my delivery stride, and I suppose I could have tried to manufacture the expression of effort that comes naturally when you're bowling, but I wouldn't have been very good at it. I'd have looked like a small child trying to do a poo. Then I'd have had to put up with seeing my face, fifteen feet high on an advertising billboard, pulling a face that made me look like a constipated toddler. Nope, I had to run in and bowl properly, however much it hurt.

And for all my pain, the bloke that I felt really sorry for was the photographer, who had to crouch down halfway along the imaginary pitch we were bowling on. His life was in our hands. We had to bowl the ball directly above his head while he tried to keep his composure long enough to take some front-on photos of us. 'Brave lad,' I thought, as another ball flew inches over his head. After the way we'd just bowled against Sri Lanka in their second innings, I'm not sure I'd have been so confident.

Mercifully, we had a week's rest before the second Test at Edgbaston and, suitably refreshed, we managed a comfortable six-wicket victory. The second and third Tests were back-to-back, so as soon as we had finished in Birmingham we travelled straight to Nottingham to prepare for the final Test of the series at Trent Bridge. That night, Sarah and I went out for a meal with Ruth and Andrew Strauss at Chino Latino in Nottingham and, as luck would have it, the Sri Lankan players were in there as well. Among them was Trevor Penney, the former Warwickshire batsman, who was Sri Lanka's assistant coach on that tour. I'd always got on well with Trevor when he worked with England as a fielding coach and we went over to sit with the Sri Lankans after we had finished our meals.

We got chatting to Trevor and the Sri Lankan lads, we'd had a few drinks, and for some unknown reason I started offering to arm-wrestle some of the Sri Lankan players. That's not something I make a habit of doing, so I'm not sure why I did it that night. It started off with one or two of them, and when I'd beaten a couple, more of them wanted a go. Jayawardena? Down you go. Muralitharan? Strong wrists but no shoulders. Malinga? No chance, pal. In the end, I worked my way through the entire Sri Lankan team, and a couple of the coaches as well. The only ones to beat me were their fitness coach, C.J. Clarke, and Kumar Sangakkara, but in my defence I'd already been through about a dozen arm-wrestles by the time I got to them. Having said that, Kumar was pretty strong and I think he might have beaten me anyway.

When I woke up the next morning, I could barely move my right shoulder. If you feel that sort of thing as a bowler, you tend to think back to what you did in the last game. 'That's strange,' I thought, 'I don't remember my shoulder hurting yesterday when I was bowling.' Then it gradually dawned on me that the pain might have something to do with the events in the restaurant the night before. 'Oh, yes, maybe it's got something to do with those fifteen arm wrestles I did.'

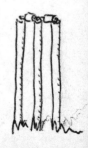

My shoulder was stiff for quite a while afterwards, but thankfully it didn't threaten my participation in the Test. I suppose people would have assumed that I had a bowler's injury if I was left out of the side at Trent Bridge with a shoulder problem. But I took a couple of wickets in each innings, so I must have made a full recovery. And Murali got his revenge on behalf of the Sri Lankan team by taking eleven wickets in the match, we lost by 134 runs and another series was drawn.

We got ourselves back on track with a good series win against Pakistan in the second half of the summer. With Fred injured, Straussy came in and did a really good job as captain, leading us to victories at Old Trafford and Headingley after we'd drawn at Lord's. We then had the bizarre situation at the Oval, where Pakistan protested about Darrell Hair and the allegations of ball tampering, and the umpires abandoned the Test. The less said about that, the better, I think. The ICC must have changed their minds at least ten times about whether we were actually awarded a win for that match, so I haven't got the foggiest whether we won the series 2–0 or 3–0, but it was great to get a series win against a decent side under our belts with the next Ashes series looming large.

As a bowler, I was able to take a bit of a back seat against Pakistan. I didn't bowl badly, just kept chipping in with wickets from time to time – you know, keeping the shop floor clean – while others grabbed the limelight. On a bouncy pitch at Old Trafford Harmy was almost unplayable, taking eleven wickets, and Monty Panesar helped him out with a very impressive five-fer. Monty then took three wickets in each innings, coming up with the goods when the pressure was on him.

Having come into the side the previous winter against India, Monty had made an instant impression, both with the quality of his bowling and with his manic celebrations, bouncing along like Tigger on happy pills whenever he took a wicket. He was like a wide-eyed schoolboy when he first came into the team: in a good way because of his enthusiasm and in not such a good way because of his dodgy fielding.

I'd played against him for Yorkshire at Northampton a couple of times and I remember him going down in a long barrier to field a ball – one knee on the ground, all his body behind the ball, just as the coaching manuals tell you – and then missing the thing completely. How on earth does that happen? We also enjoyed watching him practising his bowling while he was fielding down at fine leg. I'd look down and think: 'What's that lad doing at fine leg, running around all on his own?' And it would be Monty, practising his bowling, lost in his own little world.

But there was no doubting the quality of his spin bowling once he came into the England team. He'd bowl all day and he soon proved that he had plenty of bottle. He was quiet and unassuming off the field, perhaps more so because he attracted so much attention as soon as he came into the side. But he also asked a lot of questions, he was really eager to learn, which is always a good sign.

He is also unfailingly polite, a good bloke to stand near when we had to go to an official function on tour at a High Commissioner's residence. There's a lot of mingling to be done at these events; at least that's the theory. There are a lot of boring people to speak to, none of the players enjoy them, but I suppose they have to be done. If you're stuck in a particularly stilted conversation, it's useful to say: 'And have you met my friend Monty Panesar?' You can then sneak off and make yourself scarce, maybe have a wander round the High Commissioner's gardens for ten minutes, before coming back to see Monty still nodding away politely. Good lad, Mont, take one for the team. There are lots of different ways to make yourself popular with your team-mates and Monty was certainly getting off on the right foot.

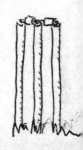

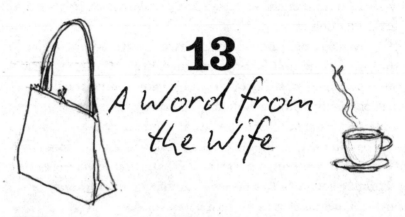

13
A Word from the Wife

Hello, it's me, Sarah, again. Matthew's let me back in the book, briefly, on the understanding that I don't reveal any more embarrassing secrets about his unpleasant habits around the house. He needn't worry. The rest of his secrets are safely tucked away down his side of the bed, along with the rest of his stuff.

You don't often hear about cricketers' wives and girlfriends, do you? Well, during the good times that Matthew has been talking about, when the England team was settled and winning lots of matches, there were a lot of good girls around as well. For those two or three years, from 2004 onwards, the bunch of lads that were playing for England were not only decent cricketers, they were also decent blokes. The players got on well together, the partners all got on together and it doesn't take a coaching genius or business guru to tell you that the lads are more likely to perform at their best when everybody's happy.

As a group, I think we all bonded that little bit more closely during the Ashes series in 2005, when we were desperately trying to stop each other from turning into nervous wrecks. My God, that series was ridiculous! I seemed to spend the whole summer either biting my nails or holding my head in my hands. And I'm not someone who usually gets particularly nervous watching Matthew play. Not when he's bowling, anyway. The times when I've been most nervous have been when he's been sent in as England's nightwatchman.

Towards the end of a day's play, I would just be preparing to make a quick getaway when a wicket would fall and I'd think: 'Oh, no, don't send the poor lad in now!' But sure enough, Matthew would emerge from the pavilion and plod out to the middle with his pads on. I would sit back down, on the edge of my seat, and hope for the best. Every time he faced a ball, I'd be taking a deep breath and hoping – desperately, desperately hoping – that he'd survive those last few minutes. 'Don't get out, Matthew, don't get out.'

I probably start with an advantage over some cricketers' wives because I grew up with the game, so I've always been happy watching. My dad had played when we were younger and I learned to score while watching him. Then when my brother was playing down at Pudsey Congs, my mum and dad used to go along, and if I wasn't doing anything else on a Saturday I'd go to watch as well. If the weather's not too bad, it's a great way to spend an afternoon. It comes to be a way of life for the summer months, and one that I was always quite happy with. Which is a good job, really, given that I ended up marrying a cricketer as well.

Does that make me a WAG? Or even a CWAG? Not likely! There have been the odd occasions when the press called us the England players' CWAGs. When I saw that the first time, I almost wet myself with laughter. The vast majority of cricketers' wives and girlfriends actually have normal nine to five jobs. Either that or we have toddlers to control or school runs to do. Rachael Flintoff has run her own promotions business, Ruth Strauss has done some acting, Nichola Vaughan has been an accountant. I used to work in advertising. There are not many Victoria Beckhams or Cheryl Coles among the cricket mob. I'm sure that most of the women who live with footballers don't really sit around in posh outfits sipping lattes all day, but we certainly don't.

In the time that we've been around the England team, Matthew and I have been lucky a far as the treatment of players' families is concerned. It's not so long ago that the ECB hardly recognised that

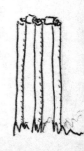

the lads had lives beyond their bowling actions or their forward defensive strokes, but thankfully that has changed for the better. When Matthew first started playing for England, I felt like a spare part much of the time when I went to watch him, and the rest of the wives felt the same. But with help from the Professional Cricketers' Association, we managed to persuade the ECB to provide us with a room on Test match weekends where we could sit together and watch our husbands play. They can be tense times, watching your other half perform in front of a crowd of thousands, so it's great to have a support network around you of people who are going through the same thing. There may even have been the odd glass of wine sampled from time to time (just to help us cope with the stress, you understand). For those few years when the England team was settled and successful, there were a lot of happy times, both for the players and for their other halves.

It can be different when the team is going through a losing spell. That is when there is chopping and changing in the side, with new people coming in and out, and that inevitably affects the partners as well. You know what it's like being the new person at work? It's never much fun. I'll never forget the first time I went on tour, to Sri Lanka in 2001[†], I've never been so nervous in all my life. It's such an insecure position to be in. You don't know quite how friendly to be because you're not sure how long your other half is going to be in the team. Or, for that matter, how long all the others are going to be in the team. You're not sure what the protocol is for wives and girlfriends. Are you expected to go the game every day? You're thrown together with a group of women you don't know and you just have to get on with it. But it goes without saying that the spirit is bound to be better when everyone knows each other well, as we did when the side was settled in Duncan Fletcher's time as coach.

[†]**HOGFACT:** In the 2001 British census, 'Jedi Knight' was classed as a religion and more than 390,000 people ticked this box. Can you imagine living in a country daft enough to do that? *Sarah: I know what you're thinking, where does he come up with this stuff?*

A Word from the Wife

Another positive about those days was that we had Fletch's wife, Marina, in our room at a Test match. And Marina is one of the loveliest women I have met. Our relationship could potentially have been quite difficult, because Matthew and Fletch just did not get on at times. I often felt that Fletch didn't treat Matthew particularly well and it would have been easy for me to steer clear of Marina as a result. But I always felt it was important that, however Matthew felt about his teammates, I would make my own decisions about their other halves. And Marina was fantastic, so it was never a problem.

One role that Marina filled, though, was that she was definitely Fletch's eyes and ears in the girls' room. Anything that was said in that room that Fletch needed to hear, he heard. And I think a few of the players' wives could forget that, from time to time. The number of times I heard someone complaining about selection or the way the team was being run and I would sit there, cringing and thinking: 'Be careful! These things can get back!'

Having said that, I don't think anybody would ever have lost their place in the side because of something that was said. Imagine that! If you were responsible for ending your husband's England career because you couldn't keep things to yourself. But I think it probably gave Fletch a pretty good insight into who was thinking what around the team.

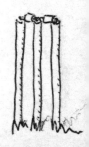

When you sign up for life as a cricketer's wife, part of the deal is that The Man of the House will not actually be in your house for long periods because he will have to go away on tour. The consolation is that you will get to see some fantastic places when you go out to visit him. Most of the countries that cricket is played around the world are lovely places and most of them have great weather. It can be tough having our husbands away for months on end, but it's undoubtedly one of the perks that I've been lucky enough to visit some wonderful places – Australia, Sri Lanka, West Indies – that I might otherwise never have seen.

I was never under any illusions about the time Matthew would spend away. Even when England are playing at home, the players will still spend umpteen weeks on the road in hotels around the country. But I remember the time when we were moving out of our first house in 2004. I was really upset to be leaving, I'd grown very attached to the place, and I couldn't understand why Matthew didn't seem bothered. 'Why aren't you upset?' I asked. 'This has been our first home together and we're not going to be living here anymore. Does that not make you sad at all?'

And he just said: 'I don't feel as though I've spent any time here.'

We then worked out how much time he had actually spent in that house in the 2½ years since we'd moved in. This was at the stage of his career when he was still playing quite a bit of one-day cricket for England, so he'd stay on tour longer, and he'd also be away for longer in summer as well. In those 2½ years, we worked out that he had actually only spent three months at home. Three months! And that included missing both the Christmases while we had been in that house. I thought to myself: 'I'm not surprised it doesn't really feel like home to him.'

In actual fact, you don't actually see an awful lot of your husband even when you are out on tour with them. They're out there to work, after all, which is fair enough. If they're having a team meal, the wives are usually not included, and if they win a Test match and are going out to celebrate, that's definitely a boys-only thing. And we wouldn't want to interfere with that!

A WORD FROM THE WIFE

But touring is another area in which things have been much better for families in the last few years. When Matthew first started going away with England, the feeling was that the players' wives would be tolerated on tour for a short while, but not much more than that. Nowadays there is a much more enlightened approach and we're usually allowed on tour for a good couple of weeks.

All that is assuming, of course, that the lads actually want to see us in the first place. There are probably some players who would prefer it if their wives left them alone for the time they were on tour. There may even be some who view their other halves as an embarrassment. I'm quite sure that Matthew wouldn't be one of them. At least I hope Matthew wouldn't be one of them. Although there was that time in New Zealand with the champagne ...

I'd better explain. This was on the tour to New Zealand in 2002 and during the first Test in Christchurch, everything seemed to be well with the world. The sun was shining, the girls had just been out for lunch and, when we went to watch the cricket in the afternoon, Matthew took five wickets. It felt like a good time to open a bottle of bubbly and, to our great delight, we discovered that there was a champagne lawn, just beyond the boundary in front of a tent, so we parked ourselves down there.

The problem was that the champagne that was being sold in the tent was a complete rip-off, so at tea, we nipped out of the ground and went round the corner to the supermarket, where they were selling the same champagne for a quarter of the price. The difference was ridiculous. It was forbidden to take alcohol into the ground, but we decided to conceal as many bottles as we could about our persons and see if we could wing it.

I had a big bag that had two bottles hidden at the bottom. Another girl had a bottle up her top (I'm not quite sure how she managed to hide that). Between us, we managed to get four or five bottles into the ground. We took them down to the champagne lawn and were feeling pretty chuffed with ourselves. But just as we were getting ready to uncork our first bottle, a security guard came over and stood above us. 'Excuse

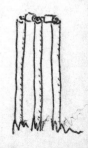

me, ladies. We have reason to believe that you may have brought some alcohol into the ground.'

We protested our innocence, pointing out that the champagne was on sale in the tent behind us. Some of the less reserved members of our party may even have attempted to flirt their way out of the situation. But he wasn't buying any of it, and he said we had to hand over our bottles or get out of the ground. At that point, we didn't have much option but to come clean and hand over our goodies.

Some of the players were mortified when they found out about our close shave. I don't think Matthew was embarrassed in the slightest.

He thought the whole thing was hilarious.

REVEALED
OVERLEAF ...

Finally, the truth about which England
player used the garden bushes at No 10
Downing Street as a toilet at our
Ashes reception in 2005 ...

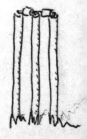

Nobody did. It was just a rumour that developed.
Sorry to disappoint.

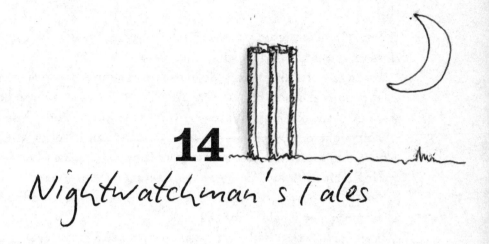

14
Nightwatchman's Tales

One of the great things about cricket is the variety of people that you meet playing the game, either on your side or the opposition. You get short blokes, tall blokes, clever blokes, thick blokes, funny blokes, dull blokes, fat blokes, thin blokes, old blokes, young blokes, loud blokes, shy blokes and even Darren Gough. It is, for the most part, a really inclusive game that anyone can play.

But no matter how much you love the game, you have to admit that cricket has more than its fair share of pretty shitty jobs. Take fielding at short leg, for example, which can be a life-threatening job at times, especially if you get stationed there for a spin-bowler who is sending down long-hops, enabling the batsman to treat you like a one-man coconut shy. Some players like to pretend that they enjoy fielding at short leg, as if to underline their tough-guy credentials, but just give them the chance to field in the slips and watch them run.

Being twelfth man is another task that nobody really enjoys; running round after your so-called team-mates all day long, ferrying drinks and fetching batting gloves, while being constantly reminded that you weren't *quite* good enough to get in the team.

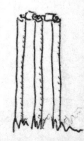

You are, in other words, treated as a slave, especially if Nasser Hussain is playing and barking the orders.

These are jobs that somebody in the team simply has to do, but everybody is secretly hoping that somebody else is chosen to do them. And the one job that everyone quite blatantly tries to avoid is being nightwatchman, the bloke who has to come in to bat when nobody else wants to, a few overs before the close of play, when it's getting a bit dark and the precious, darling batsmen need to be protected. So how on earth did Muggins here end up being saddled with this job for England for so long?

It was a duty that had often been doled out to a junior member of the team. In recent years, the post had been filled temporarily by younger lads like Alex Tudor, Richard Dawson and Gareth Batty. But the first time I was asked to do it – no, the first time I was *told* to do it – was during the first Test against New Zealand at Lord's in 2004, which was my twenty-seventh match for England, so I hardly qualified as a new boy.

I don't think there was a particularly scientific process that led to me becoming England's nightwatchman. It certainly wasn't my idea, I can assure you of that. I think that Michael Vaughan and Duncan Fletcher looked round the dressing-room at Lord's that day and asked themselves: 'Hmmm, now which one of the bowlers blocks the shit out of it and which ones go out and swing? Harmy? Nah. Jonah? Nah. There's only one candidate. Get your pads on, Hog.' And so began my life as England's sacrificial lamb.

I suppose it's like the night shift at any workplace; you don't particularly want to do it, but you hope that the rewards will make it worthwhile. Except that with the nightwatchman's duties there was no extra pay for working the unsociable hours.

Maybe I should have got my agent onto that one.

The person who was most perturbed about my new job was Sarah's grandma, Dorothy. The first time she heard I was England's nightwatchman, she rang Sarah up to check she'd be alright because I wasn't going to be home for the evening.

I don't mind admitting that the first few times I did the job as nightwatchman, I was absolutely crapping myself. There's a pretty good reason why I bat lower down the order and, all of a sudden, I was having to do the work of a batsman, being sent out in conditions that the proper batsmen didn't fancy. When you go in up the order, the bowlers are fresh, the ball is often fairly new and if Matthew Hoggard arrives at the crease rather than Kevin Pietersen, the bowlers suddenly perk up and think: 'Aye, aye, another easy wicket on its way here.' I know, because I've had the same thoughts myself with the ball in my hand. That tally of Test wickets that goes against your name at the end of your career doesn't say how many top-order batsmen you've dismissed and how many tail-end numpties.

I'm not saying that I disagreed with the policy of sending in a nightwatchman, just that I found it extremely daunting to start with. In that game against New Zealand, we were, at least, doing fairly well at the time. Batting second after the Kiwis had made 386, Marcus Trescothick and Andrew Strauss had added 190 for our first wicket, with Straussy making a century on his debut. We had reached 239 for two when Straussy was out with four overs left in the second day's play, so I was sent out to join Mark Butcher at the crease, batting at number four.

NUMBER FOUR!!! ME!!! IN A TEST MATCH!!! HOW SILLY IS THAT?

Is there any other sport where somebody gets promoted specifically because they're not very good at doing something? Bizarre.

Anyway, once I'd got over the absurdity of it all, I had ten balls to face by the close of play, all of them from Daniel Vettori, the

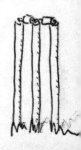

left-arm spinner. A few of the balls I left alone. Some of them I blocked with my best get-past-that forward defensive stroke. And I survived to the close, my job as nightwatchman done. Thank God for that.

But with respect to the New Zealanders, I wasn't batting then against the scariest attack in world cricket. The next time I was called on as nightwatchman, later that summer, we were playing against West Indies on a fast, bouncy track at Old Trafford and Fidel Edwards was whistling it round my earholes.

This time I went out to bat at number seven in our first innings when we were looking a bit wobbly on 227 for five. There were six overs to go until the end of play and I was batting alongside Graham Thorpe. I'm glad to say that I survived once again, but what really surprised me this time was how much I enjoyed batting the next morning.

I guess that, to a certain extent, the next day some of the pressure has been lifted from a nightwatchman who has successfully completed his night shift. Your primary task has been done and, best of all for me, you don't have to sit waiting nervously to go in to bat, the thing about batting that I hate most of all. Not that you would ever start the next morning thinking, 'Wa-hey, time to play a few shots. I'm free and easy now.' There's still a Test match to be won, after all. Having said that, Ian Botham was always keen for me to get out sharpish the next morning. He'd say, 'Don't hang around too long please, Hoggy, we don't want to be commentating on your boring batting all morning!'

I certainly wasn't feeling free and easy against Fidel Edwards at Old Trafford, because he was bowling seriously quick. It was, without doubt, one of the fastest bursts of pace bowling that I have faced in my whole career and, because of his slingy action, he's not all that easy to pick up. But I got in line – or out of line when the ball was fizzing towards my head – and I picked up runs when the opportunities came along. It was, I have to say, a hell of a buzz. My heart was thub-dubbing away in my chest the whole time, but I actually felt a degree of confidence in facing some genuinely fast bowling. Much of the time, when you're a tail-ender facing a top-class bowler, it just feels unfair. 'Shouldn't he slow down when he's bowling to me?' you feel like saying. But this time I just felt a real thrill from facing fast bowling.

I managed to stay in for almost two hours in total, making 23 and adding fifty-odd with Thorpey, which left us in a much stronger position. When I was finally dismissed by Corey Collymore shortly before lunch, I had a real sense of satisfaction, and not just because I was going to be able to enjoy my lunch properly. I even started thinking that perhaps, just perhaps, this night-watchman lark might not be too bad after all.

So the job became mine for the next few years. I won't say that I ever really, really *enjoyed* going out to bat for the last few minutes before the close of play, but I definitely started to relish the challenge and felt proud when I survived to the close. Somebody told me a while afterwards that, out of the first ten times I did the nightwatchman's job for England, I was only out once before the close. That was when Brett Lee splattered my stumps at Old Trafford in the 2005 Ashes series and it was the last ball of the day, so technically I'd still done my duty. I was never going to do like Alex Tudor, who slapped 99 as nightwatchman against New Zealand in 1999, or Jason Gillespie, who scored a double-century doing it for Australia against Bangladesh, which was just ridonculous. But I was doing the job with my own individual style (or lack of it).

Yes, it was still a mug's job being nightwatchman. But it was quite nice for this mug to add another string to his bow.

It was on the 2002–03 Ashes tour to Australia that I had started working that little bit harder to try to improve my batting. Since Duncan Fletcher had become coach of the England team, he had

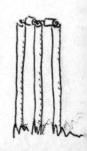

always stressed that he wanted his players to be proficient in at least two out of the game's three disciplines (batting, bowling and fielding). Runs from the tail-enders, he felt, could often be crucial to the outcome of a game, something that was all too frequently overlooked. Up to that point, I had batted at number eleven in all but one of my innings for England in Test cricket, so there was clearly some room for improvement on my behalf.

Apart from anything else, it was just nice on that tour to have the time to work on my batting. Over the course of a congested English season, you just don't get prolonged periods to work on your game in depth, especially at county level. And if you do get the chance, the likelihood is that, if you're a bowler, you'll use the time to work on your action or your run-up, rather than your batting. Throughout my first few years in county cricket, I don't think I had ever really spent a great deal of time or effort on improving my batting.

This unhealthy situation improved immensely after the introduction by the ECB of central contracts in 2002. Those of us on contracts now played less county cricket in between international matches, giving us extra time to work on areas of our game that needed attention. I still spent the majority of my time working on my bowling, of course, but now I had some time to devote to my batting as well.

On that tour to Australia in the winter of 2002–03, I found myself with more time on my hands than I had originally expected after I was dropped for the third and fourth Tests. Better put all this free time to good use, I thought. So I sought out Phil Neale, the former Worcestershire captain who was our tour manager, and spent umpteen hours working in the nets with him. We didn't have a dedicated batting coach at the time; Fletch took that on as part of his job in those days, but his time was understandably taken up with the proper batsmen.

With Phil, on the other hand, I could get plenty of time with a guy with a good cricket brain; he was happy either to throw an endless stream of balls for me to hit, or to feed the bowling machine, and we struck up a good relationship. I continued to work with Phil on my batting as long as I was involved with England.

Occasionally, Fletch would chip in with his thoughts on aspects of my technique, such as how I was sweeping or how I could manipulate the field better, and I would then go away and work on it with Phil. I had never been a complete imbecile with the bat: I had always watched the ball pretty well, it was just hitting it I had trouble with. A minor fault, that, but a fairly important one. So it was a question of trying to move my batting on to the next stage.

What I first focused on was improving my ability to survive at the crease. It was unlikely that I was going to become a pinch-hitting opener in one-day cricket – not in the short term, at least – so this seemed a sensible first step to take. Judging when to leave the ball, blocking good-length deliveries and digging[†] out yorkers – the aim was to give me more chance of hanging around at the crease while better batsmen scored runs at the other end. And maybe irritating the hell out of opposition bowlers while I was at it. As a bowler myself, I could always try to work out what the other bloke was thinking and try to use that to my advantage. I also practised ducking short balls and general evasive action, but I found that came fairly naturally. When there is a ball heading towards your skull at 90 mph, something in your brain tends to say: 'Uh-oh, time to get out of the way!'

As well as all this technical work, there was also a shift in my mentality. I became determined that I was going to be a difficult batsman to dismiss, the sort of bloke I would hate to bowl at. A lot of tail-end batsmen don't worry too much about leaving the ball, for example, but that didn't make sense to me. If I

[†]**HOGFACT:** A mole can DIG a tunnel 300 feet long in one night. But not if it comes near my garden it won't. Bloody pest, I've got traps waiting for you.

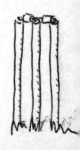

could just play out a maiden against one bowler rather than risk-ing my wicket by playing shots, somebody like KP or Freddie could be able to take advantage at the other end in the follow-ing over.

Leave – leave – leave – block the straighter ball – leave – leave. Another maiden over played out by the **WORLD'S MOST BORING BATSMAN**. There has never been an official award for that title, but I think it's high time that the efforts of stubborn tail-enders were given the recognition they deserve.

In the last couple of years, I've actually come out of my shell quite a bit and started to play a few shots. I wouldn't quite call myself a strokemaker and I don't think spectators in the front rows of the stands feel too threatened while I'm at the wicket, but I now have confidence that I'll be able to stay at the wicket for a decent length of time and if a loose ball comes along, I'll look to punish it. But all that has come from building on the defensive foundations that were laid with the help of Phil Neale.

As a result of the work I had done on my batting, on the England tour to West Indies in 2004 I found myself moved up the batting order to the dizzy heights of number nine. And this was all the way from number eleven, without stopping at number ten along the way. This was a seriously elevated position. This was nosebleed territory.

The management had decided that they wanted someone at number nine who would hang around for a while with the proper batsmen, which was precisely what I'd been working on. Steve Harmison and Simon Jones, who now had the indignity of follow-ing me in the batting order, were more likely to come in, play a few shots, and get out: they might score more runs than me, but if I could hang around for an hour and share a fifty partnership with, say, Freddie or Geraint Jones, even if I only made ten of them, my job would have been done.

The other bowlers certainly weren't jealous of my promotion. In fact, they probably thought I was welcome to it. Many's the time when I've had a dressing-room argument with Harmy over who should have the right to go in at number eleven. Depending on how fast the bowling was.

Still, as disloyal as it may have been to the fast bowlers' union, I was secretly quite chuffed with my promotion.

What I hadn't anticipated about my progress with the bat was that I would be saddled with the nightwatchman's duties as well. Some reward for all that hard work, you might think. And for some tail-enders, such a possibility might persuade them to abandon any notions of improving their batting, rather than be lumbered with the job of offering personal protection to the flash guys further up the order.

It has to be said that the whole concept of a nightwatchman is another example of why cricket is essentially a batsman's game and we bowlers are very much the poor relations. When I was doing the job for England, I was never involved in discussions about whether a nightwatchman was required. Between them, the next man in, along with the coach and captain (who is usually a batsman), would decide whether to summon the humble servant and use him as a human shield. It usually fell to Fletch to wander over and inform me of my fate, but by then I would already be strapping the pads on and chuntering away to myself about scaredy-cat batsmen.

And while I'm on a rant about bowlers being cricket's poor relations, let me tell you a bit about the convention of net-testing. This is a procedure used by England whenever we weren't sure about the quality of pitches in the practice nets. In the build-up to a game, we would usually have two adjacent nets for our practice, and if there was the merest suspicion that we might not be practising on a flat track, guess who would be sent in first? Two

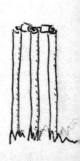

tail-enders, complete with pads, gloves, thigh pad, chest-guard, arm-guard, helmet and a message of good luck.

This could happen anywhere in the world, perhaps in some of the more remote venues on the subcontinent, or anywhere in England if it had rained beforehand. You would have thought that the more skilled batsmen would be better equipped to cope in such tricky conditions for batting, would you not? Oh no, we'll send in a pair of bowlers first so the batsmen don't break their dainty little fingers. At the start of a net session, if I saw my name down on the list as one of the first pair of batsmen, I'd think: 'Ah, the nets look a bit dodgy then, do they?' Bowlers, apparently, aren't affected by a few broken fingers. Sacrificial lambs again. Are we working in a Victorian mill or a 21st-century international cricket team?

The flipside of this comes when we practise somewhere that we're sure the net pitches will be really good. So if we were playing somewhere like Adelaide, I would stroll over with Harmy to find the list, look where we were scheduled to bat and eventually spot that we were right down at the bottom as the ninth pair.

'Ninth pair? Hang on a minute, Harmy, there are only sixteen of us in the squad. How does that work?'

So we'd look down the list of pairings again and see that some of the batsmen were going in **TWICE** before us! 'Christ,' Harmy would say, 'they must be really good tracks in there today.'

And I haven't finished yet on my batsman-beating rant. Here's another thing: if you have a two-hour net session, what do batsmen do for the whole time? Well, they bat for twenty minutes, then they might have a quick discussion with a coach about an aspect of their batting. And then they stop and chat. If they do deign to bowl at the rest of us in the nets, they usually bowl some common-or-garden variety of off-spin. Filthy, horrible off-spin, in most cases, ambling in off a couple of paces and just about managing to turn their arms over. Bless 'em, we don't want them to exert themselves too much, do we?

The problem is, who then bowls in the nets at the rest of us? What sort of practice do we get with the bat? Most likely it will be a few local net bowlers. But in a group of seven net bowlers, perhaps only four of them will be decent. You're also bound to get a leg-spinner who bowls it into the side-netting, an off-spinner who chucks it onto the roof and a budding fast bowler who steams in like Usain Bolt and then bowls as fast as Ian Bell.

And if we're down the pecking order at the net session, coming in as the ninth pair on another flat wicket, even the decent net bowlers will be knackered after bowling at the proper batsmen for an hour and a half. So what sort of preparation have we had for facing Brett Lee and Glenn McGrath?

THIS HAS BEEN A PARTY POLITICAL BROADCAST ON BEHALF OF THE FAST BOWLERS' UNION.

Anyway, rant over. For all my grumbles about being a nightwatchman, and the dubious ethics involved, I have already conceded that I did, eventually, come to relish the challenge that it presented. And on a couple of occasions, it even got me as high as number three in the batting order which, let's face it, would never have happened otherwise. My hope is that generations of the future, when they look back at the scorecards from these Test matches, will see my name up the order and think: 'My word, that Hoggard chap must have been a decent all-rounder! Batting at number three and opening the bowling? Botham and Flintoff never batted as high as that, but Hoggard never gets a mention in the history books about great English all-rounders. I wonder why not?'

And there were other spin-offs from becoming known as a reliable nightwatchman. Once I had become established as England's gloombuster, I started doing the job for Yorkshire as well, and two of my three first-class fifties (so far; I intend to add many more) came after I had gone in as nightwatchman.

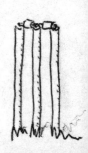

257

Against Glamorgan at Headingley in 2004, I went in at number six, reached fifty for the first time (my previous highest had been 38) and somehow went on to make 89 not out. And then, believe it or not, I ran out of partners, eleven runs short of a century. Bloody bowlers letting the batsmen down again!

Simon Jones was bowling well for Glamorgan in that game – although not well enough to get a really decent batsman out – and he was bowling in tandem with Robert Croft for quite a while. Our number eleven was Steve Kirby, and when he came in as our last man I must have been feeling full of myself because I started to push on a bit (as we all-rounders have to do when batting with the tail).[†] I'd been patting Crofty back for ages, but once the ninth wicket fell I came down the wicket and smacked him straight for four. Crofty, standing at the bowler's end, looked a bit surprised. And 22 yards away, I was trying very hard not to look too surprised myself.

Unbelievably, Crofty then decided to push both his mid-on and his mid-off back to the boundary, as though I did that sort of thing all the time. 'Crofty, I've only done it once and I've been in for two and a half hours,' I said. 'Don't be so bloody negative.'

'Oh, I don't know,' he replied. 'I thought you hit that really well.'

What a load of bollocks. He was just trying to make it harder for me to reach my hundred. Imagine the shame of allowing me to get a ton against you. He'd never have lived it down.

A short while afterwards, Kirbs, who had hung around gamely for an hour or so, was lbw to David Harrison and I was left high and dry, wondering when my next chance to score a century would come along. At the time of going to press, it is five years and counting ...

[†]**HOGFACT:** Humans have tiny bones that would once have been meant for a tail and unworkable muscles once meant to move our ears. I'm glad Andrew Caddick's ear muscles are unworkable. Imagine the draught.

The other half-century I made for Yorkshire as a nightwatch-man came against Hampshire at the Rose Bowl in 2007. If you don't mind me saying so, it wasn't a bad little innings as they had Shane Warne and Stuart Clark in their attack. It was in the second innings, I went in at number five and when I came to the wicket Younis Khan was at the other end, our new overseas player who had recently arrived from Pakistan.

This was still early in the season and none of us had played with Younis before. And because of his strong accent, some of the lads were struggling to understand his calling when running between the wickets. No fault of his – that can often be the case with an overseas player, whether they're from Brisbane, Barbados or Bombay. In the first innings at the Rose Bowl, Michael Vaughan had been run out after a mix-up with Younis and there were still a few problems in the second innings.

So I decided that a fresh approach was needed, and when I went out to bat with him we had a little chat. I'm not sure how we settled on the precise terms, but we made up a novel set of calls for running between the wickets.

'**BLIP**,' was 'Yes.'

'**BLOO**,' was 'No.'

'**BLAH**,' was 'Wait.'

Younis was most amused by the idea. He was mad keen to give it a go. You might have thought that such a daft scheme would only complicate matters further because it tends to be ingrained in a cricketer's mind to shout 'Yes', 'No' or 'Wait' after hitting the ball. But in actual fact Blip, Bloo and Blah did the job quite nicely. We put on 152 together, he hit a double-century and I got 61. And no, just in case you were wondering, I wasn't run out in the end.

So yes, it has been nice on occasions to shuffle up the order, to have the time to bat for a while and score a few runs. Perks of the nightwatchman's job, I suppose. But just think of all those not-outs I've had batting down the order at number ten or eleven – more than a quarter of my innings. If only I'd been further up the order

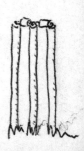

and had the batsmen to stay with me, who knows how many runs I'd have scored? I could even have requested my *own* nightwatchman ... No, that would be make me a traitor to the cause.

Without a doubt the best reward for all my hard labour as a nightwatchman was to have my own beer named after me. I don't know whether you'll have come across it in supermarkets or pubs, but when the ECB struck a sponsorship deal with Marston's to become the official beer of English cricket, the folk from the brewery seemed to think that I was a suitable type to use as their ambassador. Who was I to complain? And to thank me for my services, they decided to brew a new beer in my honour:

HOGGY'S NIGHTWATCHMAN!!!

How about that? None of the batsmen have had a beer named after them. And since you ask, the tasting notes describe my beer as 'a quaffable, pale-coloured but full-bodied beer'. If I'd known that the nightwatchman's job was going to bring such rich rewards, I'd never have moaned about it in the first place.

Pint of Hoggy's anyone? Now that's what I call a perk of the job.

15
Squashed by the Big Fat Lad

There is an awful lot of crap involved in international cricket these days, much of which has very little to do with bowling or hitting a little lump of leather. As the game has become more professional, more and more money has been spent on the way we prepare ourselves to play cricket. Much of it has been great for the players, and there's no doubt that the introduction of central contracts played a major part in our progress. But there has also been a hell of a lot of overcomplication of what should still be a perfectly simple game. Some of it is well-intentioned, harmless nonsense, such as ice vests that keep you cool but also soak you through. There are other things, though, that overcomplicate and actually get in the way of the cricket, which really is defeating the object altogether.

Possibly the worst example of something like this was at the start of our tour to Australia in late 2006, the eagerly awaited rematch of our epic series the year before. It was going to be a big series, we all had a fair idea of that. And we were certainly well aware of that by the time we had had finished our pre-tour briefing with the ECB, where Colin Gibson, the director of communications, put us in the picture about how much attention the series was going to get.

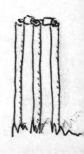

The eyes of the world would be watching us, we were told, the media would be scrutinising our every move, there would be a hundred billion trillion people (at least) watching on television, so we had to make sure we were prepared. We'd be on the back pages, the front pages, the press would be wanting to know how we slept, what we ate, what brand of toothpaste we used. Up to a point this was fair enough; no doubt the ECB felt the need to run this by us in case anyone hadn't figured it out for themselves. But I think the overall effect on the players was that, if you hadn't been feeling nervous beforehand, you definitely would be now. This was going to be **THE BIGGEST SERIES IN THE HISTORY OF THE WORLD**. If not bigger.

As part of the grand scheme to make sure that we made the right impression on the watching world, the preparations went so far as to plan the way we walked out of the airport on our arrival in Australia. First impressions are going to be important, we were told; we've got to look like a team and make sure we were all together in a group, not drifting out in ones and twos. We had to look ultra-confident in our body language and make sure we were all dressed immaculately. There was even talk of us getting a room at the airport and having showers to spruce ourselves up. Thankfully they just settled on us getting together, straightening our ties and heading out all at once.

WHAT A LOAD OF BOLLOCKS. We had just spent thirty-six hours on a plane; how the hell were we supposed to look? Did they think Shane Warne and Ricky Ponting would be watching us on telly thinking: 'Shit, Hoggy's combed his hair since he got off the plane. We're really in trouble this time!' Or maybe: 'Jeez, did you see the way that Monty Panesar strode through that airport. He must be one hell of a bowler!'

Perhaps it's just me, but when I'm preparing for a Test series in England I don't tend to tune in to watch footage of visiting teams arriving in the country to see how their hair's looking, who's holding hands with who and whether their tie knots are done up straight. If Australia came over to England when they were at their peak and arrived looking slightly scruffy, emerging from the airport in groups of two and three, we would probably have thought: 'God, they look relaxed. They must be really confident.'

What relevance this had to the cricket I do not know. As far as I was concerned, we were there to play a Test series, not to walk through airports. We'd never done anything like that before, so to do it now just seemed to add to all the unnecessary hype.

First impressions were going to count in this series, we were told. Well, we might have looked as pretty as a picture swanning out of the airport, but things turned ugly as soon as the cricket started in Brisbane. I had my own pleasant start to the series when I was told that I wouldn't be taking the first ball, as I normally did for England. It hadn't been discussed at all in the build-up to the game; I was just told by Fred, who was captain, that they wanted to make a statement by letting Harmy bowl the first over, as he had at Lord's in 2005.

It was only the difference of one over, but I just felt that we ought to be confident enough in our normal way of doing things, rather than making special arrangements for the Ashes. I was a bit narked about that, but it wasn't worth getting upset about. Anyway, there was no time to discuss it, I just had to get myself down to fine leg and make sure I was ready to bowl the second over.

As we all know now, Harmy's first ball didn't quite go according to plan and it ended up in Fred's hands at second slip. But hey-ho, it was only one ball; it's not as if it was going to cost us the Ashes. One ball can't make that much difference, can it? Can it really? Would things have really turned out much differently if Harmy hadn't bowled that wide? Well, here's how events would have

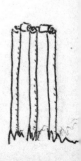

unfolded if, as usual, I had been asked to bowl the first ball of the Ashes:

1. It would have been a boring length ball, outside off stump, Justin Langer would have left it, no run.
2. We would definitely have won the first Test in Brisbane. Easy-peasy.
3. We would have won the Ashes 5–0.
4. Duncan Fletcher would have been knighted.
5. All wars would have ended and the credit crunch would have been averted.

The truth is, of course, that the first ball really only matters a tiny amount. It's a right load of twaddle to say that Harmy's first ball was the moment we lost the Ashes. Yes, it helps if you bowl a good first over, and yes, Harmy's first over at Lord's had made a very different impression, but what happens over the few thousand other balls in the remaining five days of a Test match also has some effect on the outcome. Don't forget that we got stuffed at Lord's in 2005.

Funnily enough, I had been the man asked to make a statement at the start of the previous Ashes tour in 2002. Our first game was a one-day match against an Australian Cricket Board Chairman's XI at Lilac Hill in Perth. Nasser Hussain was captain and he said to me: 'Right, Hoggy, I don't care who the opening batsman is, I want you to bowl a bouncer at him first ball and then go down the wicket to stare at him.'

Erm, right, okay Nass. Chris Rogers was the opening batsman, only a little bloke, so it wasn't hard to bowl a bouncer at him. I dug one in short, he ducked under it, and I went down the wicket a bit to stare at him. And that was it. I thought: 'Right, what happens next? Are we going to win the Ashes now? Or do I have to make another statement next ball?'

You won't be surprised to hear that my dot ball at the beginning of the match had only a slight bearing on future events. The

Aussies didn't run away screaming because that nasty Hoggy had bowled a bouncer. We lost that game in Lilac Hill and went on to lose the Ashes series 4–1. My statement had been conveniently forgotten by that time.

So I hope we've learned our lesson for the next time an England team plays an Ashes series in Australia. I hope they stagger through the airport looking like any other normal people who've just been cooped up in a plane for thirty-six hours. And then, whoever is bowling the first ball, I hope he just runs in, bowls the little red lump of leather at those three wooden things and doesn't think about anything more than that. There'll be five more balls in the over and then a few hundred more to come before any real statement will have been made.

So we were well and truly stuffed in Brisbane, not for the first time. The consolation was that our batsmen performed much better in the second innings, with KP and Colly both making nineties. And this time, at least, we had recent experience of coming back from this sort of defeat to win the series. We were beaten by 277 runs at Brisbane; at Lord's in 2005 we had lost by 239 runs, and then went on to win the next Test. We knew that all was still to play for, we just had to summon the spirit of Edgbaston and try to do the same again in the second Test at Adelaide.

We certainly started the right way. Once again, it was KP and Colly doing their stuff with the bat in a fantastic partnership of 310. Colly got 206, Kev hit 158 and we were able to declare on 551 for six, just to spare the Aussies' bowling figures. Glenn McGrath had taken none for 107, Brett Lee one for 139 and, best of all, Shane Warne had one for 167 and really looked to be showing his age.

We then sneaked a first-innings lead of 38 by bowling Australia out for 513, and the lead might have been bigger but for the odd

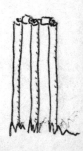

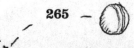

dropped catch here and there. I managed to pick up seven for 109 along the way, which was a highly satisfying performance on a flat wicket. I was chuffed to show what I was capable of in Australia, where I'd struggled four years earlier and shown my inexperience. I had a few more cards to play by now and I bowled pretty well over a tough couple of days.

By the end of the fourth day we had reached 59 for one in our second innings and we were in a strong position. We could afford to see how our batsmen fared before lunch before deciding whether we should declare to set up a push for victory.

But the important thing was that we had shown we were up for a fight again. We'd shown that we could put them under pressure, and that's when they start to struggle. Once Australia get on a roll and their confidence is sky-high they'll start to bully you and they become very, very hard to beat. It takes a massive effort to turn it around and make things even.

It's like having a fight with a big fat lad who knocks you to the floor and then sits on top of you. You've got to force him off before you can even think about throwing any more punches. From that position it takes an awful lot to get yourself back in the fight, so the best thing is not to end up getting squashed in the first place.

By the end of the fourth day at Adelaide it looked as though we would, at worst, come away with a winning draw. We would then take strength from having fought back so strongly and the pressure would be shifting back to the Aussies. They'd be thinking: 'Here we go again. We've got a series on our hands.'

On a personal level, I had been hoping for a nice, quiet start to that last day, putting my feet up after a long hard bowl and maybe loosening up later in the day if we were able to declare. At the start of the first session, I went up onto the roof of the pavilion on my own to watch for a while. The public weren't allowed up there, so it was a nice peaceful place to watch the game. After a while an Aussie bloke came up and tapped me on the shoulder and asked me to be quiet. I wasn't sure what he was on about, but I turned round and saw that I was standing near the effects microphone for the television coverage and apparently, away with the fairies, I'd been merrily singing songs to myself.

That wasn't the only interruption to my nice, quiet morning, because by lunchtime I had my pads on. Not as lunchwatchman, either. There was to be no discussion at lunch about whether we should declare, because 59 for one had suddenly become 89 for five. Warnie was working his magic again and something strange was happening to our batting. Too many batsmen were getting tied down and then trying to score off length balls. Loose shot was followed by loose shot and it's amazing how these things can snowball, with a couple of individual mistakes soon becoming a team problem. Had the pressure got to us? It's impossible to put a finger on the reasons for something like this, but by tea we were all out for 129, which had taken us seventy-three overs. The Aussies then knocked off the runs in the final session and we'd been mugged. How the hell did that happen?

I find it difficult to describe just how pissed off I felt at the end of that day. Put it this way, I don't ever remember feeling as bad after a cricket match in the whole of my career. All that we'd worked towards, all that we'd fought for, had all disappeared into thin air in the space of a few hours. It all just seemed so unnecessary.

After we'd traipsed back to our hotel and dumped our bags, a few of the lads said that they were going out to a Robbie Williams concert in town. I couldn't face that. I was far too hacked off to contemplate going out and trying to have a good time. Which is not to criticise the lads that went to the concert, everybody deals with these things in their own way, but fun wasn't on my agenda that night. Sarah wasn't coming out until we got to Perth for the next Test, so my way of dealing with the disappointment that evening was to stay in the hotel bar with Tony Finch, my mate who was over there as a spectator, and drown my sorrows in a

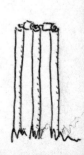

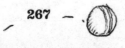

major way. There were plenty of sorrows to be drowned that night.

Sad to say, that really was the series gone. The big fat lad was sitting firmly on top of us now and we were going to get completely and utterly squashed. Who's to say how the series would have gone if we hadn't fallen apart in that second innings at Adelaide? The fact that it ended up 5–0 suggests that there was too much between the teams for it ever to have been a close contest, but you never know. It's funny how the momentum of a game or series can turn once the pressure shifts from one team to another.

So for the last three Tests we were left at the mercy of the Australian crowds to do with us as they pleased. They're never particularly friendly towards the English, as you'd imagine, and when we're getting soundly thrashed they don't offer much in the way of sympathy.

Oh, how we love those Aussie crowds. So cultured. So refined. So polite. And above all, so damn witty. In that series the abuse had begun in Brisbane before a ball had even been bowled in the series. I was the first of the bowlers out on the field to do my warm-ups on the first morning and, within seconds, the cry came from the crowd: 'Oi, Hoggard, Hoggard, Hoggard. You're the worst bowler in facking history, mate.' Nice of him to put the 'mate' on the end; that really softened the blow.

I needn't have taken it personally, because a minute later Jimmy Anderson came out to bowl. 'Oi, Anderson, Anderson, Anderson. You're the worst bowler in facking history, mate.'

Steve Harmison came out shortly afterwards, and you can guess what was said. 'Oi, Harmison, Harmison, Harmison. You're the worst bowler in facking history, mate.'

At the start of the second innings, the same bloke was there again, in the same place, and he'd obviously held a meeting with his scriptwriter in the meantime to update his material. 'Oi, Hoggard, Hoggard. Your mum's on the phone. She says she's sorry she ever had you.'

Then out came Jimmy, whose bowling had gone for a hundred and plenty in the first innings. 'Oi, Anderson, Anderson. I really enjoyed your century, mate. Almost as much as Ponting's.'

With funny guys like that in the crowd, it's a wonder that anyone saw a ball of the cricket at Brisbane. I'd have had tears of laughter[†] streaming constantly down my face if I'd been sitting near him.

There was an instance when one of our players definitely got his own back. Most of the time you just ignore whatever is said, pretend you haven't heard it, but occasionally there is the chance to have a quick word back. I won't identify my team-mate, for obvious reasons, but he was fielding on the boundary and the exchange went something like this.

Aussie in the crowd: 'Oi, Pommie, Pommie. There's only one good thing about you, and that's your wife.'

England player: 'You reckon? You ought to try living with her.'

If you're fielding on the boundary in Australia, you're unlikely to be granted a quiet day. In fact, that's another good reason why we bowlers suffer more than the batsmen. We're the ones dispatched to third man and fine leg to cop the abuse from the crowd, while the darling batsmen chat away and practise their golf swings in the slip cordon.

Anyway, when we went to play at the MCG in the fourth Test of that Ashes series, I was fielding on the boundary at fine leg and a group of spectators behind me suddenly started making a funny noise. It took me a while to work out what they were doing, but it only came when I started moving. Every time I walked in as the bowler was running up to bowl, I'd hear: *'Duh! Duh! Duh!'* in time with each footstep. Then the same thing happened when I turned round and walked back towards the rope between balls. *'Duh! Duh!*

[†]**HOGFACT** In Alabama, it is illegal to wear a false moustache that causes laughter in church. Quite right too.

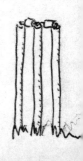

Duh! Duh! Duh!' Even if I just strolled a couple of steps, the noise would follow me: *'Duh! Duh!'* They were clearly dedicated to their task. And then, if I had to run to chase a ball, they'd start really shouting, frantically trying to keep pace: *'DuhDuhDuhDuhDuh-DuhDuhDuhDuhDuh!'*

I think it was supposed to piss me off, but I found it quite funny. Which is unusual for something coming from an Aussie crowd.

Give me the English crowds and the Barmy Army any day. I've always got on really well with the Barmy Army. The players really enjoy the support they give us. They don't stop singing when we're struggling, either. And they sing some very nice songs about me. I found that a bit weird at first, but I soon got used to it. If you're not familiar with them, here are a couple of the best:

KING OF THE SWINGERS
(To the *Jungle Book* tune)

♫ *Now Hoggy's the King of the Swingers, an England VIP,*
He has a bowl, we have a song, the Aussies are out by tea.
Ooh, ooh, oooh, I wanna bowl like you-oo-oo
Don't wanna bat like you, just bowl like you do-oo
Oh yeah, it's true-oo-oo, I wanna bowl like you-oo-oo
Don't wanna bat like you, just bowl like you-oo-oo. ♫ ♪

A bit harsh about the batting, perhaps, but I can forgive them that much. And I would usually respond with a monkey impression, which only seemed fair. Then there was this, to the tune of 'Alouette':

♫ Oh how we love our Yorkshire boy.
Oh how we love our Yorkshire boy.
Your floppy hat
Your straggly hair
Your two cross-eyes
Your loping gait
Your smelly farts
Your knobbly knees
Your pigeon toes
Your swing bowling
Your straight batting
Our hat-trick boy
Our nightwatchman
Ohhhhhh, Matthew Hoggard, Matthew
   Matthew Hoggard (etc.) ♫ ♪

To which I would respectfully doff my cap. Much more pleasant
and refined than all that nonsense spouted by those Aussie oiks,
I'm sure you'll agree. But perhaps my favourite chant dates back
to the early days of my England career, when I used to wear briefs
under my cricket trousers. (Apologies if this is too much detail,
but there is a point to it.) When I was fielding, my pants always
used to go up my bum, so while I was fielding on the boundary I
was constantly having to fish them out, which didn't go unnoticed
in the ranks of the Barmy Army. Ever since, I've been honoured
by the song (to the 'Bread of Heaven' chorus tune that the Welsh
rugby fans sing):

♫ Scratch your ar-arse, Scratch your ar-
   arse,
Scratch your arse and we will cheer (we
   will cheer)
Scratch your ar-arse and we will cheer ♫ ♪

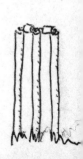

Okay, so perhaps that wasn't so refined and cultured. But it kept me amused on many a lonely afternoon down at fine leg. So thanks for your support, folks.

For players and supporters alike, the Ashes series in Australia in 2006–07 was a long and painful experience. The defeats just kept coming and coming and, once we'd been whipped in Perth and Melbourne, my body decided it had had enough. I missed the fifth Test in Sydney due to an irritating muscle strain around my ribs,[†] so my run of playing forty consecutive Test matches had finally come to an end. If you think back to the state I was in over Christmas in 2003, fretting over my place for the tour to the West Indies, it was pretty remarkable that I then ended up playing in every Test match for the next three years. Sooner or later as a fast bowler, your body is going to ask for a bit of a break.

The funny thing was that I had just turned 30, so there were more than a few jokes coming my way about being over the hill. The ECB were good enough to arrange a very enjoyable 30th birthday party at the Flying Fish restaurant near Sydney Harbour, and as my birthday is New Year's Eve there were plenty of fireworks to help us celebrate. During that Ashes series, any excuse for a bit of light relief was gratefully accepted.

I didn't know it at the time, but by that stage I had already played my last Test match under Duncan Fletcher. He hung on in his position until the World Cup a few months later, and then he was gone.

[†]**HOGFACT** Apparently, one in twenty people is born with an extra rib, that's thirteen instead of twelve. Chinese families often cut theirs out to make the delicacy known as spare ribs. (I made this last bit up.)

It was a strange feeling for me because he had been the coach for the whole of my time as an England player.

Fletch had been a very good coach in terms of technical analysis and planning for games. If you asked him a question, he'd go away and think about it and come back the next day with a detailed answer, rather than saying something to shut you up. That always really impressed me.

As a bloke, you never really knew what he was thinking. He'd sit quietly in the dressing-room, looking from side to side and making notes in his little black book. He had his favourites in the team and, if you weren't one of the chosen few, that could make life hard at times. I was never sure how much he rated me and Troy Cooley told me that Fletch was my biggest detractor in the England set-up. I haven't spoken to him since the end of that Ashes series. We still get a Christmas card, but I think that's more from Marina to Sarah than from Fletch to me.

By the end of that series, Sarah had joined me out in Australia. The pain of the 5–0 defeat and that injury was eased considerably by the three relaxing weeks we spent on holiday in Noosa, up on the Queensland coast, which is a lovely part of the world. It was an exciting time for us, because Sarah was four months pregnant. The Ashes had gone, which from a professional point of view was devastating, but on a personal level I had a lot to look forward to.

273

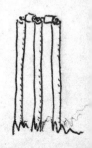

FIVE NOT-SO-GREAT THINGS ABOUT BEING A CRICKETER

BORE DRAWS

So I slogged my guts out for six hours a day, five times in a row, and we still don't know who's won? I can understand how non-cricket folk would be puzzled at that.

OUCH!

Playing in the cold at the beginning of the season: a hard ball against cold hands hurts. And it takes about ten overs to get loose, just as you're getting to the end of your spell.

LONG HAUL

Having to turn up at 9.30 in the morning and not get away until 7.30 for four days in a row. When am I supposed to get my super-market shopping done?

FAST BOWLERS

Putting health and body on the line when you go to the crease. Especially if batting is not your strong point.

NOT BEING A FOOTBALLER

Ninety minutes into the first session of a match, I'll sometimes think: 'Bloody hell, we're still half an hour away from the end of the first of three sessions today, then we've got another three days after this. If I was a footballer, I'd be going home now.'

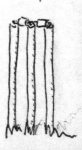

16
Press-ganged

It wasn't all doom and gloom during that complete and utter stuffing the Aussies gave us in the Ashes. The cricket was fairly gloomy, that goes without saying; we just had to be thankful that we weren't playing any more than five Tests. There was some talk of the Aussies introducing a sixth Test match for the next Ashes series down under, which would just be greedy. Then if we lost every match it would look like a tennis score. Sends a shudder down my spine.

Luckily there are always a few lighter moments along the way. You can't just walk around with your bottom lip trailing along the ground for two months. And strangely enough, one of the funniest episodes in Australia was made out by some to be a deadly serious situation. Just goes to show how the world turns against you when you are losing a few cricket matches.

This was the ridonculous situation in Melbourne when our bowling plans were nicked and leaked to the Australian media. We always have a few copies up around our dressing-room, on the walls, in the loos, it's just something to look at if you're having a tough time on the toilet. They could be nicked at any time really, if there was a cleaner who was particularly interested in how Justin Langer played a short ball.

So it wasn't a huge surprise when one of the sheets went missing, but it wasn't a great drama either, really. At Test level these days, most batsmen know what a bowler is trying to do to them, where their weaknesses lie and how the opposition will try to exploit them. They ran something like this. Justin Langer: line off/4th (off stump or imaginary fourth stump line); man on drive at extra cover confuses him; short leg if swing or turn, spin outlet is loft over mid-on. Ricky Ponting: line in the channel outside off stump; tries to impose early with drive – yorker? pulls in front of square in air; fifth slip when first in; cover early on, backward point deeper if set. This sort of thing goes on all the time in international cricket and if you're not aware of your weaknesses you're probably not going to last long at the top level anyway.

But to judge from the reaction you would have thought that someone had stolen a plot to kidnap Dame Edna Everage. Not only were we losing the Ashes, we were losing the plot as well, or so ran the general tone. For some reason I was chosen by the management to do the next press conference, when we were inevitably going to be asked about the leaked bowling plans. Whether they chose me because I was fairly experienced at this sort of thing by now, I'm not sure, but the whole thing seemed a pretty ludicrous situation, so I treated the press conference accordingly.

Andrew Walpole, our press officer, was sitting next to me and he read out a very straight-laced ECB press statement. 'There are seven copies of the team bowling plan which are pinned up in the dressing-rooms and a copy of this plan has ended up in the media's hands, and we are continuing our investigations.'

I was then asked who exactly was conducting our investigations and what the possible punishments would be. 'We are continuing our enquiries, and when we find the culprit we're going to string him up by his ding-dang-doos and chop them off,' I said. 'We've got our finest detectives on the case – Inspector Morse, Sherlock Holmes and Miss Marple.'

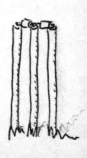

What else was I supposed to say? To my mind, it was a daft situation and it called for a daft response. Now I think about it, there was a very good reason why they chose me for that particular press conference.

A few years earlier I would never have had the confidence to relax like that in front of the press. In my first few years playing international cricket I hated that part of the job. Hated it, absolutely hated it. I always referred to the blokes who worked in the press as a cunch of bunts and I was convinced that they were all out to get us.

Now that I'm older and wiser, I know that this was just my own lack of confidence. When you first come into the England side, press conferences can be an extremely daunting business, extremely nerve-wracking. It's one thing going out onto the field to perform in front of 30,000 people, but that's what you do for a living, that's what you're good at, or at least that's what you're supposed to be good at. Sitting in front of a room of twenty or thirty journalists firing questions at you is something else altogether, especially if you're convinced that they're out to get you. If you say something wrong, or even if you say something that can be taken the wrong way, it can be there for the world and his wife to read in all the newspapers the next morning. When you're starting out, that can be a fairly scary thought, so you really don't want to mess up.

But like anything else, dealing with the press is just a case of going through the whole thing a few times until you get your confidence. I slowly realised that the journos weren't necessarily out to get us, they were just doing their jobs and sometimes that meant writing positive stuff, other times it would be more negative. Just like any other group of people, there were probably a few bunts among them, but on the whole they weren't actually such a bad cunch. Basically, I realised that doing the press was part of my job and I had to make the best of it.

There was one interview in particular that showed how much I hated doing media duties in those early days. It was in New Zealand, during the Christchurch Test when I'd just taken seven wickets, and it was an interview with Pat Murphy for Radio Five Live. Pat was someone that I'd never really seen eye-to-eye with after a misunderstanding we had in a hotel in Pakistan a couple of years earlier. That had been over something and nothing, but the feeling of mistrust seemed to linger between us for quite some time. So, adding that air of tension to my general feelings of suspicion towards the press, this clearly wasn't going to be the jolliest of interviews, even though I'd just taken seven wickets.

Predictably enough, it turned out to be a lot less than jolly. Pat has a tendency to shove his microphone right under your nose and that just irritated me further. In the space of three-and-a-half minutes he asked me 21 questions and I did little more than grunt in response to most of them. Credit to Pat, he kept going, coming up with new questions and trying to keep the interview going, only to get yet another monosyllabic answer. It went out on Five Live as well, so I wouldn't have thought I came across as the world's most intelligent person during that particular piece of radio.

Pat and I settled our differences not long afterwards, had a few drinks together and we've got on well ever since. He told me a while later that our painful encounter in Christchurch had ended up being used during BBC training sessions on interviewing techniques, serving as an example of how to deal with a difficult interviewee. So at least some good may have come of my grunting.

As time went on, this part of the job became much less daunting once I had grown accustomed to dealing with the media and developed my confidence. When I was being interviewed, whereas I used to try to answer whatever questions I was asked (unless I

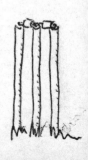

was in grunting mode), I gradually realised that if I thought a question was stupid or repetitive there was no harm in saying so. There are some questions that I have been asked time and time and time again.

'So Matthew, how does it feel to be the most experienced member of England's attack?'

To which the response should be: 'It's 2007 now and you've been asking me that question since 2004, so if you look back through your notes you'll find your answer there. And when you've finished doing that, will you please get a new question!'

To look after the players and hold our hands during our media duties, we have an ECB press officer who is with the team at all times. Before a press conference or an interview on radio or television, our press officer will make sure that we are happy with whatever we're going to talk about. Most of the time it will just be about cricket, which is unlikely to be particularly complicated. But if there are any controversial or sensitive issues that are likely to crop up, they will brief us beforehand. The trickiest situations arise when there is a bit of politics involved, such as whether we were going to fulfil our tour to India shortly after the 9/11 bombings. In those cases it will always be an experienced player who is chosen to face the media and our press officer will say beforehand: 'These are the areas to be careful of. This is our stance on such-and-such an issue. And if you're asked about the politics, just say "no comment".' They'll then come and sit in the press conference with us, and if the press try to overstep the mark they can just say: 'You don't need to answer that one, Hoggy.'

Our main press officer for most of my time in the England team has been Andrew Walpole. He's a decent bloke, Wally, but it's a pretty thankless task being our media man, coming into the dressing-room at the end of a day's play to tell us who would be made available for interview that evening. It's a bit like being a fitness trainer: he always has to make people do stuff that they would rather not do.

In those circumstances he is an inevitable target for abuse, and I'm slightly ashamed to say that I handed out a lot of stick to Walpole. For a couple of years around the middle of my career, whenever he walked into the room, whatever the circumstances, I would shout: 'F*** off, Walpole!' It might have been half an hour into a day's play and he would just have come into the dressing-room to say hello, and he'd get: 'F*** off, Walpole!' Or he could have been stepping onto the team bus at the end of a day's play. 'F*** off, Walpole!'

Wally used to hate me, and I'm not really surprised. Most of the time he treated my abuse with the contempt it deserved. Other times he got the hump. There was one time in particular when he flipped and said: 'Just piss off, you misanthropic moron!'

'Pardon?'

'I said piss off, you misanthropic moron.'

'Wally,' I said, 'I'm sure I'd be offended by what you've just called me if I had the faintest idea what it meant.'

So he explained it to me, and now I know what it means. I came out of that little exchange a slightly wiser man, having increased my vocabulary by one fairly long word. I can't say I've used it too often, but I'm sure I will do some time. Maybe when I get some idiot shouting 'F*** off, Hoggard' every time I walk into a room.

As well as having Wally and his cohort of press officers to help us in our encounters with the press, England players are also given fairly comprehensive media training. Most counties will offer some sort of training as well to their younger players these days because, as I've mentioned, it can be a daunting part of the job early in your career. Much of the training is fairly straightforward stuff about making sure you engage your brain before opening your mouth.

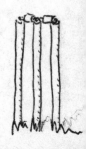

But it also gives you the opportunity to practise interviews in a mock-up situation in a closed environment, free of the threat that if you say something wrong your mistakes will be there for everyone to see in the papers the next day.

The trouble is that in those role-play situations it can be hard to take things seriously. In one of my first media training sessions I did a mock interview where I was asked how I was feeling after taking five wickets. 'Yes, it was a good day, the ball swung for me, I got a few nicks and the lads in the slips took some **ORGASMIC**† catches.' That is not the sort of answer that would go down particularly well on live television, a few hours before the watershed, while people are trying to have their tea.

We also did a role-play a couple of years ago in which we were taught how to deal with doorstepping. I'm sure most people will have seen examples of this on the telly, but for those not familiar, it's a tactic used by some of the less respectable media outlets where they camp outside somebody's house. When the person in question emerges from their house, they do so to a barrage of questions about whatever scrape they may (or may not) have got themselves into.

There were eight people in our group for this role-play, so when I was playing the hunted party, there were seven others acting as the crowd of journalists. Ottis Gibson, the bowling coach, was one of them, and Jimmy Anderson was another. The advice we had been given was that we could either blank the reporters completely, act really cheerful as though nothing had happened, or deny all knowledge of the situation. My task was to get from one door to another with those seven reporters scuffling around me. 'Could you get out of my way, please? I'd just like to get to my car, please.

---

†**HOGFACT:** In Connorsville, Wisconsin, a man shall not shoot his gun while his female partner is having an orgasm. So if you were planning to rob his house, that might be a good time to do it.

Excuse me, excuse me. Yes, yes, my wife and I are very happy. No, no further comments. Thank you. Bye.'

I actually found it quite a scary prospect. If this was happening for real, and you really had got yourself into a sticky situation of some sort, you'd be feeling pretty pissed off anyway. And then you get all these twats shoving cameras and microphones in your face, jostling you as you came out of your front door, and maybe standing in front of your car so you couldn't get in. I think I'd be hard pressed not to give them a good clout. I'd be with Prince Harry on that one.

Thankfully cricketers don't attract much of that sort of attention from the press. And you generally have to do something wrong to end up in a situation like that, so I've never had to worry about it. I've also got a big Doberman at home who would be happy to help if I needed him. Never mind all that media training, all I'd need would be two words: 'Billy, attack!'

So with all the help we get from training and from press officers, we really ought to be able to carry out our media duties without putting a foot wrong. Every word carefully chosen, every comment perfectly judged. Oh, if only it was that simple. I'm afraid to say that there have still been times when I've got myself into trouble for speaking out of turn in an interview. Often, the problem was that I had been too honest. If I admitted in a press conference that I hadn't bowled well, I would be told by the press officer that it sounded too negative. But I didn't want to be seen to be making excuses. If I'd bowled like a trollop, I'd be happy to say so.

I got into bother with Fletch once for something I said in a press conference. This was shortly after Andrew Strauss made his debut in 2004, having come into the side for the first Test against New Zealand at Lord's when Michael Vaughan was injured. Straussy

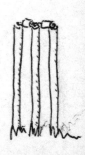

had scored a load of runs opening the batting and so created a problem for the selectors for the next Test, when Vaughany was due to return.

I did a press conference in the meantime and was asked my opinion whether I thought Straussy should stay in the side as an opening batsman, which was where Vaughany had been batting, or whether he should be accommodated elsewhere in the order. I said: 'I think he's going to have to wait his turn. He played really well at Lord's, but Vaughany has been doing a great job opening the innings. He had to wait his turn when he came into the side before he was promoted to open, so Straussy might have to bat down the order for a bit.'

When those comments appeared in the papers the next day, Fletch had a right old go at me. 'Excuse me, Hoggy, but since when were you a selector?' he said. 'You're going to make us look idiots now when we pick Straussy to open the batting and Vaughany drops down the order. In future, it would be better if you could keep your opinions to yourself.'

Oops. Time to wear that dunce's hat again, Hoggard.

That business of engaging brain[†] before opening mouth is not always as straightforward as it seems. One time you do have to be really careful is when you're coming off at the end of a long day in the field and you're asked for an interview live on telly. Now those interviews can be bloody annoying. If you've been bowling all day, you're hurting by the close, and you're just looking forward to getting back in the dressing-room for a nice sit down. Then you see someone walking towards you with a microphone, and think: 'Uh-oh, I've got to think of something to say.' And you're hot and sweaty and you're brain's feeling all fuzzy and you've all of a sudden

---

[†]**HOGFACT:** The human brain is capable of recording over 86 million bits of information daily. In my case, that will include at least 85 million bits of completely useless information.

got to try to concentrate and do a bit more than grunt into the camera. In those situations, it's advisable not to try to say anything too complicated, or to use long words that you don't know the meaning of (like misanthropic). Just stick to **THE CAT SAT ON THE MAT**.

If you've only had a short session in the field, or you've bowled the opposition out and you're coming off on a high, you don't tend to mind those interviews in the slightest. They can often be quite a laugh. During one televised game we were playing for Yorkshire, Sky wanted to interview Steve Kirby, our fast bowler, at the end of an innings. Kirbs was quite new on the scene and he was due to be interviewed by David Lloyd, or 'Bumble', as everyone knows him. Everyone, that is, except Kirbs. He didn't know what Mr Lloyd's nickname was, so we told him it was 'Womble'. So the interview began:

'Well bowled, Steve, you must be really pleased with that performance.'

'Yeah, thanks very much, Womble, it went quite well.'

'Pardon? Did you just call me Womble?'

'Erm, yes ...'

Poor old Kirbs. He fell hook, line and sinker for that. I think Bumble was highly amused.

Most of the time, the television people usually try to pick someone who's done well and has something nice to talk about. But there are times when everybody has been smashed around the park, nobody has done particularly well, and you just hope that the microphone doesn't come your way when you're wandering off the field.

Other than that, I don't generally mind doing telly at all. When there's just you, the interviewer and the cameraman, it's much less nerve-wracking than sitting in front of a room of thirty journalists. And now that every former England captain seems to be going and working for Sky, it can be quite funny doing an interview with a former team-mate. I remember when Nasser Hussain retired

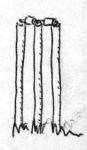

and went straight over to Sky, I had the honour of being one of his first interviewees. So of course I helped him out in the best way I could: by ripping the piss out of him.

We were standing out on the field, waiting around for Nass to get the word in his ear that we were ready to go live on air. It was taking some time, so I took the opportunity to offer Nass a few calming words: 'I know you're new at this telly lark, Nass, but try not to be nervous. A lot of people are going to be watching and seeing how you do with this, so you mustn't f*** it up. I know you're nervous, but try hard not to stutter. Don't swear, don't bodge up your questions, don't ...'

'And I'm joined here on the outfield by Matthew Hoggard. Matthew, well bowled today ...'

I like chatting to Nass on the telly, it's just speaking to a mate for me. He's the one that has to be all professional and sensible, and I can be as silly as I like. And for the record, I was actually quite nice to him once the interview actually started. When it was time to bring it to a close, he'd clearly been told to be careful to use a player's proper name, rather than a nickname, for fear of sounding too chummy. But he almost forgot himself, nearly called me Hoggy and ended up saying: 'Thank you very much Hoggard.'

'It's quite all right, Hoo-sain,' I said.

There was another time, though, when he wasn't too happy with me. We were supposed to be doing an interview before play at some unpleasant time like 9.15 in the morning. I had said that I didn't want to do it at that time. I can barely communicate with my wife at that time in the morning, let alone millions of people watching on telly. But they made me do it anyway (F*** off, Walpole), and I reluctantly arrived for the interview at about 9.45. It was a very cold day and Nasser had been waiting for me, standing outside in just his light blue, short-sleeved Sky Sports shirt.

The man wasn't happy. 'Nice of you to turn up, Hoggy. It's f***ing freezing here I've been standing here ages waiting for you to get your arse out of bed. Where the hell have you been? Piss poor effort, this. Piss poor.' I was tempted to turn round and walk off. But I hung around because it's always funny listening to Nass have a good rant. He was still ranting at me about ten seconds before we went on air.

While he was interviewing me, I couldn't help but notice that his lips were turning blue. I was trying to listen to what he was asking me, but all I could think was: 'You really must have been a bit chilly, Nass. Your lips are turning blue.' Poor old Nass, I almost felt sorry for him. Still, there was something strangely reassuring about knowing that he was still capable of giving me an almighty bollocking even though he wasn't my captain any more. I imagine that I'll be able to bump into him in thirty years' time, hobbling round some cricket ground with a walking stick, and Nass will still be coming up and giving me a bollocking for some reason or other. Good to see that some things will never change.

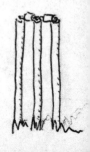

HARDEST HITTERS

ADAM GILCHRIST (AUSTRALIA)

Hit me for some of the biggest sixes of my life, including a monster back over my head at Trent Bridge in 2005.

CHRIS GAYLE (WEST INDIES)

He's a big lad and not many of his innings are dull; there are usually a couple of big blows to keep the crowd entertained.

M.S. DHONI (INDIA)

Now he does bash it, often straight back at you. I once had the pleasure of being hit in the neck by one of his straight drives in my follow-through.

NATHAN ASTLE (NEW ZEALAND)

One day in Christchurch in 2001, he hit the ball a very long way, very many times. We got stiff necks that day watching the ball go out of the ground.

YUVRAJ SINGH (INDIA)

When he hits the ball, it stays hit. Big backlift and big follow-through, he gives the ball some serious licks.

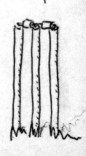

Tuna mayo.

17
It's all Gone Haywire

For most of my cricketing career, I have bobbed along on a fairly even keel. There were a few spectacular moments along the way – Barbados, Jo'burg, Trent Bridge – and a few low times as well. That's just the way it is in sport, but mostly I have managed to fulfil my unspectacular role as the bloke sweeping up on the factory floor, grafting away enjoying my job, steady as she goes. That all changed after the 5–0 Ashes defeat in Australia and, from the start of the 2007 summer onwards, everything started to go haywire. Within the space of a year and a bit I was to experience the happiest and saddest times of my life.

It was always likely to be a time of change from both the personal and professional points of view. On the cricket field, the England team were about to enter the first stages of life after Duncan Fletcher. At home, more importantly, Sarah was not too far away from being ready to give birth, so our lives really were about to change for ever.

The little 'un was due to arrive in May, neatly scheduled between the first two Tests of the summer against West Indies, which were back-to-back games at Lord's and Headingley in May. The plan was that if he arrived early, while I was playing down in London,

I would have to miss the birth. But once the first Test had finished, I'd be back up at home for the couple of days between the games, then playing in the second Test at Headingley, which was only a ten-minute drive from Leeds General Infirmary, where the big event was due to take place.

If Sarah went into labour[†] while we were batting at Heading-ley, I would be allowed to leave the ground, as long as I wasn't at the crease (which is never for long anyway). And I wouldn't have been the first Yorkshireman to make a hasty departure in the middle of a Headingley Test match for these reasons, because Michael Vaughan had done so three years earlier. It would have been uncanny if Sarah and Nichola Vaughan, who are best mates, had both managed to give birth when their husbands were play-ing just down the road.

If we were bowling at Headingley, the plan was that I would have to stick it out for the day, stay on the field and then go along to meet the new arrival in the evening.

After a side injury had broken my run of forty consecutive Tests in Sydney, I was back in the side for the first Test at Lord's. I'd taken a hatful of wickets for Yorkshire in the first few matches of the County Championship and I was feeling in great nick. We batted first at Lord's and I spent Thursday and Friday with my feet up, watching our batsmen cruise their way to 553 for five, with centuries from Alastair Cook, Paul Collingwood, Ian Bell and Matt Prior, on his debut. I spoke to Sarah on the Friday evening, just before I went out for a meal. She said that she was feeling tired and that she'd be going to bed early, so we arranged to speak again in the morning. In actual fact, she had gone into labour and would shortly be driving to hospital, but she knew that I would be

---

[†]**HOGFACT:** A female mosquito can produce 3,000 offspring in a six-week life cycle. No wonder they don't last for long. How do you cope with that many kids?

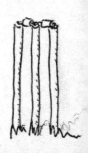

bowling the next morning, so didn't want me to be worrying all night.

I did indeed sleep soundly in my hotel bed that night, having left my mobile phone on silent. The next morning I was disturbed about 7.30 a.m. by the landline ringing in my room. Because my mobile was still on silent, Sarah was having to ring through via reception.

'Are you not even going to leave your phone on for me then?' she said.

'It is on, it's just on silent,' I replied. 'Why? You're not going into labour, are you?'

'Not at the moment, no.'

'Well, what's up then?'

'He's here, Matthew. He's already here.'

At which point I started crying like a baby myself. Our son had arrived at 3.37 that morning, 19 May, and everything had gone okay. I was a daddy to a little boy. Wow. It takes a while for that sort of thing to sink in. He was either going to be called Henry or Ernie.

'We're definitely going to call him Ernie,' Sarah said. 'He definitely looks like an Ernie.'

'Why? Has he got Ernie tattooed on his arse?'

'Yes, he has.'

'And has he got "Made in Taiwan" on the other cheek?'

'Yes, how did you know?'

Once I'd put the phone down, I just sat there in shock for a few minutes. I then remembered that I had a Test match to play, so I tried to pull myself together, got dressed and went downstairs to try to have a bit of breakfast. Even if I didn't eat anything, at least it would give me something to do. The first people I saw on my way downstairs were Andrew and Ruth Strauss. I started trying to tell them my little piece of news, and promptly burst into floods of tears again. I did a lot of crying that day, soft sod that I am.

Whether or not this state of emotional upheaval affected me a few hours later when I was bowling, I can't be sure. When I bowled

the first ball of my eleventh over that morning, just before lunch, I felt a yanking pain in my groin and had to go off the field to get some treatment. Perhaps my body was coming out in sympathy with Sarah for all the pain she'd gone through that night. I expected the pain to have gone when I woke up after a night's sleep, as is often the case with these things, but it was no better on Sunday morning.

When I told Sarah about my groin, she didn't know whether to believe me or not. 'Are you really injured, or are you pulling a fast one so you can come up to see Ernie?' she asked. She knew me better than that really, but the injury did provide me with an unplanned opportunity for a quick getaway from Lord's. When it became clear on Sunday that I wasn't going to be able to bowl in the second innings, I asked Straussy, who was captain, whether I could shoot off. We were still batting in our second innings at the time, looking to set up a declaration after building on our first-

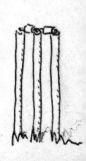

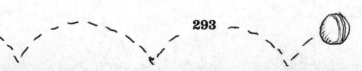

innings lead of 116, so Straussy initially asked me to hang on, just in case we needed a few extra runs.

A short while later he came back to me and said: 'We've had another think about it, Hoggy. You can pack your bags and go.' I'm not sure if it's the effect that Straussy has on me or what, but suddenly the waterworks started again and I found myself blubbing in the middle of the England dressing-room at Lord's. For God's sake, what was happening to me? If I was like this before I'd even seen the little blighter, what was I going to be like when I actually met him? Or, more worryingly, when I was left looking after him?

As quickly as I could, I started to pack my bags and get changed out of my cricket gear. While I was getting dressed, Kirk Russell, our eagle-eyed physio, noticed that I hadn't put a Tubigrip bandage on my injured thigh, and was going to suggest that I put it on for the drive home. In return I just gave him a killer stare, and said: 'Don't even think about it.' I wanted to get home as fast as I could and I wasn't about to get undressed and dressed again just for the sake of some poxy bandage. A few days later Kirk said to me: 'Sorry, Hoggy, I think I might have misread that situation.'

Before long I was on the M1, trying to break the world land speed record on my way back up to Yorkshire, while at the same time reminding myself to be careful, because I was now supposed to be a grown-up who was responsible for a small person as well as my big ugly self.

By the time that I arrived that Sunday evening Sarah and Ernie were back at home. Colin and Carole, Sarah's parents, had been there as well to help out, but they made themselves scarce when I drove through the gates. Sarah opened the door with Ernie in her arms, I gave her a hug, then took hold of Ernie. I expected the waterworks to kick in again at this point, but there were no tears at all. I'd been crying on and off for the last twenty-four hours, but now there was nothing. Why wasn't I crying now? Was there something wrong with me? We went inside, I sat down with Ernie and gazed at him for a while, then came that feeling that every new parent must get. Right, here he is. What do we do with him now?

A couple of hours later Sarah was upstairs feeding Ernie in the bedroom. I wandered upstairs too and when I poked my head round the door to see them, all of a sudden the floodgates opened again, completely without warning. There I was, bawling again. Strange thing, a bloke's waterworks. I'm not sure who controls them, but it certainly doesn't seem to be me.

That groin injury I picked up at Lord's was the latest in a series of irritating injuries that were starting to interfere with my bowling. These things go with the territory as a fast bowler, but I'd been free of injuries for so long that it was frustrating now to be picking up all sorts of strange niggles. Was it because I was over 30? Was it the responsibilities of fatherhood taking their toll? Or was it all the fault of Peter Moores?

The Lord's Test against West Indies was Mooresy's first as coach of the senior England team, having been named as Fletch's successor. But it wasn't the first time that I'd been injured in a game when he was my coach. In fact, up to this point, every time I'd been involved in a game with Peter Moores I'd picked up an injury. It was uncanny. The previous year I'd played for England A against Pakistan at Canterbury, with Mooresy as our coach, and I came a cropper before I'd even bowled a ball when Tim Bresnan kicked my hand during a pre-match game of football.

Then, in the first game of the 2007 season, Mooresy was in charge again when I played for MCC at Lord's. That time I dropped a catch and hurt my finger. So the groin injury completed an unwanted hat-trick of accidents in my first three games with the new England coach. It was beginning to look as though we were jinxed.

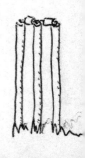

The injuries didn't stop there, either. I made a brief comeback for the fourth Test against West Indies at Chester-le-Street, but then started suffering from a back injury that ruled me out of the whole series against India in the second half of the summer. It just showed how lucky I'd been to stay fit for those forty consecutive Test matches. Four would have been nice at this stage.

The back problem had eased by the end of the summer and I managed to stay out of trouble for the first couple of weeks of our tour to Sri Lanka in November, but only just. I had a decidedly hairy moment in our first warm-up game, against a President's XI in Colombo, when I tried to introduce myself to a local snake that was lurking just beyond the boundary while we were fielding. He was green, about six feet long and looked friendly enough. Some of the local spectators were shouting 'Naya, naya', their term for a cobra. I've always fancied myself as a bit of a Steve Irwin type, so I picked him up by his tail to say hello. I'm not sure if he didn't speak English or he just wasn't in the mood, but he didn't say hello back, and he looked as though he was going to try and bite me, so I quickly plonked him back down and legged it back onto the field. If I was becoming increasingly accident-prone, as seemed to be the case, perhaps I should have been trying a little harder to stay out of trouble.

Perhaps the strangest injury of the lot started to bother me during the first Test match in Kandy. I'd bowled really well in the first innings, taking four for 29 as we shot them out for 188. Towards the end of that innings I felt a shooting pain going from my back right round to my belly-button. It only happened a few times, but it was incredibly painful and felt like I'd wrenched every muscle around my stomach. Every time I really put everything into a delivery, it would hurt, and in the second innings I had to bowl within myself. I still picked up a couple of wickets but Sri Lanka scored 442 for eight and then skittled us out for 261 in the last innings to win the match.

We still didn't know what the problem was with my stomach, but it wouldn't go away. Other than it being something to do with my spine, we never found out exactly what the problem was. I missed the second Test in Colombo, which was drawn on a flat wicket (no, I wasn't suffering from flatwicketitis again). I then returned for the third Test in Galle, but the stomach problem was still bothering me occasionally. It wasn't the only thing on my mind, either, because my granddad had died two days before the game.

We needed to win the third Test to square the series, but we performed abysmally. Even though the wicket was offering plenty of assistance, we let their batsmen score 499 for eight. We all bowled poorly, myself included. A late call had been made on whether I should play in that game, but I was fit to play, so I had no excuses. The shooting pain came back two or three times, like someone was stabbing me in the stomach as I bowled, but by the time I had walked back past the umpire it would have gone completely.

Looking back, though, I'm not sure whether you can ever really put that sort of thing out of your mind. I'll repeat that it wasn't an excuse for a poor performance, but I wonder whether it meant that I was bowling within myself more than usual.

Whatever the reasons, I bowled crap, so did everyone else, and then we were bowled out for 81, so it was a poor effort all round. Chaminda Vaas bowled as we should have done, making the most of some helpful conditions, and our chances of drawing the series had gone. We salvaged a draw thanks to the rain, but that was little consolation. That had not been a good Test match, or a good series. And when we got to New Zealand after Christmas, things were about to get much worse.

From the tour to New Zealand in 2002, when I was just making my way in international cricket, I had nothing but happy memories of the place. It's one of the most beautiful countries on the planet, the people are great, they love their rugby, they love the

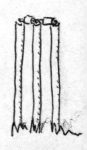

outdoors. For a seam and swing bowler, the pitches are often help-ful, as close to English conditions as you'll get, and I'd had a good tour there first time round. All of which suggests that I should have had an enjoyable six weeks or so on tour there from Febru-ary to March in 2008. Unfortunately, nothing could have been further from the truth.

It all started with a dodgy tuna sandwich, which gave me rotten guts during a warm-up game in Dunedin. Apologies for the detail, but I was feeling so rough that I actually had to dash from the field to throw up into a big oil drum. Pity the poor spectators who were sitting nearby. Other than that, I performed reasonably well in the two warm-up games in Dunedin, taking three for 30-odd in the first game and one for not too many in the second, so I wasn't bowling too badly in the build-up to the first Test in Hamilton. But there was a lot more going on in my mind at that time than bowling a cricket ball.

The background to this is that Sarah and I had been having prob-lems at home. Sarah had not been at all well. She had been suffer-ing with depression for some time before we had Ernie, then she got post-natal depression on top of that, which hit the poor girl as an awful double whammy. I hadn't been coping with that partic-ularly well, and when I left for New Zealand things weren't right between us and Sarah's depression was getting worse. Inevitably, we were unable to make any progress while I was away. Problems like that aren't easy to solve over the phone from the other side of the world.

During the first Test, Sarah was due to fly out with Ernie and her parents to join me in New Zealand. In her condition, that was the last thing in the world that she wanted. She got to Heathrow airport with her parents, and when she got to the check-in desk she said that she didn't want to get on the plane. In the end, she was pretty much forced onto the flight by her parents, who said that Ernie needed to see me, I needed to see her, and that she really had to go to New Zealand.

Meanwhile, I was playing in the first Test in Hamilton and bowling like a wet lettuce. My figures from the first innings there pretty much tell the story: 26–2–111–1. I should thank Jacob Oram for giving me one wicket by edging a wayward drive to gully. That dismissal was certainly more his doing than mine.

Before the game, I'd thought that playing a Test match would help to take my mind off my problems away from the cricket. If there had ever been anything in my life that I'd wanted to get away from, I'd always been able to lose myself in the contest of a cricket match. But all of a sudden, when I was walking back to my mark one time at Hamilton, it all just hit me. As I got back towards the end of my run-up, I felt as though I wanted to cry. Remember what I said about the mysterious functioning of a bloke's water-works? Well, somebody was trying to turn them on for me again, this time in the middle of a Test match.

As I stood by my marker, I turned to Michael Vaughan, who was standing at mid-off, and said: 'Vaughany, I think I'm going cuckoo, I'm doing a Tres.' This was a reference to Marcus Trescothick, who had broken down with depression not so long before. I'm not sure what Vaughany thought of that, but at the time it was true. The only previous time I'd felt like crying while playing sport was when my dad hit me in the chops with a hard ball, or we were playing football and I couldn't get the ball off him. This time it just came out of the blue.

Anyway, I fought back the tears and kept on bowling. What else are you supposed to do when you're live on television? New Zealand scored 470, then bowled us out for 348. In their second innings I didn't take any more wickets, but I felt that my bowling had improved. I was more myself and my rhythm was coming back. New Zealand declared on 177 for nine before bowling us out for 110 to win by 189 runs. By that time, everybody in our team must have felt like crying.

Despite everything that had been going on between me and Sarah, I was really looking forward to seeing her and Ernie when

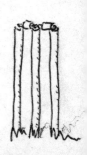

299

we moved on to Wellington. I suppose I was just hoping that the chance to get our heads together for a while, spending some time away from home, would somehow miraculously make everything all right. But I was underestimating the extent of Sarah's illness, not for the first time and not for the last.

Brave as ever, Sarah managed to put on a happy face in public for the next couple of weeks. But privately she was really suffering and, as anyone who has suffered from depression will know, that can affect everything.

And then, joy of joys, to add to our problems, two days after Sarah had arrived, I was dropped for the second Test. They say that bad things happen in threes. They seemed to be happening in thirty-threes on that tour. Although I knew I'd bowled poorly in the first innings at Hamilton, this still came as quite a shock. I'd been bowling pretty well since, especially in the nets in Wellington, where I had an encouraging chat with Peter Moores. He said I was looking fit, the bowling was looking good and the coaches felt I was hitting the gloves hard. And Wellington would be a much different pitch to the slow surface at Hamilton, much more suited to swing bowling. I was desperate to rectify my performance from the previous Test.

But while I was sitting in the players' gallery at Wellington, looking through some videos from that Hamilton game, Michael Vaughan and Peter Moores came up to me and told me that I wouldn't be playing. They said they wanted to go for the bit of extra pace that Jimmy Anderson would give them. Harmy had been dropped as well, and they were bringing in Stuart Broad. They won the Test and Jimmy got five wickets in the first innings, and good for him, he's had more than his share of disappointments in his career. But it hurt like mad to be ditched by England. It was the first time I'd been dropped since the tour to Sri Lanka in 2003 and it didn't hurt any less for having another 200 Test wickets under my belt.

So why was I dropped? Did my comment to Vaughany about going cuckoo make him doubt my ability to deliver in the next game? I wouldn't be at all surprised if it did. I've never asked him, because that wouldn't be fair, but I'm sure it didn't help my cause. But my personal hunch is that there was an agenda, from Peter Moores in particular, to move out the old guard and bring in the new. There was an opportunity to get rid of both me and Harmy and it was swiftly taken, even though the batsmen had just been bowled out for 110. The fact that Vaughany was no longer captain by the end of the next summer may have had something to do with that agenda as well.

Why were they so keen to get rid of us? I really don't know. England won that series in New Zealand, but has it paid off in the long run? That's not really for me to say. Nobody, absolutely nobody, has a right to a place in the England side, and I never took my place for granted. But from a purely personal point of view, it felt extremely harsh to be binned after one bad Test, maybe two if you take in Galle as well. Mooresy said to me that if I didn't want to come into the dressing-room and do twelfth man duties for that game in Wellington, I didn't have to. Nice thought, but how would that have looked to the rest of the lads? It wouldn't have looked good, not good at all.

Once I had been dropped, Sarah begged and pleaded with me to go home. She wasn't getting any better, and for the sake of her health she wanted to be back in England. We had always put my cricket first and she had fitted in with that, now she wanted me to give a bit back, especially if I wasn't going to be playing in the last two Tests.

But I didn't want to go. I didn't want it to look as though I was taking my bat and ball home as soon as I'd been dropped. I'm not a quitter, so I wanted to stick it out. I didn't want to run away and hide. I wanted to stay and fight for my place.

When it came to the third and final Test in Napier and I wasn't playing again, Sarah pleaded again for us to leave. By this stage I didn't think another five days would make such a big difference, so I thought we may as well see the last week through. But in the middle

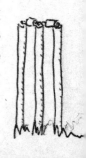

of that Test in Napier we had a horrendous falling-out. Sarah fell out with her mum and dad, the two of us fell out with each other. I stormed out of the hotel and wandered off down the street.

When I came back, Sarah said that I'd done things on this tour that she never thought I would do. I'd failed to back her up when she needed me the most, and it was making her question our marriage. We needed to go home and evaluate where we stood, she said, because we needed to see whether our marriage was broken, or whether it could be fixed.

Shit. It had come to this. I was in danger of losing everything. As soon as I was on the plane home, and I was away from the cricket circus, I suddenly realised just how tough things had been for Sarah. I hadn't really understood before, or at least I hadn't allowed myself to understand. I'd been on the other side of the world while things were getting worse for her at home, and since she'd been in New Zealand I'd been too preoccupied to appreciate the serious-ness of the situation. Believe me, if I'd realised, I would have been on the first plane home.

Depression is a very difficult disease to understand, and it took me some time. In many people's eyes, Sarah has the life of Riley. She doesn't have to work, she has a nice house, nice car, she's got enough money, a lovely son and we go on nice holidays. But all this means nothing if you're not happy deep down. And depression makes being happy very, very hard at times.

When she said she needed to go home, I should have backed her up straight away and said that, whatever it took to get her better, we would do it. To the England team I could just have said, 'Sorry, lads, I need to go home. My family is more important.'

Instead, I let my pride, my ego, my Yorkshire bloodyminded-ness – whatever it might have been – get in the way and rule my brain. It was my job, that was all. It might have been playing for England, it might have been fulfilling a childhood dream. But if the person you love and have married, the mother of your child, says, 'I'm not well and I really need to go home,' it shouldn't be a difficult choice. But I chose cricket. *It's a f***ing game.* And I put a game before my wife and my marriage and my family.

With hindsight, I should have realised that people in the England team and beyond know me well enough to understand that I wasn't the sort of person to run away, just because I'd been dropped. I'd played international cricket for seven years, and by that stage I should have felt secure enough in myself to do that. But in actual fact I had never really felt secure in the England team, not even when I was playing forty consecutive Tests. Still, I should have been big enough to say: 'Look, this is what I need to do. I've got to go home.'

If I could turn back time, that is something I would change instantly. I would have gone as soon as Sarah wanted. But I'm hopeless at talking about this sort of thing and I suppose I was just hoping it would be swept under the carpet. There are some things that are too big to be swept under the carpet. Depression is one of them.

As you would imagine, the pieces from that car-crash of a cricket tour took some time to pick up once we got home. Illnesses like that take time to heal and Sarah was still in a bad way, blaming herself for everything that had happened, and I was starting to suffer as well. It didn't help either of us that there were only a few weeks between us arriving home and the county cricket season starting again. At that time, I wanted to play for Yorkshire like I wanted a hole in the head.

For the first three months of the 2008 season I was nowhere near a cricket field. I might have been standing on a cricket field, I might have been playing cricket, but in my mind I was nowhere near the game. After a while I asked Yorkshire if I could be excused from one-day games because I needed to save my marriage. Thankfully, they agreed. I played in the Twenty20 Cup

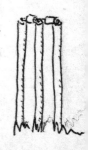

games in June, but otherwise I stuck to four-day championship cricket.

When I was playing for those few months, I was just going through the motions. The funny thing was this was a time when everybody was wondering whether I would get my England place back. In public I had to say that I was keen to get back in the England side, and in theory that was true, but in fact I was extremely relieved that I didn't get recalled. I had actually been picked in the squad for the first Test of the summer, against New Zealand at Lord's, but I was released on the first morning and that was a good job, because playing for England wouldn't have been a good idea at the time. I was ruled out of the next couple of Tests anyway when Steve Harmison broke my thumb[†] while I was batting for Yorkshire against Durham.

For Yorkshire, I was getting through games but little more than that. I felt as though I was acting most of the time. My figures weren't fantastic, but I was doing enough. I took a reasonable amount of wickets, but I'd have taken a lot more if my heart had been in it. There's a difference between running in, putting your back into your bowling and trying to hit the keeper's gloves hard, and jogging in, turning your arm over and knowing that the ball will end up there or thereabouts. That in itself shows what a state I was in, because I have never, never, never given less than my all in a competitive game before or since. But at that time I couldn't have cared less.

Away from the field, while we were batting, I did a lot of work on my own batting against a bowling machine fed by Martyn Moxon, the Yorkshire coach, and that was something I really enjoyed. It felt like a real release, much better than sitting in a

---

[†]**HOGFACT:** The middle fingernail on each hand grows the fastest. The THUMB-nail grows the slowest. Mine grew even slower after Harmy had hit it, the lanky git.

room full of people when I wasn't in the right frame of mind for small talk or banter. I could just stand in a net on my own and smash a few balls.

The real low point came in early July when, in the space of three days, we had two important one-day games, both of which I'd agreed to play in. The first was the semi-final of the Friends Provident Trophy against Essex at Chelmsford, when I didn't turn up. Well, I played, and I bowled six overs for 41 runs, but I wasn't really on the park. Two days later we had a quarter-final of the Twenty20 Cup against Durham at the Riverside, but Goughie knew how things were going for me, so did Martyn Moxon, and they decided not to take me up to Chester-le-Street. I'm sure that was the right decision, but I was unable to see that at the time and it just made me feel like a complete and utter failure.

I was in tears on the living room floor at home. Sarah was telling me to pull myself together, to start fighting again and to do what I wanted to do, but I just felt as though I'd reached the bottom. Until then, there had never been a time in my life when I hadn't stood up and fought my corner. Whatever the situation, I've always stuck up for myself.

But at that particular time, lying on the living-room floor, if anybody had wanted to kick me, I'd have said, 'Go on, kick me. Give me your best shot. I'm down.' I didn't give a toss and I didn't want to play cricket any more. It felt as though the world had won.

I'm not sure if I was ever clinically depressed. I think there's a fair chance, although what I was feeling was nothing like as bad as Sarah has been through. A fortnight after I had that unpleasant encounter with the living-room floor, I arranged to see Steve Bull, the ECB's sports psychologist, during the Headingley Test match, which was a step in the right direction. And as the weeks went by I gradually started to feel better. There wasn't a particular turning point, as far as I'm aware, but the most important factor was that things were improving between Sarah and me.

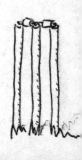

We had reached the stage where we knew that our marriage was going to work. Once a lot of rubbish had been cleared out of the way, it became clear that we still loved each other as much as ever. The problems we had been going through hadn't changed that at all. We just realised that we had been dealt a hell of a lot of crap over the last year: Sarah's depression, the further strains brought on after Ernie's arrival, then that grim time in New Zealand followed by my emotional problems in the summer. Those sort of things would have tested any marriage, but they hadn't changed the way we felt about each other.

Inevitably, one spin-off of my improved state of mind was that I started performing a bit better on the cricket field. I was no longer just going through the motions, and by the end of the summer I was pretty much my old self again. All was well at home, I was enjoying playing cricket and I was bowling as well as I had done since I was dropped by England. And just for the record, I finished the 2008 season with 42 wickets in the county championship at an average of 24.69, which isn't bad considering I was performing without my brain in gear for half the season.

But the thing that really astounded me about those few months after I was dropped was the staggering lack of interest in my welfare shown by the ECB, who were, after all, my main employers. From the time that I broke my thumb in mid-May, when Geoff Miller commiserated with me on my bad luck, to the day I was told that my central contract would not be renewed, which was 22 August, not one single person from the England set-up talked to me. There was not one iota of communication.

Peter Moores, the coach, had known about Sarah's illness since the tour of New Zealand. Still no contact, no phone call to see how things were at home. Not even a message of encouragement to ensure that I was striving to get back in the England team. Regardless of my own personal issues, if I'd been coach of the England team and I had a bloke who had taken 248 Test wickets, and was still only 31, I think I'd have wanted to keep tabs on him.

Even if they only had me in mind as back-up, would it not have made sense at least to see how I was feeling? And these are people given highly paid jobs because of their supposed ability to manage people. To go from having one bad Test in New Zealand to losing my central contract five months later, and to barely have any contact for the five months in between, was a joke. Did they really think so little about what effect being dropped might have on a player? Apparently so.

Even during the fiasco at the Headingley Test against South Africa, when they said they needed a pitch-it-up swing bowler and they selected Darren Pattinson, an Aussie who had only played a handful of first-class games, they didn't offer me the courtesy of an explanation as to why they hadn't picked me instead, a centrally contracted player, in helpful conditions, on my home ground. As I've already mentioned, I wasn't in the right frame of mind to play Test cricket anyway, but how were they to know that? I was still on the payroll, I was being blatantly ignored, and there was no explanation. Bizarre.

As Sarah has said to me, with England you go from having this incredible network of support around you, when you can't so much as fart without anybody knowing about it, to being absolutely on your own as soon as you're dropped.

Given this treatment, it came as little surprise when I was told on 22 August, during the one-day international against South Africa at Headingley, that my central contract wouldn't be renewed. Hardly shocking news since they had barely bothered to speak to me for the last five months.

I sat down with Geoff Miller and Hugh Morris, the managing director, to hear my fate. I told them about the state I'd been in earlier in the season, how I hadn't wanted to be near a cricket field. I also told them I was staggered that nobody from the ECB had so much as phoned me up to see how things were going after being dropped.

Geoff said: 'It's a two-way street, Matthew. You could have phoned me.'

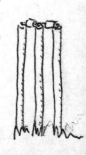

I said: 'Have you been listening, Geoff? I said that I didn't want to be near a cricket field.'

Yes, I could have phoned them myself, but that doesn't alter the fact that they had failed to check on how I was feeling after being dropped. They want you to strive to play for your country with everything you've got, and then when they decide to take it away at the drop of a hat you're just expected to deal with it.

These dealings reminded me of an exchange I'd had a year before with Geoff's predecessor, David Graveney. He had met me at Head-ingley to tell me that I was being lowered by one salary band on my central contract because I'd been injured a few times during the summer. There were three bands: 'A+' for senior players play-ing both Test and one-day cricket, 'A' for senior players in one or the other form, and 'B' for the more inexperienced. They were lowering me from A to B but were unable to come up with a convincing reason why. That seemed a bit rough to me because my form had still been good. I protested that it was unfair to cut my wages when I had become injured doing the job they were paying me to do. We went round in circles in search of a justifiable reason, but in the end Graveney's blunt explanation was: 'We're doing it, Matthew, because we can.'

They certainly can, and it seems that frequently they do. You'd have thought that the players would be the most important people to an organisation like the ECB, but half the time you're made to feel like a piece of clothing that can be worn and then thrown away. If the ECB don't improve their man-management, and start to treat players a bit more like human beings, the edge could easily be taken off the thrill of playing for England.

Every cloud has a silver lining and all that, and the positive aspect of not being involved with England was that I could spend my first full winter at home with Sarah and Ernie. For the first time I was able to enjoy the build-up to Christmas 2008 with my family, rather than arriving back on Christmas Eve with jetlag and watching people open presents from me that I didn't know anything about. It's even given me time to write a book. You might like to read it some time.

It's been nice just to do normal things, especially being able to help out with Ernie. As any parent will know, it can be tiring looking after children, and, if you're doing it constantly without a break, you can feel as though you're not doing it to the best of your ability.

So I've enjoyed getting up early in the morning, having time to play with Ernie, watching episode after episode of *Peppa Pig*. I know some of them off by heart now. And yes, I've even enjoyed the early mornings, although I'd better admit that there's been the odd time when I've been playing with Ernie downstairs and sneakily tried to nod back off to sleep. But he spots it every time, comes and jumps on me and tells me to wake up. Serves me right, I suppose.

But I've enjoyed the feeling that comes with having the time to pull my weight as a dad and as a husband. And that's the most important thing of all.

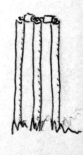

THE FASTEST SPELLS I EVER FACED

1. BRETT LEE, THE OVAL, 2005

It was the final day, the Ashes were already won and he was steaming in with an angry look on his face. I asked politely if I'd done anything to upset him. 'No, I'm just pissed off,' he said. Fair enough.

2. FIDEL EDWARDS, OLD TRAFFORD, 2004

Hard, fast, bouncy pitch, slingy action, serious pace. I was ducking and weaving all over the place. But it was good fun.

3. SHOAIB AKHTAR, PAKISTAN, 2005

He seemed to get especially wound up playing against England and he was very fiery in that series. Calm down, lad, I'm only a tail-ender.

4. ALLAN DONALD, FREE STATE NETS, 1998–2000

I don't think he ever bowled at full pace at me, and thankfully, as we were mates, he always pitched it up. Still plenty quick enough for me, though.

5. DAVID BYAS ON A BOWLING MACHINE, 1997–2006

Hang on, he's not a bowler. No, but when he was feeding a bowling machine, he suddenly thought he was a Nasty Fasty. Without telling you, he'd crank up the pace, set it onto in-swingers, out-swingers and basically do whatever he could to get you out.

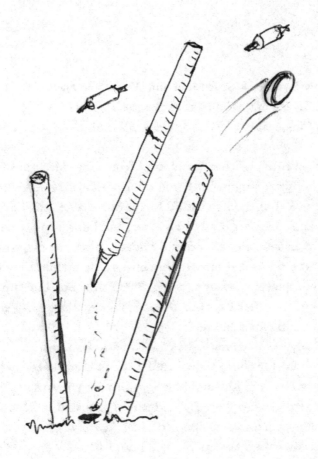

EpilogueHog

Interviewer, to Morecambe and Wise: *What would you two have been if you hadn't been comedians?*
Eric Morecambe: *Mike and Bernie Winters.*

I always think of that funny line from Eric Morecambe when anybody asks me what I would have done if I hadn't become a cricketer. What the hell would I have done? Who the hell would I have been? Yes, I wanted to be a vet, but I don't know whether I would have been clever enough. I never got to the stage of thinking about alternative careers much more than that. Would I have been a completely different person? Probably not, but I just thank my lucky stars that I've been able to play cricket as my job. It sure beats working for a living.

Anyway, such serious questions are not something I need to worry about for the time being. I've been a cricketer for quite a few years now and I intend to keep going for a few more, until the body starts groaning loudly and telling me that it doesn't fancy running up hill and into the wind five days a week any more. You never know when that point will come, but I'm only 32 and I'm hoping to keep playing for another five or six years yet.

One of the great things about cricket is that you can learn something new about it every day. Just before Darren Gough packed up playing for Yorkshire recently, at the age of 38, I heard him asking one of our younger bowlers, Richard Pyrah, to teach him a new slower ball that he had noticed Richard using in one-day cricket. This is one game in which an old dog can always learn a few new tricks.

And as long as I'm playing cricket for a living, I will want to play for England. From the example of my own career, and from watching so many others over the years, I know how valuable experience can be in international cricket. You learn how to survive when things aren't going your way; you learn how to cash in when things are going well. Coaches could be paid all the money in the world to sort out players' techniques, but cricket games are won and lost between the ears of the players.

I've got plenty of experience, I've had a lot of success and I still think I've got plenty to offer to England. Every single time I have pulled on an England shirt, it has been an honour and a privilege and I would love to have that feeling again. But of course, if the chance comes to resume my international career, I will have to make sure it is the right thing for my family at the time. I won't just be going in blind and doing it for my own sake this time.

If the opportunity doesn't come up again, it won't be the end of the world. I'll keep running in for Yorkshire, all guns blazing, and I'll do exactly the same if I'm playing club cricket. And when I finish playing professionally, I've got no idea how I'll feel about keeping my hand in with the game. I can't imagine hanging my boots up completely, but I've never been one of life's great planners, and I suppose it depends what I'm doing for a living then. If I'm working Monday to Friday, nine to five, I probably won't want to be playing cricket every Saturday and Sunday because I'll be looking forward to spending my weekends with Sarah and Ernie.

No doubt Ernie will keep me pretty well occupied and entertained for the next few years of my life. When he's a bit bigger, I'm

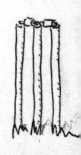

looking forward to him coming with me to walk the dogs, stopping off to see how many creepy-crawlies we can find in the undergrowth, looking for moles, foxes and maybe even devil's coach-horses. We'll have plenty of company on our walks as well, because there has recently been a new addition to our family with Walter, a new little puppy, moving in to join us. He's a very cute black mongrel and he wees all over the place. So there's something else to keep me busy for a while yet.

I'll also look forward to playing sporty games with Ernie – golf, cricket, rugby, football – but only if he wants to. We won't be pushing him in a particular direction. The lad can do what he likes. If he wants to be a bookworm rather than an outdoor type, that'll be fine by me.

I suppose that there will come a point in the next few years, a time in my life when I am confronted by the awful truth and I have to get **A PROPER JOB**. Aaaaarrrrggghhh!

What am I going to do then? Write books? No, I can't see them letting me do that any more after this. How about being a bin-man? I've always quite fancied that as a job, but I imagine it would involve some fairly early starts, so I'd better rule that out as well.

I guess my dream job (make that *second* dream job, as I've been doing my first-choice dream job for the last umpteen years) would be to work with animals in some way. It's probably a bit late to become a vet, but maybe I could open a safari park or something like that. How about a big game reserve on the outskirts of Bradford? That might surprise a few drivers passing by if they suddenly see a pack of lions strolling along the side of the ring road. I might have to run that one by the local council.

But what sort of proper job does playing cricket prepare you for? When I sketch out a CV, what sort of skills can I take into the real world? Let's see ...

1. Likes working outdoors
2. Prefers flexible working hours, ideally with late starts

3. Used to unsociable hours and working away from home

4. Enjoys job with a lively social scene

5. Needs regular drinks breaks

Doesn't really bring a load of jobs to mind, does it? Actually, there is one job for which I'll be as well qualified as anyone: Underwater Wood Welder. Never heard of one of those? Well, that is often the job title that I give to complete strangers that I meet in a bar on tour. Unless they happen to be cricket fans, I never think they'd believe me if I said that I played for England. But you'd be amazed how many people believe that I'm an Underwater Wood Welder.

'What does that involve?' they'll ask.

'Oh, you know, making sure the structures are sound on oil rigs, that sort of thing.'

I don't think there should be too much competition in the underwater wood welding business, given that it's technically impossible to weld wood. But I see that as a small problem to overcome and a great career opportunity. And maybe I could set up my headquarters just off the coast of Barbados. Not too far from shore, though, because I'm not such a great swimmer, and I wouldn't want to be too far from the beach bars.

Whatever the future holds, I just feel incredibly lucky to have spent so much time being able to play a game I love for a living. And I love the game as much now as I did when I first started. Even spending the last winter at home, when I had my first few months away from the game for ages, I still enjoyed watching any cricket that happened to be on the telly: India against England, South Africa against Australia, whatever.

Cricket has been great to me, it's taken me to some fantastic places and I've met a lot of amazing people. My only complaint is that the game hasn't been played in America in my time as a player, so that's one place I've never been.

All those experiences are what will stick in the memory, but it's also been a bit of a bonus that I'll have a small place in the record

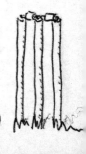

books as well. I've never been a big one for stats (they all say that, don't they?), but to stand sixth in the list of all-time Test wicket-takers for England, out of all the hundreds of bowlers that have played, is something that makes me very proud. Every England victory I played a part in made me feel just the same way. If nothing else, it will give me something to tell the grandkids about.

'Daddy, Daddy, please can I do some words for your book?'
'Go on then, Ernie, just a few. Don't bash the computer too hard.'

*Dear readers, please bear with Ernie here, he's only little and this is
his first time at the keyboard ...*

WCJHBJCHBAJ HSCB JAHXBJS ASCAC
DADDY WRESTLE ICUNDAICSXJ
DCHJDCA VKNJSC CDAC LASXNCKAS
DON'T WRESTLE DOGS DON'T LIKE THAT
JUST ME AJCHBA OICAWIU IXBJXxk
WJCHCNCK SXOIQWUYDN XKJNASX
SAKSXNASX SAXHBC WATCH PEPPA PIG
ADKCNKADNJC CAKCSNAJS OWPDKRYU
GIKJERABSXH ALEEEES ALEEEES
NOONOO NOONOO AJSXHBCNE
AUXSYBKJV JSJAHCBJHSC ACSJHBASY
WURBUEXNJK AXSHJIUERFH DON'T
WASH MY HEAD WAAAAAHHH ASXBH
WRFIHIEWF WIVBJCCDSKN
AISCUNASIC EWCNQEIC KSXNJAS PEPPA
PIG EWCMCOEW PSJSCBFKK
ASIUXCNSA ASIUCSN DADDY DANCE
AKIDNID EONELCASHC WEBQUILXMSAK
CNAISUCNS DADDY DAFT EKMFRN
WENWICN OPWRGJ CISDCJNK.

Good lad, Ernie. That's probably the most sense that anybody's written in the whole of this book. Now off you go upstairs to bed ...

Acknowledgements

I'd like to thank everyone who has read this book, because otherwise there wouldn't have been much point in writing it. I'd also like to thank all the local takeaway establishments who have helped throughout the process of working on the book: Rupali curry house, Wok This Way and Webster's Fish & Chips, where would I be without you all? The same applies to Marston's for all the beer. I hope that everybody who has helped me throughout my career has had a mention somewhere in these pages. If I've forgotten you, I owe you a pint. Finally, big thanks to all the guys at HarperCollins, for helping me to get the thing done, and to John Westerby, for listening to me spout my nonsense and drinking all my coffee.

Hoggy Stats

Full name: Matthew James Hoggard
Born: 31 December 1976, Pudsey, West Yorkshire
Nickname: Hoggy
Bowling: right-arm fast medium
Batting: right-handed
Height: 6ft 2in (1.8m)
Family: father John, mother Margaret, sisters Karen and Julie; wife Sarah; son Ernie; dogs Billy, Molly, and Walter

England's Leading Test Wicket Takers

	Matches	Ave	Wickets
1. I.T. Botham (1977–1992)	102	28.40	383
2. R.G.D. Willis (1971–1984)	90	25.20	325
3. F.S. Trueman (1952–1965)	67	21.57	307
4. D.L. Underwood (1966–1982)	86	25.83	297
5. J.B. Statham (1951–1965)	70	24.84	252
6. M.J. Hoggard (2000–2008)	67	30.50	248
7. A.V. Bedser (1946–1955)	51	24.89	236
8. A.R. Caddick (1993–2003)	62	29.91	234
9. D. Gough (1994–2003)	58	28.39	229
10. S.J. Harmison (2002–2009)	60	31.90	217

Best Strike Rates for England (min 100 wickets)

	Matches	Wickets	Ave	SR
1. G.A. Lohmann (1886–1896)	18	112	10.75	34.1
2. S.F Barnes (1901–1914)	27	189	16.43	41.6
3. J. Briggs (1884–1899)	33	118	17.75	45.1
4. C. Blythe (1901–1910)	19	100	18.63	45.4
5. F.S Trueman (1952–1965)	67	307	21.57	49.4
6. D. Gough (1994–2003)	58	229	28.39	51.6
7. R. Peel (1884–1896)	20	101	16.98	51.6
8. R.G.D. Willis (1971–1984)	90	325	25.20	53.4
9. M.J. Hoggard (2000–2008)	67	248	30.50	56.0
10. I.T. Botham (1977–1992)	102	383	28.40	56.9

Uncovered wickets? Or were these lads seriously good?

Hat-tricks for England

1. W. Bates   v Australia, Melbourne, 1882–83
2. J. Briggs   v Australia, Sydney, 1891–92
3. G.A. Lohmann   v South Africa, Port Elizabeth, 1895–96
4. J.T. Hearne   v Australia, Headingley, 1899
5. M.J.C. Allom   v New Zealand, Christchurch, 1929–30
6. T.W.J. Goddard   v South Africa, Johannesburg, 1938–39
7. P.J. Loader   v West Indies, Headingley, 1957
8. D.G. Cork   v West Indies, Old Trafford, 1995
9. D. Gough   v Australia, Sydney, 1998–99
10. M.J. Hoggard   v West Indies, Bridgetown, 2003–04
11. R.J. Sidebottom   v New Zealand, Hamilton, 2007–08

Sneaks in everywhere, doesn't he? Get your own book, Goughie!

Bowling in Test Matches

Matches	Balls	Runs	Wkts	Ave	Econ	SR	4-wkt	5-wkt	10-wkt
67	13,909	7,564	248	30.50	3.26	56.0	13	7	1

Best bowling (inns): 7–61, v South Africa, Johannesburg, January 2005.
Best bowling (match): 12–205, v South Africa, Johannesburg, January 2005.

No wonder I'm knackered.

Record in First Innings of Test

Overs	Mdns	Wkts	Ave
1,457.5	305	150	31.56

Record in Second Innings of Test

Overs	Mdns	Wkts	Ave
860.2	188	98	28.86

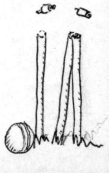

Breakdown of Test Dismissals (248)

Caught by fielder	99 (40%)
Caught by wicketkeeper	48 (19%)
Bowled	36 (15%)
LBW	65 (26%)

Yes, but how many were DROPPED, please? They never tell you that.

Dismissals of Right-Handed Batsmen (157)

Caught by fielder	64 (41%)
Caught by wicketkeeper	32 (20%)
Bowled	21 (14%)
LBW	40 (25%)

Dismissals of Left-Handed Batsmen (91)

Caught by fielder	36 (40%)
Caught by wicketkeeper	15 (16%)
Bowled	15 (16%)
LBW	25 (28%)

Bowling in First-Class Cricket

Balls	Runs	Wkts	Ave	Econ	SR	4-wkt	5-wkt	10-wkt
32,686	16,802	622	27.01	3.08	52.5	32	20	1

Best bowling (inns): 7–49, v Somerset, Headingley, September 2003

Mostly edges through the slips.

Bowling in One-Day Internationals

Matches	Balls	Runs	Wkts	Ave	Econ	SR	4-wkt	5-wkt
26	1,306	1,152	32	36.00	5.29	40.8	0	1

Best bowling: 5–49, v Zimbabwe, Harare, October 2001.

Batting in Test Matches

Matches	Innings	Runs	HS	Ave	4s	6s
67	92	473	38	7.27	42	0

Proper batsman, you see, doesn't need to hit the ball in the air.

Batting in First-Class Matches

Matches	Innings	Runs	HS	Ave	50s	100s
179	229	1,458	89*	9.00	3	0

There's still time ...

Record as Nightwatchman in Tests

Match	Position	Score at close	Score when out
v New Zealand, Lord's, 2004	4	0*	15
v New Zealand, Trent Bridge, 2004	7	0*	5
v West Indies, Old Trafford, 2004	7	3*	23
v South Africa, Cape Town, 2004/05	6	0*	1
v South Africa, Johannesburg, 2004/05	6	0*	5
v Australia, Edgbaston, 2005	3	0*	1
v Australia, Old Trafford, 2005	6	4†	n/a
v Pakistan, Multan, 2005/06	5	0*	1
v Sri Lanka, Lord's, 2006	5	2*	7
v Sri Lanka, Edgbaston, 2006	5	2*	3
v Australia, Perth, 2006/07	6	0	n/a
v West Indies, Riverside, 2007	4	0	n/a
v New Zealand, Hamilton, 2007/08	3	2	n/a

† dismissed with last ball of day

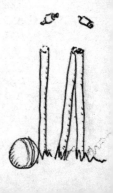

Bowlers Dismissed by Most in Tests

Shane Warne   6
Glenn McGrath   4
Brett Lee   3
Harbhajan Singh   3
Anil Kumble   3
Shahid Afridi   3

Warnie's proudest achievement, I imagine.

Test Series Record

	M	O	R	W	Ave	Econ	SR	BB	Result
2000 v WI (h)	1	13	49	0	–	3.76	–	–	W 3–1
2001 v Pak (h)	1	48	172	6	28.66	3.58	48.0	3–79	D 1–1
2001/02 v Ind (a)	3	101.5	281	9	31.22	2.75	67.8	4–80	L 0–1
2001/02 v NZ (a)	3	119.2	402	17	23.64	3.36	42.1	7–63	D 1–1
2002 v SL (h)	3	133	449	14	32.07	3.37	57.0	5–92	W 2–0
2002 v Ind (h)	4	160	533	14	38.07	3.33	68.5	4–87	D 1–1
2002/03 v Aus (a)	3	103.3	375	6	62.50	3.62	103.5	4–92	L 1–4
2003 v Zim (h)	1	33	59	3	19.66	1.78	66.0	3–24	W 2–0
2003/04 v Bang (a)	2	82	204	9	22.66	2.48	54.6	4–48	W 2–0
2003/04 v SL (a)	1	29	82	1	82.00	2.82	174.0	1–33	L 0–1
2003/04 v WI (a)	4	106.4	326	13	25.07	3.05	49.2	4–35	W 3–0
2004 v NZ (h)	3	109	385	9	42.77	3.53	72.6	4–75	W 3–0
2004 v WI (h)	4	126	492	16	30.75	3.90	47.2	4–83	W 4–0
2004/05 v SA (a)	5	200.3	663	26	25.50	3.30	46.2	7–61	W 2–1
2005 v Bang (h)	2	50.1	181	14	12.92	3.60	21.5	5–73	W 2–0
2005 v Aus (h)	5	122.1	473	16	29.56	3.87	45.8	4–97	W 2–1*
2005/06 v Pak (a)	3	110	407	11	37.00	3.70	60.0	3–50	L 0–2
2005/06 v Ind (a)	3	106.5	232	13	17.84	2.17	49.3	6–57	D 1–1
2006 v SL (h)	3	136	36	15	24.60	2.71	54.4	4–27	D 1–1
2006 v Pak (h)	4	138	473	10	47.30	3.42	82.8	3–117	W 3–0
2006/07 v Aus (a)	4	141	486	13	37.38	3.44	65.0	7–109	L 0–5†
2007 v WI (h)	2	47.1	115	5	23.00	2.43	56.6	3–28	W 3–0
2007/08 v SL (a)	2	64	205	7	29.28	3.20	54.8	4–29	L 0–1
2007/08 v NZ (a)	1	38	151	1	151.0	3.97	228.0	1–122	W 2–1
TOTALS	67	2318.1	7564	248	30.50	3.26	56.08	7–61	

* Look! We won the Ashes!
† Oh dear, we lost them again!

Index